Intifada

Bookmarks
London, Chicago and Melbourne

Intifada

Zionism, imperialism and Palestinian resistance

Phil Marshall

Intifada / *Phil Marshall*
First published November 1989.
Bookmarks, 265 Seven Sisters Road, London N4 2DE, England
Bookmarks, PO Box 16085, Chicago, IL 60616, USA
Bookmarks, GPO Box 1473N, Melbourne 3001, Australia
Copyright © Bookmarks and Phil Marshall

ISBN 0 906224 52 7

Printed by Cox and Wyman Limited, Reading, England
Cover design by Peter Court

Bookmarks is linked to an international grouping of socialist organisations:
Australia: *International Socialists*, GPO Box 1473N, Melbourne 3001
Belgium: *Socialisme International*, 9 rue Marexhe, 4400 Herstal, Liege
Britain: *Socialist Workers Party*, PO Box 82, London E3
Canada: *International Socialists*, PO Box 339, Station E, Toronto, Ontario M6H 4E3
Denmark: *Internationale Socialister*, Morten Borupsgade 18, kld, 8000 Arhus C
France: *Socialisme International*, BP 189, 75926 Paris Cedex 19
Greece: *Organosi Sosialistiki Epanastasi*, PO Box 8161, 10010 Omonia, Athens.
Holland: *Groep Internationale Socialisten*, PO Box 9720, 3506 GR Utrecht.
Ireland: *Socialist Workers Movement*, PO Box 1648, Dublin 8
Norway: *Internasjonale Sosialister*, Postboks 5370, Majorstua, 0304 Oslo 3
United States: *International Socialist Organization*, PO Box 16085, Chicago, IL 60616
West Germany: *Sozialistische Arbeiter Gruppe*, Wolfgangstrasse 81, 6000 Frankfurt 1

Contents

Acknowledgements
Thanks to the friends and comrades whose advice and criticism have helped in the writing of this book: Tony Cliff, John Rose, Clare Fermont, Peter Marsden and Kim Thomas.

Phil Marshall is a journalist specialising in the Middle East. He is the author of **Revolution and Counter-revolution in Iran** (Bookmarks 1988) and a member of the Socialist Workers Party in Britain.

This book is published with the aid of the Bookmarks Publishing Co-operative. Many socialists have some savings put aside, probably in a bank or savings bank. While it is there, this money is being loaned out by the bank to some business or other to further the capitalist search for profit. We believe it is better loaned to a socialist venture to further the struggle for socialism. That's how the co-operative works: in return for a loan, repayable at a month's notice, members receive free copies of books published by Bookmarks. At the time this book was published, the co-operative had more than 300 members, from as far apart as London and Malaysia, Canada and Norway.
Like to know more? Write to the Bookmarks Publishing Co-operative, 265 Seven Sisters Road, Finsbury Park, London N4 2DE, England.

Introduction

WHEN THE *INTIFADA* began in December 1987 it won the
support of millions worldwide. For all who identified with the
struggle against imperialism this new mass movement of
Palestinians under Israeli occupation was a confirmation that
economic and military domination do not guarantee political
control; that wealth and power are not enough to destroy the
collective will to resist.

After 70 years of confronting Zionism and its supporters in
the West the Palestinians had raised their struggle to a new level.
Israel was thrown onto the defensive, the Palestine Liberation
Organisation (PLO) received unprecedented backing, and the
declaration of a Palestinian state in territory still occupied by
Israel was hailed by scores of countries. Among Palestinians
scattered across the world there was talk that their dream of
al-awda—the return from exile—was to become a reality.

Many Palestinians were certain that an independent
Palestinian state would now be established. They argued that it
would be a state born of struggle, for the might of Israel's military
machine had not stopped the strikes and demonstrations of the
intifada. Despite Israel's policy of repression—the beatings,
shootings, mass arrests and deportations, an 'iron fist' to crush the
Uprising—the people of the West Bank and Gaza had not been
cowed. According to such a view the 'revolution of stones' had
finally turned the tables on Israel.

But an independent Palestinian state remains an aspiration.
Although courage and determination have brought the idea of
such a state onto the agenda it is far from becoming a reality.
Israeli prime minister Yitzak Shamir says: 'A Palestinian state will

not arise and will not be.'[1] In May 1989 Shamir promised that 'peace talks' would be accompanied by an intensification of repression. He declared: ' The [peace] initiative does not rule out suppression of the *intifada*. We extend one hand for peace and have the other free to strike at the rioters.'[2]

Can the idea of a Palestinian 'ministate'—one which would share the territory of Palestine with Israel—become a reality? If so, can such a state satisfy Palestinians' long-held hopes for liberation from Zionist domination?

Many Palestinians, especially those of the West Bank and Gaza, believe that it can. They argue that the level of self-organisation achieved during the *intifada* means that Israel will never re-establish full control over the Occupied Territories and that the network of committees that has led the Uprising will be the basis for a new democratic state. Others raise doubts: has the *intifada* done enough to force Israel to make a territorial compromise? Will Israel's friends in the West ever really pressure the Zionist state to make concessions? Will the Arab regimes allow an independent Palestinian state?

This book tries to answer some of these questions. Its premise is that the problem of Palestine can be understood only in the context of the history of imperialism—the social force from which Zionism emerged and which the Zionist movement has sought to serve. It looks at the origins of Zionism, at its efforts to create a settler colony in Palestine and at the first Palestinian response. It also examines the development of the relationship between Israel and its main Western backer, the United States, the emergence of the modern Palestinian national movement and the strategies the PLO has pursued. It looks at the achievements—and problems—of the *intifada*, and the hopes which it has raised for an independent state.

Finally it considers the greatest obstacle facing the Palestinian movement—its isolation from the wider mass struggles of the Arab world.

Chapter One
Intifada

ON 8 DECEMBER 1987 hundreds of Palestinians returning to Gaza from a day's work in Israel witnessed a gruesome killing. The driver of an Israeli army tank transporter aimed his vehicle at a line of cars carrying Arab workers—four passengers were crushed to death and seven seriously injured. Three of the dead men were from nearby Jabalya refugee camp; their funerals that night turned into a demonstration of 10,000 camp residents. The *intifada* had begun.

The following day another demonstration in Jabalya was attacked by Israeli troops who killed a 20-year-old man. His funeral too became a protest against Israeli occupation; within hours marches throughout Gaza were being met by Israeli troops, repeated killings and renewed demonstrations. A tide of anger swept across the area: tens of thousands joined demonstrations that carried forbidden Palestinian flags and chanted nationalist slogans. Israeli forces declared curfews in refugee camps and closed schools. Schoolchildren took to the streets to build barricades and hurl stones and bottles at the army.

Two days into the Uprising an international relief worker described the situation in Gaza City:

> Gaza is totally closed. The roads are blocked, the streets are strewn with debris. The black smoke of burning tyres hangs over the city.[1]

All over the area protesters defied the Israeli army. Groups of teenagers assembled at street corners, marches were organised, huge demonstrations assembled in the camps. Twenty years of frustration and bitterness at unemployment, overcrowding,

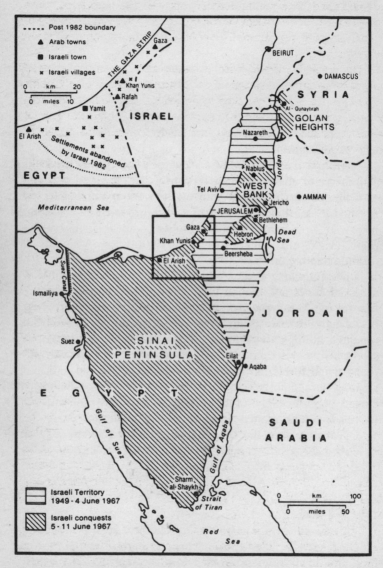

Israel and the Occupied Territories after 1967.

poverty and repression was exploding in a collective rejection of the Israeli occupation. Everywhere Gazans demanded that Israeli troops must go and called for Palestinian rights and national independence. One young activist captured the combined sense of rage and hope that gripped the protesters: 'We were waiting to do such an uprising,' he said. 'Everyone here has a demonstration inside his heart.'[2]

The *intifada* spread with extraordinary speed. A hundred miles away a demonstration at Balata refugee camp near Nablus in the West Bank was attacked by Israeli troops. Four Palestinian teenagers were killed and 30 people wounded. Now the cycle of protests, funerals, killings and further demonstrations began to sweep the West Bank.

Haidar Abdel-Shafi, head of the Palestinian Red Crescent Society in Gaza—the organisation which collected the dead and wounded—noted that 'the slightest spark ignites a fire'. A 'chain of confrontation' had begun in the Occupied Territories, he said.[3]

The Iron Fist

The Israeli government saw the protests as the work of a small minority which sought 'to disturb the peace and way of life of most residents of the territories'.[4] Defence minister Yitzak Rabin declared that the movement was inspired by Iran, Iraq, Syria and the PLO. He ordered reinforcements into Gaza and the West Bank with the promise that Israel would use all means to crush disruptive elements. In the first ten days of the Uprising 27 Palestinians were killed and more than 250 injured.

But already the Uprising had a momentum that could not be halted by such measures. On 21 December the Palestinian Arab population of Israel joined a general strike in solidarity with the people of the Occupied Territories. Israelis were stunned: for the first time since the 1930s all Arab communities in Palestine had mobilised to support their national rights. In towns such as Jaffa, Acre and Lod, 'Israeli' Arabs fought police during demonstrations which proved that 40 years of life under Zionist repression had not destroyed their Palestinian identity.

The evident spontaneity of the movement in Gaza and the West Bank and the reassertion of a Palestinian identity among 'Israeli' Arabs produced a first hint of official anxiety. The Israeli government had believed the PLO to be dead—crushed by Israel's

1982 invasion of Lebanon and the expulsion of Palestinian guerrillas from Beirut. Now a new wave of nationalist activity seemed capable of reviving the PLO and of threatening Israeli control over the Occupied Territories. Israeli defence minister Yitzak Rabin declared:

> Gaza and Hebron, Ramallah and Nablus [all in the Occupied Territories] are not and will never become Beirut, Sidon and Tyre [formerly PLO strongholds in Lebanon]... here we shall fight united and with all our strength, and it is great, against every force that tries by violent means to undermine our full control of Judea, Samaria and the Gaza Strip.[5]

Rabin announced a further intensification of repression in the territories: an 'iron fist' policy, similar to that which he had initiated in Lebanon, would be put into operation in Gaza and the West Bank. Israeli forces were to use 'force, power and blows' against demonstrators. 'We will make it clear who is running the territories,' Rabin insisted. 'We are adamant that the violence shall not achieve political ends.'[6]

But the 'iron fist' met opposition which the Israeli army was all but helpless to resist. Trained to fight 'conventional' wars against the armies of neighbouring Arab states and PLO guerrilla fighters, Israeli forces were unable to contain mass demonstrations or the swift attacks on military vehicles or Israeli buses mounted by youths armed only with stones. By January 1988 the Israeli press was forced to admit that the army was ineffective. **The Jerusalem Post** observed:

> The streets, both in Gaza and the West Bank and in East Jerusalem, are thus in effective control of the youth. It is a situation of our 20-year-olds battling their 20-year-olds —ours using armour, helicopters and guns; theirs, clubs, rocks and primitive Molotov cocktails.[7]

Israel's leaders tried a new tactic: they would starve the Palestinians of Gaza into submission. From mid-January long curfews were imposed on the eight Gaza camps. Soldiers were stationed at the entrances and patrolled the camps at night; no one was allowed outside. Food and water became scarce and Israeli forces increased pressure by searching houses, beating residents, firing tear-gas into homes and dropping gas canisters by helicopter. When injured Palestinians were taken to hospital they were often pursued by troops and dragged from their beds. Thousands of Palestinians were taken into detention.

The death toll mounted—by mid-January at least 50 Palestinians had been killed by gunshots or the effects of tear-gas used at close quarters.[8] But the Uprising could not be crushed. PLO leader Yasser Arafat had already dubbed the movement 'a revolution of stones'; in the battle for the streets, stones triumphed over helicopters and guns. For the first time in a generation Palestinians had turned the tables on their Zionist enemy.

Israel's bantustan

The youth who battled with Israeli forces had known only occupation. Gaza and the West Bank, including East Jerusalem, had come under Israeli control in 1967 when, in the war between Israel and its Arab neighbours, the two areas had been seized from Egypt and Jordan respectively. But neither the West Bank nor Gaza were part of Arab states. They were part of historic Palestine—a country which extended from Lebanon in the north to the Sinai Desert in the south, and from the Mediterranean Sea to the River Jordan. This country had been dismembered in 1948 when the militias of the Zionist movement of settler Jews seized large areas of land while Arab armies, ostensibly fighting on behalf of the Palestinians, occupied the West Bank and Gaza.

When Israel seized these territories during the 1967 war it acquired a valuable resource. The two areas were a useful strategic asset: they provided buffer zones which, Israeli strategists argued, would help to give protection in future conflicts with the Arab states. In addition they provided land which might be used for settlement in territories the Zionist movement had long aimed to control—and which contained water resources that could be diverted into Israel. The West Bank and Gaza also contained human resources: in 1967 there were 820,000 people in the West Bank, 80,000 in East Jerusalem and 450,000 in Gaza.[9] Tens of thousands fled the prospect of Israeli rule but the bulk of the population remained to provide the Zionist state with a valuable market for its goods and a large pool of labour which might be mobilised to serve its industries.

Israel pillaged the Occupied Territories. Its hydraulic

engineers pumped water from the West Bank to the farms and towns of Israel, massively reducing local water resources. The traditional economy, based on agriculture, suffered badly; in some areas whole communities were killed off when water supplies were drained into the Israeli water system or the Israeli authorities shut off pumps.

A programme of land seizure forced tens of thousands of Palestinian peasants and labourers from areas their families had worked for generations. As part of their attempt to 'Judaise' the territories Israeli leaders initiated a new process of colonisation. Settler communities were established throughout the West Bank and Gaza with the aim of eventually integrating some or all of the territories into the Israeli state. By 1988, 55 per cent of land in the West Bank and 30 per cent of land in Gaza was in Israeli hands.[10]

These policies increased the large numbers of unemployed in the West Bank and Gaza. The expulsion of Palestinians from areas seized by the Zionist militias in 1948 had resulted in the establishment of refugee camps in the territories in which for 20 years many had been unemployed; after 1967 unemployment rose sharply. There was now a large pool of labour which Israeli employers were quick to exploit. Palestinians were soon being employed by Israeli industry and agriculture—but in the most menial jobs at the meanest of wages. Workers from the Occupied Territories did not enjoy the protection of Israeli trade unions and unions organised in the territories were not recognised in Israel. This employment apartheid meant that by 1977 the wages of workers from the West Bank and Gaza were on average only 40 per cent of those paid to Israelis.[11] In 1987 the average income in Israel was ten times higher than that in Gaza and four times higher than that in the West Bank.[12]

There were enormous benefits for the Israeli economy. Palestinian labour fuelled its industries—by 1981 more than 110,000 labourers were travelling from the Occupied Territories to work in Israel each day while the large number of those still unemployed in the West Bank and Gaza helped to keep their wages low.

Meanwhile the West Bank and Gaza became vital markets for Israeli goods. Despite limited purchasing power, their 1.3 million people provided a much-needed boost for Israel's fragile economy.

By 1986 the Occupied Territories had become Israel's second largest 'export' market.[13]

The occupation generation

Life under occupation was a constant reminder that Israel was intent on eliminating the Palestinian identity. Israeli troops controlled movement to and from the Occupied Territories and patrolled camps and towns; Israeli administrators ran educational and legal institutions. Independent Palestinian organisations were banned. It was illegal to fly the Palestinian flag, to read 'subversive' literature, or to hold a press conference without permission.

Between 1977 and 1982 the number of incidents of Palestinian protest averaged 500 a year. Between 1982 and 1987 protests averaged 3,700 a year.[14] They were ruthlessly suppressed. Schools and university campuses were among the key battlegrounds; here many students were killed by Israeli troops or were seriously wounded. Thousands of protesters were arrested and beaten, hundreds were placed in administrative detention (imprisonment without trial) and scores were deported. Between 1985 and 1987 alone more than 100 homes of Palestinian activists were demolished.[15]

The situation was especially intolerable in Gaza. Close to the centres of Israeli industry, the area had been first to supply cheap labour to factories, hotels and restaurants, and to Israel's highly commercialised agriculture. By the early 1980s, 43 per cent of Gaza's labour force worked in Israel. Banned, South Africa-style, from staying in Israel overnight, tens of thousands of labourers travelled daily to and from their homes, passing through Israeli checkpoints at the edge of the Gaza Strip. Most young Gazans knew no other routine of work. One Israeli organisation described the area as 'the labour camp of Tel-Aviv... the Soweto of the state of Israel'.[16]

But jobs in Israel were often casual and many Gazans remained unemployed. As a result many families, especially new households, had no effective breadwinner. The rate of population increase was high—among the 525,000 people in Gaza by the mid-1980s, 5,000 new households were created each year. Many lived in poverty, dependent on wider family support.[17]Employed and unemployed alike faced intolerable overcrowding. Gaza's population was crammed into an area 28 miles long and five miles wide in which population density of 3,754 people per square mile was about the same as that of Hong Kong.[18] Though Israel could show massive economic benefits from its control of the area, it was unwilling to make any but the most basic provisions there for health, education or housing. Less than 40 per cent of new households were housed each year.[19]

Israel's settlement policy in Gaza increased Palestinians' anger. By 1987, 65,000 Israeli Jews had been settled in the West Bank and 2,500 in Gaza. The Jewish population of Gaza thus constituted a mere 0.4 per cent of the population of the area. But each settler had on average 2.6 acres of land; their Palestinian neighbours had on average 0.006 of an acre. And Jewish settlers, living in purpose-built accommodation and benefiting from Israeli government services, consumed, on average, 19 times more water than the slum-dwellers of the Palestinian camps, most of whom had no regular water supply and no main drainage.[20]

For Gazans the settlement policy was an outrage which made the problems of employment, housing, education and welfare all the more unbearable. But every attempt at a response was obstructed: efforts to organise independent trade unions, university and school students' organisations and, above all, independent political parties, met with the same intimidation and violence. The Israeli approach was obsessive—even those religious and community leaders who sought to defend Palestinian rights but who sought an accommodation with the occupying power were treated with suspicion.

Israel's strategy bore a bitter fruit. As the level of resistance began to rise in 1986 it was evident that a new spirit of defiance had developed. The Israeli army's policy of arresting, beating and detaining demonstrators had less and less effect. By December 1986 Haidar Abdel-Shafi could comment that the youth were no longer retreating from Israeli troops: 'The kids are drawing different conclusions. They are becoming more daring and they are not running away,' he observed.[21] When the *intifada* erupted in December 1987 it revealed the existence of a generation of young activists prepared to match the violence of the Israeli state with a determination to free themselves of its control.

The 'occupation generation' had grown up under Israeli rule. By 1987 it constituted the greater part of the Gazan population:

the number of people aged 25-34 in the area had doubled in a decade; those under the age of 14 made up almost half of all local residents.[22] Many of these young people had lost the fear of authority which had held back their parents. Steeled by a life under Zionist oppression and with nothing to lose, the *shabab*— 'the guys' or 'the youth'—stood their ground against the Israeli army. As one middle-aged woman observed: 'Our generation failed. It is the children who now show us how to fight.'[23]

Two months into the Uprising the reality of the new situation dawned on some Israelis. **The Jerusalem Post** admitted that a new Palestinian movement had emerged, first in Gaza, then in the West Bank. This was under the leadership of 'a young and dynamic local Palestinian leadership' which had enjoyed 'almost unbelievable success'.[24] The paper went on:

> The Palestinians we are fighting now are not the same as the Palestinians we met 20 years ago. They have not been cowed by two decades as refugees under Egyptian and Jordanian rule, or humiliated by the defeat inflicted on the combined Arab armies by Israel in 1967... They are a generation who have grown up under Israeli occupation...[25]

Striking for freedom

By February 1988 the young activists had succeeded in stimulating a movement which had grown to encompass the whole population of the Occupied Territories. It wielded the weapon of the strike—one not seen in Palestine since 1936, the year of the great strike against the British colonial occupation and the Zionist movement. On selected days the majority of workers from Gaza and the West Bank remained at home. A new industrial working class was able to demonstrate that Palestinians now had an impact on the Israeli economy. In some areas of the Occupied Territories workers remained at home for weeks, their Israeli employers appealing to the government to find labour which would run their hotels and restaurants or save the fruit harvest.

Such coordinated action showed that the movement, which had begun spontaneously from below, had rapidly developed a formal leadership. Many of its members were young activists; others were experienced nationalists whose activity had been curbed by Israeli repression. Local committees, organised across the West Bank and Gaza as the Unified Command of the Uprising, quickly expressed their allegiance to the PLO. Israel's leaders, who had believed that the Occupied Territories had been purged of direct PLO influence, discovered that the national movement had been reborn on a massive scale.

The Unified Command organised strike days, 'commercial strikes' and boycotts involving the whole community. Shops closed in defiance of the Israeli authorities, opening only at agreed times to supply necessities. Israeli goods disappeared from many shops as Palestinians sought out goods produced locally. Consumption of the most popular Israeli cigarettes declined by 80 per cent in the first eight months of 1988 and Israeli textiles were largely replaced by those produced in the West Bank.[26] Consumption of Palestinian fruit, vegetables and dairy products rose sharply. As part of the boycott and as an attempt to ensure that Palestinian communities would be able to survive curfews and Israeli blockades, a campaign for Palestinian self-sufficiency took hold throughout the Occupied Territories. An observer described the impact:

> The campaign... has a role for every Palestinian—the shopper who chooses a Palestinian product over an Israeli one, the merchant who adheres to the strike schedule of the national leadership, young people working on family or neighbourhood garden plots, women pickling their own produce. This multiplicity of modes of struggle politicises the most mundane aspect of life and expands enormously the number of active participants in the *intifada* beyond those directly engaged in stone-throwing or formal political organising.[27]

Meanwhile, a call for Palestinians to withhold taxes paid to Israel and to resign their positions as police and local administrators met with striking success.

The people of the Occupied Territories had risen against the forces of occupation. By mid-1988 even the most remote hamlet of the West Bank was engaged in the movement and everywhere young Palestinians continued to confront the Israeli army. 'Elite' Israeli troops were brought in to deal with the most intransigent opposition. Often they had to reconquer camps and villages, sometimes more than once, sometimes using hundreds of troops.

In May 1988 Major General Amram Mitzna, Israeli commander in the West Bank, was asked if there were 'still any so-called liberated villages'. He replied that there were still 'a few villages, which I would not call liberated, but places we enter more infrequently'.[28]

By December 1988, after 12 months of resistance, Israeli deputy chief of staff General Ehud Barak revealed that the army had used an average of 10,000 troops a day in the West Bank and Gaza and that 3.5 million working days had been 'invested' in putting down the *intifada*.[29] They had failed to do so—but the army had taken a heavy toll among the people of the Occupied Territories: by December 1988, the first anniversary of the Uprising, at least 30,000 Palestinians had been held by Israeli troops. Many had been beaten during arrest, hundreds had been tortured, some had been executed.[30] By February 1989, 450 Palestinians had been killed by Israeli troops—one murder for every 3,300 inhabitants of the West Bank and Gaza.

Israel in the dock

Israel's attack on the Palestinian movement in Lebanon in 1982 had been stimulated largely by its desire to destroy PLO influence in the Occupied Territories, where efforts to control the population had met with a rising level of resistance. The expulsion of the PLO from Beirut led many Israelis to believe that the movement had been fatally disabled and that the West Bank and Gaza were open for annexation. As a result the scale of land seizures in the territories increased and the pace of Israeli settlement was stepped up.

The Uprising of 1987 showed that Palestinian nationalism was far from dead—it also demonstrated the impossibility of sustaining Israel's programme of expansion in the territories. By February 1988, after three months of *intifada*, Israeli historian Shlomo Avineri emphasised the seriousness of the situation for the Zionist state. He told the **New York Times**:

> In 1967 the Israeli army needed fewer than five days to gain control over the West Bank and Gaza. In 1987 to 1988 the same army—much stronger—cannot restore order when faced with stone-throwing turbulent youths. A Greater Israel is not more secure but less secure for Israeli Jews.[31]

Avineri pointed up the real contradiction in Israel's

colonisation strategy: though it had taken the West Bank and Gaza by force it could not impose control on the mass of the population. 'Turbulent youths' made a 'Greater Israel'—one which embraced the Occupied Territories—a threat to Israel itself. Four months later Shlomo Maoz, economics editor of **The Jerusalem Post** repeated the warning. 'The dream of having *Eretz Israel* [Greater Israel] at a bargain price has been shattered,' he wrote.[32] Israel's occupation of the West Bank and Gaza could be achieved only at a heavy price to Israel itself.

Liberal Zionists argued that the people of the West Bank and Gaza could not be battered to defeat and that it was time to withdraw from the territories. Former chief of military intelligence Yehoshafat Harkabi warned: 'We cannot rule another people for long and annex the territories. Our problem is not that we will be an apartheid state, but that we will not be.'[33]

As more Israelis criticised military strategy in the Occupied Territories the very basis of Zionist land rights in Palestine came under examination. Deputy prime minister David Levy pursued such criticisms to their conclusion. Making concessions to Palestinian pressure in the West Bank and Gaza meant that Israel's rights on all the land it controlled would be in question, he argued. 'If turmoil should erupt among the Arabs of Galilee [occupied by the Zionist movement in 1948] will anyone advocate giving up Galilee too? Where do they draw the line?' he asked.[34]

Political opinion in Israel began to polarise. A minority called for an accommodation with the Palestinians; a majority agreed with the government's 'iron fist' approach. Among those appalled by the treatment meted out to Palestinian protesters were reserve soldiers called up to serve in the Occupied Territories. In 1982, soldiers opposed to Israel's invasion of Lebanon had formed Yesh Gvul ('There is a Limit'); 2,000 soldiers requested not to serve in the army.[35] In 1988 the organisation took a new initiative, producing a petition which declared:

> The Palestinian people are waging an uprising against the Israeli occupation in the territories. Over 20 years of occupation and oppression has not prevented the Palestinian struggle for national liberation. The uprising in the territories and the brutal oppression by the Israeli army establish clearly the terrible price of a continued occupation and absence of a

political solution. We, reserve soldiers in the Israeli Defence Forces, announce that we cannot share any more the burden of cooperation with and the responsibility for this moral and political deterioration. We hereby declare our refusal to participate in the suppression of the uprising in the Occupied Territories.[36]

Within a few weeks 600 people had signed the petition. By September 1988, 37 members of Yesh Gvul had been jailed for refusing to serve in the West Bank and Gaza.[37]

But the majority of Israelis swung behind the government and in a climate of anti-Palestinian feeling far-right parties gained a new audience. Aggressively racist organisations such as Kach and Eretz Israel, with their demands for the expulsion of Palestinians from all areas under Israeli control, became especially popular among Jewish settlers in the Occupied Territories. Eretz Israel activist Zvi Shiloah told a meeting in Tel-Aviv that 'transfer' of the Palestinians would mean that Israel's 'Arab problem' would be at an end. 'We won't have to wake up in the morning and ask how many Arabs were born during the night,' he commented.[38] When a general election was called in November 1988 the right-wing Likud group again won a controlling influence.

Israelis became increasingly preoccupied with the Uprising: its cost to the defence budget, the economy and the stability of the political system. But more damaging was the cost to the Zionist movement abroad. Among its supporters abroad, especially in North America, Israel had been seen as a stable democratic state—the embodiment of the 'the national liberation movement of the Jewish people'. News of Israeli repression of the *intifada* brought a rapid change of approach. Daily television coverage of the beating and shooting of unarmed Palestinians by Israeli troops brought howls of outrage from some of Israel's most loyal backers. One Israeli newspaper correspondent in Washington told his readers:

The television images of the territories have been both poignant and devastating and Israel has suffered greatly in the process...

Instead of acknowledging that the situation in the territories has deteriorated to the point of civil rebellion—as it apparently has—Israeli spokesmen and their American

Jewish counterparts find it easier to lash out at the messengers of this bad news. But they do so half-heartedly. Deep down, they know the truth.[39]

For 40 years Israel had depended on massive financial backing from Western governments and Zionist organisations, especially those in the US. Although there was no question that its ties with Western powers would be broken, the level of financial support from pro-Israeli organisations might come under threat. Among the first to understand the seriousness of the situation was former US secretary of state Henry Kissinger, long a friend of Israel. In March 1988 he told a meeting of American Jewish leaders:

> The insurrection [in the Occupied Territories] must be quelled immediately, and the first step should be to throw out television, à la South Africa... The Palestinian Uprising must be suppressed brutally and rapidly.[40]

Israeli leaders' views were in accord with Kissinger's. Despite the damage done to Israel's image—with its possible consequences for dollar transfers and for Jewish migration to Israel—repression continued at an increased pace. More troops were mobilised: by mid-1988 Israeli troops on service in the Occupied Territories, together with their back-up units, accounted for an estimated 20 per cent of the total strength of the Israeli army.[41] Army commanders doubled reserve duty for most Israeli Jewish men from 30 days to 62 days. Some Israelis refused to serve, but the majority took their place in units which continued to implement the government's hard-line policy. The whole Jewish population of Israeli was being mobilised against the Uprising.[42] By April 1989 more than 500 Palestinians had been killed in the West Bank and Gaza; by July this had exceeded 600.

The *intifada* and the 'ministate'

For 25 years the PLO had rejected the legitimacy of the Israeli state. Though its component groups differed on strategy for the liberation of Palestine, all opposed the Israeli occupation of Palestinian land. All agreed that the PLO's eventual aim should be the establishment of a state throughout Palestine in which Arabs and Jews could live as equals. The Uprising brought a change of direction. The people of the West Bank and Gaza demanded the removal of Israeli forces and the assertion of Palestinian rights—in short, they called for the immediate establishment of a Palestinian state in the Occupied Territories.

The demands of the *intifada* were reflected in the PLO, which united behind the call for a 'ministate' in the Occupied Territories. On 11 November 1988, after almost a year of the *intifada*, the Palestine National Council (PNC) meeting in Algiers asserted that the Uprising had provided a basis for Palestinian national aspirations to be formalised. It declared:

> The massive national uprising, the *intifada*, now intensifying in cumulative scope and power on occupied Palestinian territories, as well as the unflinching resistance of the refugee camps outside the homeland, have elevated consciousness of the Palestinian truth and right into still higher realms of comprehension and actuality... The *intifada* has set siege to the mind of official Israel, which has for too long relied exclusively upon myth and terror to deny Palestinian existence altogether. Because of the *intifada* and its irreversible revolutionary impulse, the history of Palestine has therefore arrived at a decisive juncture...
>
> The Palestine National Council, in the name of God, and in the name of the Palestinian people, hereby proclaims the establishment of the state of Palestine on our Palestinian territory with its capital Jerusalem.[43]

The PLO initiative was timed to achieve maximum impact. The movement in the West Bank and Gaza was solid and Israel was facing a rising tide of international condemnation for its policy in the territories. The PLO hoped that those states whose interests were best served by stability in the Middle East would bring pressure on Israel to enter negotiations leading to Palestinian self-determination in the Occupied Territories. Above all, it hoped that the US, Israel's main backer, would convince the Israeli government that the West Bank and Gaza were now ungovernable and that the only way to end the Uprising was to accept Palestinian self-rule.

The declaration of independence therefore made clear that the Palestinian national movement was prepared to accept a state in only part of the land of historic Palestine; in effect, the PLO had set aside the aim of liberating the whole area occupied by Israel and was now advocating a 'two-state' solution to the problem of Palestine.

Within a fortnight 60 countries had recognised the new Palestinian state.[44] But in those capitals where the PLO most eagerly sought recognition there was a lukewarm reception. In the US Palestinian officials were told that further steps were needed: before there could be any public dealings with the Palestinian movement the PLO must formally recognise Israel and renounce 'terrorism'. The movement's leadership accordingly made a huge concession: Yasser Arafat accepted the legal status of Israel and told the United Nations that he condemned terrorism 'in all its forms'. Despite furious Israeli opposition, US officials now declared themselves willing to enter talks.

PLO leaders announced that a breakthrough had been made. They anticipated that the continuing strength of the *intifada* would keep Israel on the defensive, while Israel's friends in the West would bring pressure that would lead to concessions by the Zionist state. Salim Tamari, a leading Palestinian academic, summed up PLO expectations:

> One would hope the US Congress would be affected by the current mood both in Israel and the world at large, so as to make a more realistic assessment of what the Palestinians want...[45]

Though talks between US and PLO officials continued, there was no sign of such a new assessment, nor of pressure on Israel. Israeli leaders canvassed the idea of 'limited self-rule' in the West Bank and Gaza but asserted that there would be no involvement of the PLO and specifically that there would be no Palestinian state on territory controlled by Israel. Prime minister Yitzak Shamir insisted: 'We will not give the Arabs a single centimetre.'[46] Meanwhile trade and industry minister Ariel Sharon called for Israel to 'eliminate' Yasser Arafat, who only weeks earlier had been elected president of the PLO's new state of Palestine.[47]

The level of repression was again increased. In July 1989 Israeli troops carried out sweeps of the Occupied Territories and imprisoned hundreds of Palestinians said to be members of local *intifada* committees. Defence minister Yitzak Rabin reported that more than 13,000 people from the Occupied Territories were in custody—one for every 100 inhabitants of the West Bank and Gaza.[48]

It seemed that Israel could live with the *intifada*. Despite the damage to its economy, the cost of its military operations, disagreements about policy and its increasingly ugly image abroad, the country's leaders would not concede to the Palestinians. On 4 July 1989 Israeli chief of general staff Dan Shomron issued a new order. Henceforth Palestinians with their faces covered in the traditional *kuffiyeh* headdress could be shot on sight. The symbol of the Uprising was itself to become the target of Israeli repression.

Twenty months after the start of the *intifada* the people of the Occupied Territories still showed the energy and determination which had been evident during its earliest days. But still they were far from the independent state they wished to establish: the forces of occupation still controlled the camps of Gaza and the towns and villages of the West Bank; curfews were imposed and reimposed; houses demolished; activists deported. A solidarity movement had emerged abroad which had shaken the complacency of the Arab rulers, leading some to fear that the Palestinian issue might stimulate mass action against their own regimes. But still there was no sign of pressure from Israel's allies which could bring concessions from the Zionist state.

How could the Uprising go forward? Should activists commit themselves to a long war of attrition? Would the US wring concessions from Israel? If not, why had it entered talks with the PLO? Was the prospect of a 'ministate' a real one and could such a 'state' satisfy the aspirations of the mass of Palestinians? If not, which strategy should be adopted? As the Uprising moved towards its third year the questions mounted.

Chapter Two
The imperialist connection

THE *INTIFADA* expressed all the problems which had afflicted the Palestinian people for over 70 years. During this period there had been repeated attempts by Palestinians to struggle free of the domination of Britain and the Zionist movement, and later from Israel and the Arab regimes. On each occasion the Palestinians had met with the same response—the use of overwhelming force to crush their movement. But Palestinians had never displayed such energy and determination as that shown during the Uprising and for the first time it seemed that brute force might not be enough to destroy the movement. How was this momentum to be carried forward?

The problems of strategy which emerged during the *intifada* could be solved only by examining events which had taken place long before. The future of the Palestinian movement could be understood only by looking into the past, above all by looking at the relationship between the Palestinians, the Zionist movement and the force which has dominated the modern Middle East, that of Western imperialism.

The fate of Palestine has been inextricably linked to the interests of imperialism. The Zionist movement's ambition to control Palestine had its origin in imperialist assumptions about the process of colonisation. Its success in implanting a settler community in Palestine was a result of its relationship with the powers that controlled the region and its ability to win their backing. Its triumphant establishment of the state of Israel and its victories over Arab armies in a series of wars were likewise a function of Zionism's link to the ruling classes of the West.

Correspondingly, the Palestinians' plight was an expression

of their status as the colonised. Imperialism armed the Zionist movement; it disarmed the Palestinians. By so doing it created an antagonism at the heart of the imperialist system in the Middle East. The Palestinian struggle to assert an independent identity became a central feature of political life in the region—and this struggle too was shaped by the structures of imperialism, for the nationalist and communist traditions to which the Palestinian movement looked had their own contradictory relationships with the imperialist powers.

At every turn the Palestinian struggle confronted the structures implanted by imperialism. Of these the most significant was the Zionist movement.

Zionism and imperialism

The Zionist movement was a product of the crises of nineteenth-century European capitalism. As a strand of Jewish nationalism, it was a reaction to conditions imposed on Jews by the ruling classes of Eastern Europe, a region which by the 1880s was in the process of rapid change.

In the more advanced countries of Western Europe, such as France and Britain, Jews had largely assimilated into economic and political life, but the empires of Russia and Austria-Hungary were far more backward; here Jews remained outside the mainstream. As capitalism advanced into Eastern Europe Jewish communities which had depended on their role in the feudal economy came under threat. At the same time, as capitalism fell into crisis and local ruling groups sought to deflect mass anger at unemployment, shortages and political repression, Jewish communities became the target of sustained racist attacks.[1]

Jewish nationalism was a reaction to the instability and insecurity of such a society; it also mirrored that society. Thus although Jewish nationalists sought to defend the Jewish community they emphasised its separation from the wider society and leading Jewish nationalists emphasised the need for separate Jewish organisation.[2] The fullest expression of the nationalist idea was political Zionism. This maintained that Jews and non-Jews were incompatible; that while Jews remained a minority among a non-Jewish population they would always be persecuted and that therefore it was necessary to withdraw from Gentile (non-Jewish) society. The Zionists advocated mass Jewish emigration to a region where they could establish an exclusively Jewish state; only here would Jews be safe from persecution.

In 1896 Theodore Herzl crystallised the Zionist viewpoint in his pamphlet **The State of the Jews**. He argued that an exclusively Jewish state could be established in an 'undeveloped' country—one outside Europe, to which Jewish emigration could take place unhindered. The main aim of the Zionist movement, he insisted, should be to win the approval of the great powers who dominated the world system, for unless Zionism could win such backing it would not be allowed to acquire the territory on which to found the new state. Herzl intended that once having gained imperialist approval, the Zionist movement should conduct itself like other colonising ventures: it should establish a 'Jewish Company' along the lines of the British colonisation companies, such as the East India Company. This would pioneer settlement and act as the basis for the new state. Herzl was quite conscious of the implications of this approach: Zionism, he asserted, was 'a colonial idea'.[3]

Herzl's approach was consistent with that of the other European nationalisms. In a period when European empires were still competing to colonise huge areas in Africa, Asia and the Middle East, the idea of establishing a new state as an act of occupation did not disturb the Zionists or their potential backers. Indeed, though the State of Zion was to be entirely distinct from all other states, Herzl stressed its similarity to the nations which were emerging in Europe. He argued that the new state should form 'a portion of the rampart of Europe against Asia'.[4] It should be 'an outpost of civilisation as opposed to barbarism'.[5] Though an exclusively Jewish state, it would also be a 'European' state, for although its founders rejected the racism of European society they intended that their new home should imitate its other features.

Herzl was not specific about where the new state should be. Unlike some Jewish religious figures who had long viewed Palestine as a spiritual home, Herzl was more concerned that the Zionist movement should win the backing of the imperial powers and was willing to consider any 'empty' territory they might concede. Thus during the 1890s he canvassed the idea of emigration to Argentina, Uganda and even Madagascar.[6] But Herzl seemed to underestimate the strength of feeling among *religious* Jews, whose influence on the Zionist movement finally directed it towards Palestine—the Biblical 'Promised Land'. In 1897 the Zionist Congress decided that the movement's first objective was 'to create for the Jewish people a home in Palestine'.[7]

The choice of Palestine did not affect the method of securing territory. Once the movement had settled on a site for the State of Zion it bent every effort towards winning imperialist backing. According to Max Nordau, one of Herzl's closest associates, the Zionists decided that since 'Our aspirations point to Palestine as a compass points to north, therefore we must orient ourselves towards those powers [Germany and Turkey] under whose influence Palestine happens to be.'[8]

Herzl first courted the Turkish Sultan, ruler of the Ottoman Empire. Failing to persuade him—largely for want of money[9]— Herzl turned to Germany, which had a strong relationship with the Sultan and trading interests in the region.[10] Herzl's death in 1904 brought these efforts, temporarily, to an end. But a strategy had been adopted which was not to change for over 80 years. The Zionist movement, which had emerged as a response to social crisis in Europe, had elaborated a solution to anti-Semitism which bore all the marks of that same society. It was highly conservative; it was exclusivist; it was colonialist. Above all, it was wedded to the notion that its future lay with the imperial powers.

Weizmann's strategy

The Zionist movement agreed that its future rested with the imperial powers, but it disagreed about which held the key to Palestine. Thus there were factions which argued the case for France, for Germany, for Britain, for the US and even for Turkey —largely depending on the nationality of those concerned. Each group sought close co-operation with the favoured government, usually promising the backing of the Zionist movement and the Jewish community in return for support in the settlement of Palestine. But the First World War soon narrowed the options: for Britain took control of Palestine. It became increasingly likely that its future would be decided in London.

Among the most prominent Zionist leaders was Chaim Weizmann, a scientist working for the British government. At the beginning of the war he argued:

Palestine will fall within the influence of England... we could easily move a million Jews into Palestine within the next 50-60 years and England would have a very effective and strong barrier and we would have a country...[11]

As the war went on he became convinced that Britain's interests in the region dictated a need for local allies who would help secure imperial control. He argued that Britain should declare a protectorate in Palestine and then permit the settlement of European Jews—who would form a community committed to defend British interests. Weizmann was convinced that the strategic location of Palestine and the eagerness of Zionist Jews to settle the country presented a unique historic opportunity. 'A Jewish Palestine,' he told British cabinet minister Sir Robert Cecil, 'would be a safeguard to England, in particular in respect to the Suez Canal.'[12] Both parties would gain from this 'providential coincidence of British and Jewish interests.'[13] Weizmann became impatient with British politicians who did not understand the complementary nature of Zionism and imperialism. He told a fellow Zionist leader: 'The British have to learn to protect the jugular vein of the British Empire.'[14]

War created conditions which gave Weizmann a more attentive audience. Strategic considerations dictated that the British win the support of the small Jewish community in Palestine, of the far larger Jewish population in North America and especially of Jews in Eastern Europe. Germany had declared that it was liberating Jews from Tsarist control and had established relations with the Zionist movement, among which some elements were sympathetic to German aims.

But Britain had other concerns, which were to prove of more lasting significance. War had emphasised the strategic importance of the Eastern Mediterranean. The region lay on the sea route to Britain's key imperial possessions—India, South East Asia and East Africa—and was close to the newly developed Persian oilfields, which were proving of immense importance to the Allied war economy.[15] It was also adjacent to Egypt, site of the Suez Canal and a country with a vigorous national movement which Britain had already had difficulty bringing under control.[16] Furthermore the French had secured Syria and Britain needed its own local base to ensure that its imperial rival did not win wider national influence.

It had become necessary to integrate the area into the imperial plan. British strategists favoured the method of 'indirect rule', which used sections of the indigenous population to secure control over the masses. Establishing a client government—which could always be backed up by brute force—was a tried and tested method all over the empire. One possibility in the Middle East was the establishment of an Arab government in the area of Syria, Palestine and northern Arabia on the basis of independence from the Ottoman Empire but closely tied to Britain. British intelligence agents such as T E Lawrence ('Lawrence of Arabia') played a key role in setting up an Arab army which could form the basis of such a state under the Arabian King Faisal. Among the 'Arabist' section of the Foreign Office there were those who feared that moves towards the Zionists would prejudice Britain's relations with the Arab world. But Weizmann's offer—a client Jewish government in Palestine—began to win over British policy-makers.

Weizmann could not simply deliver the Zionist movement to Britain. He had to argue his case against those such as the head of the Zionist Executive, Nahum Sokolow, who wanted an agreement on Palestine to be negotiated with France. But growing British interest in Weizmann's position greatly strengthened his hand and by 1917 he was able to arrange for American and Russian Zionists to support 'the policy eventually determined on by Great Britain'.[17]

Weizmann had now been adopted by the British government as, in effect, 'their' representative in the Zionist movement. He was seconded from his job as a government scientist officially 'to work for a British Palestine'.[18] So deep was his involvement in the British cause that 'Weizmann's activities as a Zionist leader became merged with the stratagems of British diplomacy.'[19] His biographer comments that 'Weizmann performed his function as a faithful servant of an England at last entangled with his own cause.'[20]

Weizmann still did not have the full backing of the British government—until revolutionary change in Russia gave a final impetus to his argument. The February revolution of 1917 deepened British fears of the spread of revolutionary activity in Europe. Backing the Zionists, who were assertively anti-Marxist, was seen as one way of containing revolution.

In November 1917, on the eve of the Bolshevik revolution in Russia, Weizmann won the British Cabinet to the view that Zionist settlement in Palestine should receive at least cautious endorsement. On 2 November 1917 British foreign minister Lord Balfour issued a statement to the Zionist Federation. This declared that 'His Majesty's Government views with favour the establishment in Palestine of a national home for the Jewish people, and will use their best endeavours to facilitate the achievement of this object...'

The colonising process

The Balfour Declaration was a turning point in Zionist history. It did not establish a Jewish state—Britain still wished to keep its options open—but it did encourage the Zionist movement to believe that 'a national home' in Palestine might become just such a state. And in declaring British support for Zionist settlement the Declaration legitimised the colonisation of Palestine. Over the next 20 years the settler community—the *yishuv*—built a base on which the state of Israel was to be constructed.

The settlers who arrived in Palestine after the First World War found a country which had little in common with the 'land without people' of the Zionist leaders' rhetoric.[21] With more than half a million Arab inhabitants it was more densely populated than any other part of the Eastern Mediterranean.[22]

There were also between fifty and sixty thousand Jews already living there. Some of these belonged to small communities which had survived for centuries; others had emigrated from Europe over the previous 30 years, establishing pioneer Zionist settlements.[23]

Following the Balfour Declaration the pace of immigration stepped up rapidly. Between 1919 and 1923, 34,000 settlers joined the *yishuv*, and in 1925 another 34,000 immigrants arrived. By 1927 the Zionist community numbered 150,000 —some 16 per cent of a population in Palestine of now almost one million.[24]

Several factors account for the consolidation of the community over this period. First, it had established a stable base by buying large areas of land from Palestinian absentee landlords. The need to acquire territory had always been the key to the

Zionist venture and a preoccupation of the early settlers; in the wake of the Balfour Declaration access to land became far easier. In 1920 the first British High Commissioner to Palestine was appointed. Sir Herbert Samuel was a Zionist and had been one of the architects of the Declaration. He immediately issued a series of Ordinances which recognised Zionist organisations and

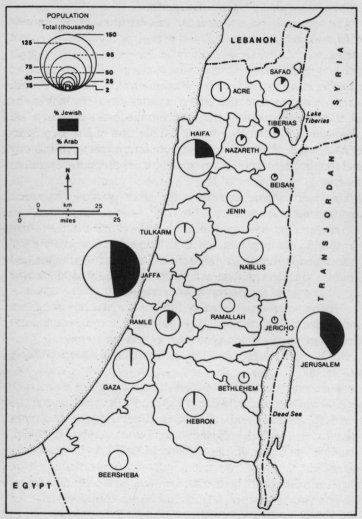

The Jewish and Arab population of Palestine in 1931

formalised the process of colonisation—for example, facilitating land transactions from Arabs to Jews.[25] This permitted organisations such as the Jewish National Fund to bring swathes of land under Zionist control. As a result, whereas by 1922 three decades of Zionist colonisation had brought 594,000 *dunam* of land under the control of agricultural settlements, by 1931 the figure had reached 1,058,500 *dunam*.[26]

The second factor was that the Zionists built an exclusively Jewish 'enclave' economy. This was organised around the general confederation of Hebrew workers in Palestine, the Histadrut, which was less a trade union than the leading institution of settler life in Palestine. Its two main principles were those of Jewish labour—ensuring that the settler community was served by Jewish labour alone—and of Jewish produce—the boycott of all Arab goods. On the basis of an explicit division of Jew from Arab the Histadrut separated the settler population from the majority of Palestinian Arab society, producing a relatively independent economy.

These developments helped the *yishuv* survive the major threat to its existence during the 1920s—the sharp fall-off in immigration. This was a response to economic crisis in the settler community and a rapid rise in Jewish unemployment. By 1927 net migration was static and the whole Zionist enterprise seemed in doubt.[27] But the rapid growth of the early and mid-1920s had given the community a certain momentum—that characteristic of all colonising ventures. It continued to acquire land and to tighten its racially defined economy. The *yishuv* hung on and within a few years was again experiencing dramatic growth.

By the mid-1930s immigration figures had moved sharply upwards: in less than ten years the Jewish population had increased almost threefold to 443,000.[28] The impulse for the new migration had its origins in the world crisis of capitalism and the rise of fascism.[29] In Europe there was a huge movement of Jews away from those countries under fascist control or in which fascism had influence. In the two years following Hitler's rise to power in 1933, 150,000 Jews left Germany, Poland and Central Europe for Palestine.[30] Nazi pressure increased until a policy of systematic elimination was devastating Jewish populations. Over the next eight years a further 2.5 million Jews left Germany and neighbouring states.

The racist policies of countries such as the US and Britain meant that only small numbers were admitted.[31] Most Jewish emigrants—some 75 per cent—fled to Russia. Despite the best efforts of Zionist leaders, whose eagerness to ensure migration to Palestine often exceeded their desire to see European Jewish communities survive, the number who travelled to Palestine was small—8.5 per cent of the total migrants.[32] But such numbers were enough to make a difference to the health of the *yishuv*.[33]

The new migrants were of a different character to earlier settlers, most of whom had been of petit-bourgeois origin and many of whom were motivated by a commitment to Zionist ideals. The new wave contained many bourgeois and professionals able to mobilise large amounts of capital: between 1925 and 1929 Jewish capital invested in Palestine had amounted to one million Palestinians pounds; between 1933 and 1939 this figure reached seven million.[34] At the same time large sums of money were generated by Zionist organisations outside Palestine, much of which was used for continued land purchase. By the late 1930s the settler community was far stronger than a decade earlier—its population had grown rapidly, it had consolidated a shaky economy, and had much increased the area of land under its control.

These developments stabilised the Zionist community—but they were still not enough to guarantee its existence. For this, British approval was necessary.

Divide and rule

In the period after the First World War Arab nationalism swept the Middle East. In Egypt, Syria and Iraq mass anti-colonial movements demanded independence: in Palestine a similar current hoped for union with Syria. But in Palestine the anti-imperialist movement found itself in conflict with a second colonial force—the settlers.

In 1920 nationalist demonstrations ended in battles with Jews. The protests were suppressed by the British, who dismissed Arab national claims. The following year, when British cabinet minister Winston Churchill visited Palestine, there were further Arab demonstrations which also ended in battles with Jews and which were similarly crushed by British forces. A pattern was developing: Arab nationalism—a movement of opposition to imperialism—was being expressed most sharply in opposition to the Zionist presence.

Publicly, British administrators adopted an 'even-handed' approach to events in Palestine. For example, they declared elements in both camps responsible for inter-communal clashes and commissions of inquiry recognised Arab concern over land losses and Arab aspirations for greater autonomy. Proposals were even made to protect some Arab land and to limit Zionist immigration. But Britain continued to facilitate Zionist land purchases, helped establish a Zionist militia, and made concessions to Jewish separatism by treating Jews differently to Arabs—for example, by paying Jews higher wages than Arabs for equal work.[35]

There were some differences over policy within the colonial administration. Not all British strategists had been won to the idea of the Zionist state. Some were adamantly opposed to the project on the basis that it would prejudice relations with the Arab states; most favoured British control over a country with relatively autonomous Arab and Jewish populations. But almost none questioned the settlement process itself, for backing the establishment of a 'national home' for the Jewish people remained British government policy. Administrators who saw dangers in the British approach were removed. Sir Ronald Storrs, military governor of Palestine, commented: 'It cannot be denied that there were amongst us two or three officers in high positions overtly against the declared policy of His Majesty's Government. In due course these were eliminated...'[36]

Britain's approach to the political leadership of the two communities was starkly different. On the one hand it maintained formal relations with the national and local representatives of the Zionist colony.[37] On the other hand, British administrators courted the most backward elements in Arab society and recognised its most reactionary figures as a formal leadership. These they used to deflect anger away from British policy and towards the settlers, cynically sharpening legitimate Arab anger over landlessness and unemployment. In 1921, for example, they fixed the 'election' of Hajj Amin al-Husseini as Mufti of Jerusalem, effectively leader of Palestinian Arab society.[38] Husseini was a landowner and right-wing nationalist who could be relied upon to channel the anti-imperialist sentiments of the masses in an anti-Jewish direction. Such divide-and-rule had been well tested throughout the the British empire and was second nature to experienced administrators such as Storrs.

Meanwhile rural Palestine was being transformed. A decade of land purchases by the Zionist movement had driven tens of thousands of Palestinian peasants from their fields. A British report concluded that in 10 per cent of villages a third of families had no land at all and another 40 per cent of families possessed holdings smaller than the minimum required for subsistence.[39] The inevitable result was mass opposition among peasants and increasing numbers of rural and urban unemployed—and in 1929 conflict erupted again, with Jewish communities the main target.

Britain again declared that it recognised Arab fears, but went on to make further concessions to the Zionists.[40] These came at a time when Jewish immigration was increasing steadily; with the spectre of Nazism in Europe, tens of thousands of migrants were arriving each year. This relentless pressure produced a new Palestinian reaction. A long series of strikes and demonstrations began, this time largely aimed at the British. These were on a far higher and more effective level than those of the 1920s—a function of the more developed character of Arab society.

The Revolt

By 1935 Palestine was in turmoil. Arab anger expressed years of frustration at the hands of a cynical British administration and the ineffectiveness of the Arab leadership. It was also stimulated by a new wave of nationalism in nearby Syria—where a general strike had succeeded in putting the French on the defensive—and in Egypt, where the British were forced to make concessions to the Wafd Party.[41] In April 1936, under enormous pressure from below, the Palestinian leadership reluctantly called a general strike. It demanded an end to Jewish immigration, a ban on the sale of land to Jews, and the replacement of the British mandate regime by a government drawn from the majority population.

The 'strike'—in reality a mass movement of non-co-operation with the British and the Zionists—lasted six months. It mobilised workers, peasants, the urban petit bourgeoisie and even the merchants and landowners, who for a while gave financial support to the activists. The British responded with great brutality. From the first days of the dispute they used martial law, collective punishment and internment. Whole sections of cities were demolished[42] and villages blown up. By the end of the strike Britain had brought in 30,000 troops—one for every 30 Arab inhabitants.[43]

In October 1936 the nationalist leadership surrendered, bringing an end to the strike but not to Palestinian resistance. Activists took to the hills in a campaign of guerrilla warfare and for a time it seemed that Palestine had fallen from British control. But force of arms and the bankrupt character of the traditional Palestinian leadership allowed the colonial authorities to restore military rule. The cost to the Arab resistance was high: the British air force strafed villages, captured guerrillas were executed, and there was large-scale demolition of insurgent villages.

From 1936 to 1939 the settler community profited handsomely. With the Arab economy paralysed, Jewish producers extended operations into areas of activity hitherto beyond their influence. In particular, they were able to entrench their role as suppliers to the colonial administration and the huge British military presence. The British military authorities also employed large numbers of Jews, partly resolving the serious problem of Jewish unemployment.[44] The infrastructure of the *yishuv* was strengthened: more settlements were built[45] and roads and ports constructed.

The leading Zionist Norman Bentwich, who was also attorney-general of Palestine, described how the settlers exploited the effectiveness of the general strike:

> In 1936, when the Arab lightermen, stevedores and porters of Jaffa [one of the two main ports of Palestine] joined in the Arab revolt, Tel-Aviv was for a time cut off from the import and export trade which was its life-blood; and its citizens then took the sea, as it were, into their own hands. In a few weeks they had built a wooden jetty from which it was possible to discharge cargo. They went on to replace the wooden by a permanent steel jetty, protected by a breakwater... Then the government agreed to use the port for the landing of passengers, and immigrants, as well as goods...[46]

Economic activity during the Revolt greatly strengthened the settler community *vis-à-vis* the mandate authorities, but more important, from the Zionist viewpoint, was the opportunity to serve Britain militarily.

British administrators had long encouraged the settler militia, the *haganah*, which from the early 1920s they had helped to arm.[47] Openly using the *haganah* during the 1936 strike was judged too provocative, but British administrators formed the Jewish Settlement Police, which by 1939 numbered 21,000—one for every 20 of the Jewish population.[48] They also enlisted underground Zionist militia in various special police units; one way or another the *haganah* and extreme right-wing Irgun Zvai Leumi militia were given official backing, the latter taking the opportunity to pioneer terrorist tactics which later became its hallmark.[49] In addition, the British army officer Charles Orde Wingate organised 'Special Night Squads'. These were joint Jewish-British patrols which carried out attacks on Arab guerrillas and protected strategic installations, notably the railways and the vital oil pipeline from Kirkuk in Iraq to the Palestinian port of Haifa.[50]

Wingate's role during the Revolt summed up the real relationship between the British and the Zionists. Wingate was an intelligence officer delegated to incorporate the Jewish Settlement Police into British counter-insurgency operations. He became a passionate supporter of the Zionist cause, telling officers under training for the militia: 'We are establishing here the foundations of the Army of Zion.'[51] According to Maurice Edelman, he 'transformed *haganah* from a purely static and defensive force into one which could seek out the aggressor and destroy him.'[52] 'The aggressor', of course, was the Palestinian resistance, fighting against a British army of occupation.

While Britain trained its militias the settler community stockpiled arms. During 1937 its supporters in Europe smuggled in 2,750 rifles, 225 machine-guns, 10,000 hand grenades and some 700 tons of explosives. Meanwhile local production of arms and ammunition went on inside Jewish-owned factories and workshops.[53]

By the end of the Revolt the settler community, though still numbering less than 450,000,[54] had been immensely strengthened. This had been achieved by serving Britain, at the expense of the Palestinian Arab anti-colonial movement. The Zionists had secured a double bonus: not only had they gained new strength, they had been able to participate in a war which had battered the anti-imperialist forces to defeat. The Palestinian Arab economy had been devastated, its political structures wrecked and its best activists excecuted or imprisoned. The damage done to Arab society had been sufficient to ensure that it would not be able to resist the pressures of an increasingly confident settler movement.

In 1921 the British Zionist Israel Zangwill, who disagreed with Weizmann's strategy for building up a Jewish settler presence in Palestine, had complained bitterly:

> We behold... the curious phenomenon that a moment when Hindoos, Egyptians and Irishmen vie with one another to shake off the British yoke, the Jews are equally frenzied to put their neck in it. They are like castaways at sea, rejoicing to be picked up even by a slaver.[55]

By the late 1930s Weizmann and the Zionist mainstream had their answer to Zangwill. The movement they led had indeed put its neck into the imperialist yoke. Its reward was a position of strength in Palestine which had been unthinkable 20 years earlier. The symbiotic relationship with imperialism had at last brought the establishment of a Jewish state onto the agenda.

The *yishuv* grows stronger

Following the general strike of 1936 the British government's Peel Commission presented proposals for the division of Palestine. These underlined the difference between Arabs and Jews, suggesting the partition of the country with the British retaining an enclave around Jerusalem. The notion was anathema to the Arabs, who would lose scores of towns and villages and huge areas of land. For those Zionists intent on a state in the whole of Palestine it was unsatisfactory, though for the Zionist movement as a whole it marked another step in the recognition of an independent settler presence.

In 1939 the Peel proposals were revamped in a government White Paper. This marked a shift in policy—its partial concessions to the Arabs reflected Britain's recognition that a major effort had been required to crush the Revolt and British fears that regional disputes such as that in Palestine might prejudice imperial interests at a time when Europe was again on the brink of war.

There were two main economic concerns. First, Britain was anxious to maintain a firm hold on the Suez Canal, through which most of its trade to the East passed and which would be of enormous strategic importance in a new world war. Second, Britain was determined to secure the Persian Gulf oilfields. These had increased in importance since the original oil finds in Iran had been followed by discoveries in Iraq and the Arabian Peninsula. Whereas in 1921 Middle East oil production had been 16.8 million barrels a year, by 1939 it had reached 114 million barrels.[56]

Much of the investment in the region had been carried out directly by the British government through its majority holding in the Anglo-Iranian Oil Company—later to become British Petroleum (BP)[57]—but US companies had also come onto the scene, notably in Saudi Arabia, where Standard Oil of California

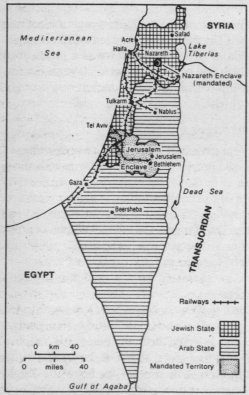

The 1937 Peel Plan for partition

had just made its first finds.[58] Pipelines already crisscrossed the area from the Iraqi oilfields to the Mediterranean coastlines of Syria, Lebanon and Palestine.[59]

The White Paper also reflected Britain's wish to 'freeze' the situation in the region. Britain feared that the impact of war might stimulate new national movements capable of threatening its interests. Following the First World War the Egyptian national movement had caused major problems and Britain had been forced to concede quasi-autonomy. But Egypt was still unstable and Britain did not want a repeat of the earlier events which might stimulate further difficulties in Palestine. Further afield Britain did not want to alienate Muslim leaders in India, who were heading a strong independence movement of their own and had already warned of their concern for Muslim rights in Palestine. Finally, Britain did not want to drive an embittered Palestinian population into the hands of Germany and Italy, with whom Palestinian leaders such as Hajj Amin al-Husseini had already had contact.

The White Paper therefore made gestures towards the Palestinians. It called for independence within ten years and limits to Jewish immigration and land purchases. But independence was made conditional on the Zionists' agreement—and the settlers were vehemently opposed to Arab majority rule. On the Zionist side there was fury that Britain had shifted to a position far less favourable to the settlers than that of the Peel Commission just two years before. There were large Jewish protest demonstrations and strikes, and terrorist groups began operations against the British forces. Nevertheless, the Zionist leadership, which had already seen its strategy of alignment with Britain proved successful, assured London that, in the words of Weizmann: 'We wish to... place ourselves, in matters big and small, under the coordinating direction of His Majesty's Government.'[60]

Declaration of war between Britain and Germany in September 1939 produced more statements of Zionist support and even the extreme right-wing Irgun swung behind Britain.[61] In line with the White Paper, Britain had restricted Jewish immigration and land purchases but the level of economic and military cooperation now stepped up sharply. Palestine became a major military base with a huge budget: from 1939 to 1944 British military expenditure was estimated at £113 million—a massive injection into the local economy. There was a major building programme and military and public works took up much unemployed Arab and Jewish labour. In addition, there was a massive boost to local agriculture, from which both communities benefited.

However, in industry it was the Jewish economy that raced ahead. The value of Jewish industrial production rose from nine million Palestinian pounds in 1937 to 20.5 million in 1942; exports rose from under a million pounds to 4.5 million.[62] In the years 1940-1943, 400 new factories and workshops were established by Jewish entrepreneurs using the skilled labour available in the immigrant community. Many factories were in relatively advanced manufacture: 55 were for metal-working, 78 for textiles, and 48 for chemicals.[63] Bentwich comments: 'All manner of articles were produced for the Forces, ranging from water-bottles to precision instruments, lorries and parts of weapons. Ships were repaired at Haifa. Spinning-mills made cotton-drill for uniforms. Leather factories turned out 100,000 pairs of boots each month.'[64] Nowhere else in the region except Egypt was industrial growth so rapid.

The war put Jewish capital on the map in the Middle East. But capital was not only recirculated, or diverted into consumption for the few, as it would have been elsewhere: part was channelled into operating of the Zionist enterprise itself. Thus during the first three years of war Jewish capital invested in Palestine was estimated at £15 million, of which one-third was given to national and public funds.[65]

On the military level the impact of war was even more dramatic. Whatever the reservations shown in the 1939 White Paper, Britain was prepared to use Zionist military resources for its war effort. *Haganah* units were soon being trained by the British and were undertaking attacks on Syria, then under Vichy French rule. By 1942, 43,000 Jews had enlisted as volunteers; by 1944 it was estimated that the *haganah* 'had a potential strength of 100,000 men and women, of whom 25,000 were armed, first-line troops.'[66]

By the end of the war the whole settler community had been brought into the Zionist military apparatus. According to the report of the Anglo-American Committee of Inquiry in 1946, out of a total Jewish population in the *yishuv* of 590,000, around 120,000, or 20 per cent, were armed and trained to fight. They had access to light and heavy weaponry and even a small force of aircraft.[67] By contrast, the Palestinian Arab community had been disarmed and politically paralysed, many of its leading figures killed or imprisoned. On the impact of the Second World War, Nathan Weinstock comments:

> The economic boom... facilitated the completion of Palestine Jewry's economic infrastructure. With its industry, its agriculture, its language, its social and cultural institutions, the *yishuv* now possessed unmistakable national and state characteristics. The military experience accumulated by the Palestinian Jews during the war electrified their national consciousness and strengthened their self-confidence. From that point onwards British tutelage became a yoke: Palestine's Hebrew community entered into conflict with its former protector.[68]

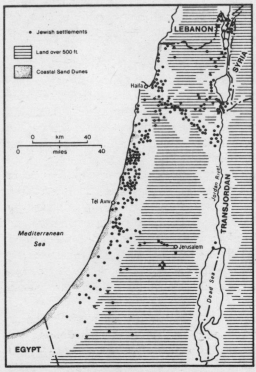

Zionist settlement during the British mandate

Chapter Three
Towards a state of Israel

THE ZIONIST MOVEMENT had been strengthened enormously since the Balfour Declaration almost 30 years earlier. By operating within the limits of British concerns in the Middle East, Zionism had won itself land and an economic and military base. The *yishuv* was a successful colony—an outgrowth of Western capitalism in a region which was still largely economically backward. However, this did not mean that Zionism aligned itself with imperial interests in every detail; as the movement had become stronger and more confident, the tensions in its relationship with Britain had become more evident. Such tensions were rooted in a conflict between the Zionists' concern to establish an independent Jewish entity in Palestine and Britain's wish to protect its interests in the whole of the Middle East.

By the mid-1940s these tensions dominated relations between the movement and the British. They are captured, from a British viewpoint, by Richard Crossman, a member of the Anglo-American Committee of Inquiry which was appointed in 1946 to recommend a solution to the Palestine problem. Crossman saw the Jewish Agency, which ran Zionist affairs in Palestine, as 'really a state within a state, with its own budget, secret cabinet, army, and above all, intelligence service. It is the most efficient, dynamic, toughest organisation I have ever seen, and it is not afraid of us [the British].'[1]

One reason the movement was not 'afraid' of Britain was that some of its leading elements understood that fundamental changes had been taking place in world and regional politics. Most important among these was a change in the balance of imperial power. On a global level Britain had given up its dominant position: American imperialism had extended its influence considerably during the war years, especially in Asia.

British India was about to break up, with enormous implications for other colonies, especially those in the Middle East which had protected the principal imperial trade route. The other European imperialisms were also on the retreat in the Middle East: France withdrew from Syria and Lebanon in 1946. In Egypt, Palestine's neighbour, Britain was under renewed pressure from a huge anti-colonial movement and in Iran a working-class movement of revolutionary potential was sweeping the country.[2]

The European retreat did not leave a vacuum; as Britain and France prepared to withdraw, the US was stepping up its involvement in the region. The main American concern was oil. Discoveries in the Arabian Peninsula had excited enormous interest in Washington, where in 1945 the State Department described the Saudi Arabian oilfields as 'one of the greatest material prizes in world history.'[3] Aware of the threat both from British oil interests based in Iran and the far more serious danger of the anti-colonial movement, the US decided it must secure Saudi Arabia at all costs. President Roosevelt declared that 'the defence of Saudi Arabia is vital to the defence of the United States.'[4]

The US decision to pay large sums of money to the Saudi King Abdel-Aziz, effectively transforming his country into a client state of the US, was a pointer to American seriousness about the region.[5] Such moves confirmed the belief of some Zionist leaders that whereas their ambitions could no longer be fulfilled by Britain's narrowing imperial interest, the US offered new opportunities. On Nordau's principle that the Zionist movement should direct itself at those powers with influence in the region, they argued for re-orientation towards Washington.

But the preoccupations of US capital were not the sole factor which influenced Zionist leaders. Developments inside the Zionist movement, especially in North America, also had an impact.

Since the 1890s the US had been the main destination for Jews seeking escape from Russia and Eastern Europe.[6] By the late 1930s there were 4.5 million Jews in the US; in New York alone there were two million—four times the number in Palestine.[7] The Zionist current had had a limited appeal in this highly heterogeneous society, but at this point it began to make headway. This was partly a result of the racist Quota Act, introduced in 1924, under which 'Anglo-Saxon' immigration was favoured over that of East Europeans, reducing the number of Jews entering the US to a trickle. The institutionalisation of racism, sharpened during the Depression, coincided with the rise of fascism in Europe and a growing awareness of the terrible predicament faced by Jews in countries under fascist control. The Zionists' argument that European Jews forbidden to enter the US must be allowed refuge in Palestine won wide backing.

As the logic of this argument became more compelling the Zionist current strengthened. During the mid-1930s Zionists captured most of the leading positions in Jewish-American community organisations and established fund-raising networks that collected huge sums for Jewish relief in Europe and for the settler community in Palestine.[8] At this period too Zionists began to exercise influence in US politics, forming lobby organisations which aimed at securing US backing for the movement's aims in Palestine.[9]

The much increased weight of American Zionism was shown by the decision of the World Zionist Organisation (WZO) to meet in 1942, not in Europe as was customary, but at the Biltmore Hotel in New York. At the Biltmore Conference, delegates passed a resolution which reflected most American Zionists' conviction that the time of accommodation with Britain was over; the Biltmore Programme demanded the fulfilment of 'the original purpose' of the Balfour Declaration, rejected the British 1939 White Paper, and called for the establishment of an autonomous Jewish military force.[10] It asserted:

> The conference urges that the gates of Palestine be opened; that the Jewish Agency be vested with control of immigration with Palestine and with the necessary authority for upholding the country, including the development of its unoccupied and uncultivated land, and that Palestine be established as a Jewish commonwealth integrated into the structure of the new democratic world.[11]

For two years the WZO organised a sustained, high-pressure lobbying campaign in the US Congress. In January 1944 Congress endorsed the aims of the Biltmore Programme. It declared that the US 'shall use its good offices and take appropriate measures to the end that the doors of Palestine shall be opened for the free entry of Jews into that country, and that there shall be full opportunity for colonisation, so that the Jewish people may ultimately reconstitute Palestine as a free and democratic Jewish commonwealth.'[12]

This was a breakthrough for Zionism on a level with the Balfour Declaration. Though the movement had yet to win the backing of the US administration, which hesitated to follow Congress, it had the support of the parliament of the West's most powerful state, one which would certainly determine the political future of the Middle East. And it had won this on the basis of commitment to a 'Jewish commonwealth'—a term understood to mean that a Jewish state should be established in all of Palestine. This triumph confirmed the position of Zionist leaders who declared that the future lay in Washington. They now concentrated all their efforts on winning US government backing for the position taken by Congress.[13]

For ten years the balance of power within the Zionist movement had been shifting towards those who insisted on the establishment of an independent state in Palestine. From the Biltmore Conference their position was enormously strengthened.

The movement as a whole had always been committed to the establishment of a Jewish settler presence in Palestine but contained rival currents with sharply differing conceptions of how it should develop. The Revisionists of Zev Jabotinsky, dubbed 'fascist' by their Zionist rivals, had argued that there could be no compromise with the Arabs, an enemy who should be driven from Palestine by force to allow the establishment of an independent state.[14] At the other end of the spectrum bi-nationalists such as Ruppin and Magnes had argued for territorial compromises which would allow Jews and Arabs to live within the same Palestinian state.[15]

Between these poles lay a number of currents, most of which had favoured an independent Jewish state but differed on how to achieve it. Since the First World War Weizmann had been convinced that a close relationship with Britain was the key; even the shock of the 1939 White Paper—which led many Zionists to conclude that Britain had become the main enemy—did not deter him. In 1942 he still argued: 'As long as British policy in Palestine permits us to buy land and bring in Jews, I am ready to put up with anything.'[16] But others, such as David Ben Gurion, concluded that the movement must realign with those willing to identify fully with the idea of a Jewish state. When the WZO agreed the Biltmore Programme it rejected Weizmann and confirmed this strategy. Those who still argued for a territoral compromise to be negotiated with Britain or directly with the Arabs were marginalised.

The change in Zionist policy decided in North America soon had its impact in Palestine. From the point at which Zionist settlers had begun sustained colonisation of Palestine the movement had been on a collision course with the Palestinian Arabs. By the early 1940s the success of the movement had given it a momentum which, further impelled by US backing, was leading to an explosive conflict with the indigenous population. Some elements in the movement, such as Jabotinsky's Revisionists, had long anticipated such a conflict, and glorified the idea of Jewish self-assertion through a triumph of arms. The mainstream of the movement had adopted a different strategy, concentrating on the acquisition of land and the strengthening of the *yishuv*. However, by the early 1940s even leading officials associated with this gradualist philosophy had accepted that it had become necessary to expel the non-Jewish population.[17] In 1940 R Weitz, head of the Jewish Agency's colonisation department, confided to his diary:

> Among ourselves it must be clear that there is no room for both peoples together in this country... With the Arabs we shall not achieve our aim of being an independent people in this country. The only solution is *Eretz Israel* [Greater Israel], at least the west part of *Eretz Israel*, without Arabs... and there is no other way but to transfer the Arabs from here to the neighbouring countries, transfer all of them, not one village or tribe should remain... There is no other alternative.[18]

At the leadership level the movement had accepted that a final, traumatic conflict with the Arab population was not only inevitable but was necessary. Its military resources, built up with British support, gave the *yishuv* a means to carry out the 'transfer' of the Palestinians. What was now needed was the wider international backing which would neutralise Britain— allowing such 'transfer' to go ahead without British military intervention —and which would guarantee backing for the Jewish state which would result.

The US government hesitated. It favoured a pro-Western presence in a region of strategic importance where there were few stable allies—certainly none with the highly developed appreciation of Western imperial needs which characterised Zionism. Added to this was the growing anxiety that Russia would pose a far greater challenge in the period after 1945 and that Communist Parties tied to Moscow were making rapid progress in the Middle East, notably in Iran, Iraq, Egypt and Syria. A Jewish state, Washington believed, might play a counterbalancing role.

But the US administration was not convinced that these advantages would outweigh the damage that might be done to relations with the Arab states. The State Department reasoned that backing a Jewish state would stimulate intense anger among Arab rulers, who might swing behind Russia, taking their oil with them. It pondered whether continued support for the British mandate in Palestine would better serve its aims.[19] But policy was also influenced by the flood of new information about the Holocaust and the politicians' wish to be seen as offering a future for what remained of European Jewry. In 1942 The Roosevelt administration had suppressed facts about the Nazis' extermination programme[20] but by 1944, aware of the impact of the issue on his election chances, Roosevelt opportunistically endorsed the idea of 'a democratic Jewish Commonwealth in Palestine'.[21]

There followed two years of diplomatic manoeuvring during which American strategists argued over the course which would best serve US interests. After failing to win British endorsement for increased Jewish immigration into Palestine, a new administration under President Truman jointly established the Anglo-American Committee of Inquiry. This set out to satisfy British wishes to maintain the mandate and US hopes to satisfy both Zionists and the Arabs: the result was a complicated fudge— a rejection of contending claims to a Palestinian state and a proposal to place Palestine under United Nations control. More Anglo-American talks followed which were equally indecisive— then, in 1947, Britain referred the issue to the UN.

Now the US swung behind the Zionists. Post-war competition between the two new superpowers—the US and Russia—was stepping up and it was clear that in the Middle East Britain was no longer capable of playing the required role alongside its American ally. Despite an increase in the British garrison in Palestine—to 100,000 men by 1946[22]—there was every sign that Britain's grip on the region was failing. On either side of the Gulf—in Egypt and Iran—mass movements threatened Western interests; in Iraq a new anti-colonial movement was on the rise.

In addition, in the US the WZO and the Jewish lobby was proving increasingly effective. As one semi-official history of the US-Israeli relationship points out, Truman cynically 'considered the advantages to be gained in the domestic political arena by adopting a course of action aiding the Jews of Europe.'[23] He opted for the Zionists and campaigned vigorously for a UN vote to recognise a partition of Palestine that would establish a Jewish state. After US lobbying that included threats to withdraw Marshall Aid from those states which did not cooperate,[24] the US position was endorsed. In November 1947 the United Nations General Assembly approved the partition plan by 33 votes to 13.[25] The Soviet Union, encouraged by the prospect of eliminating the British presence in Palestine and, it hoped, of slowing the advance of Western capitalism in the region, supported the plan.[26]

Even before the UN vote, Britain had announced that if its mandate was ended, troops would be withdrawn. The response of the Zionist movement was to declare that 'Should British forces not be available, the Jewish people of Palestine would provide without delay the necessary effectives to maintain public security.'[27] Through late 1947 and early 1948 clashes between Arab and Jewish groups in Palestine stepped up.[28]

It was an unequal battle. A few thousand ill-directed Arab volunteers faced well-armed Zionist militias prepared by years of training. The British prevaricated, supporting one side, then the other, but not bringing their forces fully into the battle; as a result the Zionist militias made rapid headway. The *haganah* strategy was to take possession of territory allotted to the Jews under the UN plan and to strike out along routes to isolated Jewish settlements in Arab areas. They quickly took many of the towns and means of communication. In these areas the Zionist state apparatus was put into place and on 14 May Ben Gurion proclaimed a State of Israel in the territories under Zionist control.

Just eleven minutes later President Truman recognised the new state.

Chapter Four
The Palestinian resistance

THE ARAB RESPONSE to Zionism reflected the economic and political backwardness of Palestinian society. Whereas the Zionist movement carried the mark of modern imperialism, Palestinian Arab politics expressed the structures of a society still emerging from feudalism and being shaped by both the experience of British occupation and Jewish settlement.

Although Palestine at the end of the First World War was more densely populated than any other part of the Eastern Mediterranean, a tiny group of families owned huge areas of the land. According to a census taken in the 1920s, 144 families owned 3.1 million *dunam* (one *dunam* was roughly a quarter of an acre); some owned hundreds of thousands of *dunam*. Two hundred and fifty families owned as much land as the entire peasant population. The average peasant family held a mere 0.46 *dunam*.[1] Although 65 per cent of peasant families owned some land, most did not hold enough for subsistence and almost 30 per cent were share-croppers or agricultural labourers.

Most important, of the 65 per cent of total land which was rented, two-thirds belonged to absentee landlords who lived in the major Palestinian towns. Although a similar pattern had existed for centuries this showed the extent to which, since the mid-19th century, capitalism had penetrated the local economy. For almost 50 years a small bourgeoisie had been speculating in land. Large areas of state land and village property, traditionally cultivated on a communal basis, had been bought under new land laws and provided income for a layer of absentee landowners, who further strengthened their position by providing credit to peasant farmers. This layer, together with the largest traditional landowning families, constituted the Palestinian ruling class.[2]

Palestinian cities such as Jerusalem, Haifa, Jaffa and Nablus were well established. They had long relied on trade routes which linked the Mediterranean to Central Asia and, like other such cities in the region, supported a population of merchants, shopkeepers and craftsmen. At its upper levels this layer was an embryonic bourgeoisie; its more prosperous members became land speculators and entrepreneurs who controlled the small Arab industrial sector. At its lower levels it merged with artisans, workers and the poor.

British occupation and Zionist settlement produced rapid changes. Both accelerated the penetration of the cash economy, the privatisation of land and the process of rural depopulation which was a result of increasingly concentrated land ownership and peasant indebtedness. From the early 1920s large land purchases by Zionist organisations from Palestinian landholders —largely from absentee landowners—resulted in the expulsion of Palestinian cultivators and produced a rapid increase in the number of landless labourers, who drifted towards the cities. Largely as a result of migration the urban Arab population grew from 194,000 in 1922 to 289,000 by 1936.[3]

The character of the 'dual economy' imposed by Zionist organisations committed to 'Jewish labour' and 'Jewish produce' made it difficult for Arabs to find work. Although the Arab working class grew steadily—mainly in traditional industries and in the British-controlled public sector—it did not keep pace with changes in the economy as whole. Craftsmen and skilled workers also suffered from the decline of the traditional economy and many moved to the cities, where some set up small workshops; most joined the ranks of the unemployed.

But development did benefit two sectors: the Arab bourgeoisie and the new professionals. In areas not wholly dominated by Jewish capital—especially trade in agricultural products and industries connected with agriculture, such as the manufacture of irrigation equipment, packaging and transport —Arab entrepreneurs fared well. Traditional industries such as textiles, food, furniture and soap production, quarrying and construction also boomed. Modernisation also stimulated the growth of a layer of professionals—administrators, teachers and lawyers—drawn disproportionately from the Christian population (10 per cent of the total, of whom 75 per cent were urbanised).[4]

A sketchy idea of the development of Arab society is given by figures from 1931. These showed that 60 per cent of Arabs were still engaged in agriculture, 22 per cent in commerce and administration and 18 per cent in construction, mining and transport.[5] But such statistics fail to convey the real pattern of development, in particular the distorting impact of the Zionists' parallel economy, which much reduced the potential for Arab industrial development. Even by 1942, when war was providing a massive stimulus to development, there were only 1,558 Arab-owned industrial establishments, employing a mere 8,804 workers. In neighbouring Syria (which then included Lebanon) where development followed a more conventional pattern, the industrial workforce in a population about twice that of Palestine was over 200,000.[6]

The politics of resistance

Political life was controlled by the landowning class. A system of patron-client relationships gave landowners influence which extended to the level of the individual household; within this system the leading families competed for leadership. The petty concerns of the most powerful landowning groups were reflected at all levels; throughout the 1920s and 1930s the feud between two of the leading families—the Husseinis and the Nashashibis—dominated national politics. Meanwhile the Arab bourgeoisie played a minor role. Restricted by settler capital, it did not have the political weight to challenge the landowning class, as in neighbouring countries.[7]

After the First World War nationalists demanded the integration of Palestine into an independent Syria. This was soon replaced by a nationalism which confronted the unique problems of British occupation and Zionist settlement. Its demands remained essentially the same until the end of the mandate: for the formation of a national government responsible to a parliament which represented all sectors of the population (Muslims, Christians and Jews) and which was independent from Britain; for abolition of the principle of a Jewish 'national home' in Palestine; and for an end to Zionist immigration until an independent government should decide on immigration policy.

These demands received widespread support, especially among peasants dispossessed by Zionist settlement, whose anger was reflected in a series of conferences which articulated rural grievances, and more directly in Arab attacks on Zionist colonies, which began as early as 1921.

The Palestinian national leadership was hopelessly compromised. Its wealthiest members had sold huge areas of land to Zionist organisations, leaving Arab villagers to face eviction, often at the hands of the colonists' militias.[8] At the same time they competed to win British approval, hoping to place themselves in positions of influence, and the leading families used the national movement to further their family feuds.[9] Their feeble, uncoordinated response to both the British and the settlers was an enormous handicap to the national movement. The Arab Executive—formed among members of the leading families—was content to petition the British and to send ineffectual lobbies and delegations. Its conduct only increased frustration among the Arab masses, who faced evictions, homelessness and daily harassment by the British forces, which brutally put down protest demonstrations and attacks on settler communities.

One result was that in 1929 frustrated activists formed the first Palestinian guerrilla group, the Green Hand, which operated in the mountainous north of the country. Within a year it was broken up by massive British police and military action but two years later Shaikh Izz ad-Din al-Qassem began more systematic guerrilla attacks on Zionist settlements through the Ikhwan al-Qassem—the Qassem Brotherhood.

By the early 1930s the country was in ferment. Strikes and protests put the Arab Executive under pressure—to which it responded with conferences which agreed a cautious programme of non-cooperation with the British. But the Executive could not contain the movement from below. It was pressured into supporting demonstrations which violated British regulations and led to clashes with settlers, notably over the question of Jewish pickets against the hiring of Arab labour and the use of Arab products. Repeated clashes showed that the situation had passed beyond its control and in 1934 the Executive dissolved.

In a new effort to control the movement the traditional leadership formed national political parties. These reflected traditional ruling-class rivalries: the Husseinis formed the

Palestine Arab Party; the Nashashibis the National Defence Party. Each drew in those clans and families owing them allegiance through tenancy or which had received favours through the distribution of local offices or other influence.

Set somewhat apart from these organisations, and a handful of other smaller parties established on similar lines, was the Istiqlal (Independence) Party. This attracted members of the bourgeoisie and of the new professional layers; as such, it was far closer to the nationalist organisations which had developed elsewhere in the Arab world, such as Egyptian Wafd, but its influence could not match that of the traditional Palestinian leadership.

After months of bickering the parties (with the exception of the Istiqlal, which distanced itself from the manoeuvring) again presented their demands to the British and were again rebuffed.

The situation now passed out of their control. The Qassemites had launched a campaign of guerrilla warfare that targeted Zionist settlements. Unlike the Green Hand, which was a spontaneous, ill-directed group operating through bandit-like attacks, the Ikhwan al-Qassem had an ideology which drew mainly on Islamic ideals. In the late 1920s al-Qassem had been president of the Haifa Muslim Society and had used his position to organise among educated youth and among the large numbers of dispossessed peasantry congregating near the city. He argued for clandestine organisation which would train cadres capable of leading a peasant revolt.[10] Al-Qassem's campaign lasted only a few days: in November 1935 he was killed in a gun battle with British police. But his followers continued to organise and in April 1936 their attack on a group of Jews, followed by revenge killings and a provocative Zionist demonstration, began an Arab mobilisation which precipitated the general strike.[11]

The General Strike

The idea of a 'general strike'—mass national mobilisation against the colonial authorities—had been stimulated by a recent seven-week mobilisation in Syria which had forced concessions from the French and by similar successes by the Wafd in Egypt. It was taken up by young activists in Jaffa and Nablus who issued a strike call, soon answered by almost every town in Palestine, and 'national committees' were set up throughout the country to coordinate action. For the first time the traditional leadership moved speedily: anxious to avoid losing all influence they established an Arab Higher Committee headed by Hajj Amin al-Husseini which attempted to coordinate the complex of local groups which had taken the initiative.

Trade unions, Muslim and Christian associations, women's committees, boy scout groups and all manner of cultural associations organised activity under the umbrella of the national committees. These met to agree a programme of civil disobedience, nonpayment of taxes and a halt to municipal government activity. Most Arab businesses and almost all Arab-run transport came to a halt.

Agricultural work continued in order to feed both rural and urban populations and food distribution centres were established in the towns. Finance came from both the urban bourgeoisie, the landowners and from *waqf* (religious endowments). Thomas Hodgkin, a British official working for the mandate authorities, described the movement:

> The strike is a spontaneous movement which has the support of almost all sections of the Arab people, the natural response to the [British] government's continued frustration of peaceful efforts of the Arabs towards independence. Its character is plain from its origin. It started as a movement from below, not from above, and it has been kept alive by pressure from below.[12]

The British response included demolishing a large section of Jaffa, imposing collective punishments and detaining large numbers of Arabs without trial.

Hundreds of men now flocked to join guerrilla bands that had moved into the mountains and begun hit-and-run attacks on the British. The British High Commissioner described the country as being 'in a state of incipient revolution' with 'little security or control of lawless elements outside principal towns, main roads and railways'.[13]

The Syrian nationalist Fawzi al-Qawuqji moved into Palestine in August, leading a band of Syrians, Iraqis and Palestinians which fought the British in the north of the country.[14] At this point there were an estimated 5,000 guerrillas in the mountains. They derailed trains, dynamited roads, sabotaged the

Iraq Petroleum Company's pipeline, ambushed British military convoys, and attacked Jewish settlements.[15]

The British stepped up repression but were unable to end the strike. Their problems were eventually eased by the Arab Higher Committee, which in October suggested to the rulers of neighbouring countries that they issue an appeal which would assist the committee to rein in the movement. The kings obliged and the committee called off the mobilisation 'as a submission to the will of their majesties and highnesses'.[16] The fighters disbanded and returned to their villages.

The national mobilisation had fractured along class lines. The ruling families' fear of losing income (especially from the threat to the citrus harvest) and of losing government payments and privileges had held back the movement from the beginning. In addition, the success of workers and of the peasant guerrillas in organising independently of the Arab Higher Committee made the movement a political threat to the traditional leadership as much as to the British. Hajj Amin al-Husseini took an ambivalent attitude towards the armed struggle, while the Nashashibis refused to support such a strategy on the grounds that armed actions might be directed towards themselves.

According to the Arab historian George Antonius their fears were well grounded, for rank-and-file participants saw the movement as a challenge to the corruption and hypocrisy of the landowning class:

> Far from being engineered by the leaders, the revolt is in a very marked way a challenge to their authority and an indictment of their methods. The rebel chiefs lay the blame for the present plight of the peasantry on those Arab landowners who have sold their land, and they accuse the leaders of culpable neglect for failing to prevent the sales... and their anger and violence are as much directed against Arab landowners and brokers who have facilitated the sales as against the mandatory power under whose aegis the transactions have taken place.[17]

Hodgkin, who had observed the conduct of the traditional leadership, wrote:

> It would be foolish to pretend that the members of the Higher

Committee are disinterested angels. Several of them would probably be willing to sell the strike, betray their followers and compromise with the government if they had the chance: the same is true of many of the local leaders. But they have had no chance. They are now being carried on the backs of the exasperated Arab people, who are determined that this struggle shall go on until either the Arabs get satisfaction from the government or are broken by the government.[18]

The enthusiasm of the bourgeoisie and the professionals, largely expressed through the Istiqlal, had waned when the movement passed beyond their influence. Workers, most of who took part in sustained strike action, and peasants, fighting in the countryside, wished to continue the struggle but lacked effective political organisation. The traditional leadership thus regained control, an outcome always likely in a movement in which no stable political current opposed them.

The Revolt goes on

But the end of the strike did not bring an end to the Revolt. In July 1937 the British published their proposals for partition, incensing the mass of Arabs. Members of the Arab Higher Committee were exiled and in the absence of a formal leadership activists again took matters into their own hands. Guerrilla attacks restarted and soon the countryside was under the control of armed bands. Strikes closed major towns such as Ramallah, Bethlehem and Nablus and the British evacuated Beersheba and had to fight a five-day battle to recapture the Old City of Jerusalem.

The British general officer commanding Palestine reported that 'the situation was such that civil administration and control of the country was, to all practical purposes, non-existent.'[19] The movement had again developed a dynamic which carried it well beyond the level of national demands. Landowners came under threat from armed peasants and prominent figures associated with the Zionists and the British were assassinated. According to Bauer many of the feudal bosses fled, 'practically disintegrating as a class'.[20]

The British brought in further reinforcements until there were 30,000 troops in the country. They initiated a new wave of repression, hanging guerrilla fighters, detaining hundreds without trial in concentration camps, imposing collective punishments, and bombing insurgent villages. Still they could not crush the movement and turned increasingly to the Zionist militias, both official and clandestine.[21] By the summer of 1938, between 3,000 and 5,000 Palestinians had been killed and thousands injured.

Under intense military pressure and still lacking any form of independent political organisation, the movement gradually petered out.

By 1939 Palestine was again under full British control and the mandate authorities had resumed relations with the traditional leaders. The Husseinis and Nashashibis (who had renewed their feud, which again dominated national politics) occupied positions of formal leadership; meanwhile hundreds of rank and file activists remained in prison. The combined action of the British and the Zionists had destroyed the anti-colonial movement.

The problem of leadership

The Revolt of 1936-39 faced the difficulty of confronting both imperialist forces and the settler community. The pattern of economic development meant that bourgeois nationalism was weak and that the landowning class, incapable even of articulating demands for national independence, played a dominant role. The influence of the landowning families reached far into the countryside; their quarrels were reflected at a local level, further weakening an already fragmented peasant society. The Arab working class was small and existed in the shadow of the more developed Zionist industrial sector.

Yet both town and countryside showed an impressive level of resistance. Why did they not produce a political current capable of providing an alternative to the traditional leaders or bourgeois nationalism?

One explanation lies in the conduct of the left. The only organisation which had formally internationalist principles and therefore organised among both Arabs and Jews was the Palestine Communist Party (PCP). The party had been formed in 1923 on the basis of splits from the left-Zionist Jewish Socialist Workers Party (known by the Hebrew acronym MOPSI). It had an exclusively Jewish membership.[22] It was recognised by the Communist International in 1924.

During the mid-1920s the PCP operated almost exclusively among Jews: its leadership argued that the development of capitalism in Palestine was advancing most quickly in the settler community and that possibilities for change lay mainly among Jewish workers. Although it formally identified imperialism as the principal enemy, the party effectively ignored the Comintern's insistence that the experience of British occupation and the colonial character of Zionism would produce an Arab national mass movement.

The party had not absorbed the approach to anti-colonial struggles adopted by the Communist International in 1920. The 'Theses on the National and Colonial Questions', drafted by Lenin, had anticipated continuing struggles in the countries dominated by the imperial powers. Here, Lenin maintained, anti-colonial movements would emerge which, although under the influence of bourgeois and petit-bourgeois ideas, had the potential to threaten imperial control in the countries concerned and to destabilise the wider imperialist system. Marxists should back such movements, Lenin argued, without giving them a 'communist colouring' and without surrendering working-class independence of the movement or independent communist organisation.[23]

Despite strong pressure from the Comintern Executive throughout the 1920s to move 'out of the Jewish ghetto' and organise among the Arab population, the party made slow progress. By 1929, when it produced its first regular Arabic publication, it had only a handful of Arab members.[24]

The PCP was ill-prepared for the Arab resistance movement which began to emerge in 1929. Its leadership took a schizophrenic approach. On the one hand it viewed the strikes and demonstrations as 'a general Arab uprising' and even 'an insurrectionary movement'. On the other hand it declared them to be a 'pogrom' instigated by reactionary Arab leaders who argued for *jihad* (holy war) against the Jews.[25] The Comintern rebuked the party for its confusion, characterising the events as 'an anti-imperialist peasant revolution'.[26]

But the Comintern, now under Stalinist leadership, had entered a phase in which it too distorted the real character of events. In its 'Third Period' it massively overestimated revolutionary possibilities and directed communists worldwide to engage in a ferocious assault on all those tendencies not aligned with Moscow. Reversing the position adopted by the International in 1920, it now declared that it was no longer possible to support national revolutions under bourgeois leadership. Rather, revolutionaries should prepare for the establishment of Soviet power. The PCP was instructed to struggle against the Arab national leadership and to argue for 'workers' and peasants' government'. The Comintern appointed a new party leadership with instructions 'to Arabise the party from top to bottom'.[27]

The PCP accordingly waged a determined campaign against the traditional Arab leadership. The Arab Executive was said to have 'entered upon the road of traitorous competition with the Zionists in bargaining for concessions from British imperialism'.[28] Bourgeois and petit-bourgeois elements such as those grouped around the Istiqlal were characterised as having turned to 'counter-revolution and capitulation'.[29]

The strikes and demonstrations of 1933 seemed to confirm the party's approach: the Arab working class had grown and was becoming more militant and the traditional leadership was no longer capable of exercising control. But the party overestimated the possibilities; in line with the Comintern approach, it characterised the situation as one of 'revolutionary crisis'.[30] At the same time it modified its attitude to the Istiqlal: the organisation was praised as having become 'more revolutionary'—its radical wing was commended as containing 'true anti-imperialists'. This attitude may have been prompted by a realisation that the Arab Executive had, in fact, been forced to offer some formal opposition to the British; it was a hint of further change. The party abandoned calls for workers' and peasants' power and began to put greater emphasis on the Arab national struggle.

A further change in direction dictated by the Comintern now led the PCP into uncritical support of the Arab leadership. In 1935 the Seventh Congress of the Communist International declared that its slogans of 'workers' and peasants' revolution' and 'Soviet government' had been 'ultra-left'.[31] Instead, the Comintern maintained, Communists should adopt a theory of stages in which that of 'national liberation' dictated the formation of an anti-imperialist 'people's front' with 'progressive' elements of the 'national bourgeosie'.[32]

The PCP turned accordingly: it called for 'the abandonment of the policy of class struggle' and emphasised the need to lead the national movement against the British and the Zionists, without giving up the effort to organise Jewish workers.[33]

The party declared that the *yishuv* had a 'fascist' role in an imperialist plot to prevent the advance of the Arab nationalist movement. It called on Arabs to set up 'committees and associations to struggle against the privileges granted to Zionism'[34] and called on 'all patriotic groups' to participate; such groups included 'merchants or artisans, shopkeepers or factory owners, bankers or professional persons'.[35] The PCP's Arab members were urged to work alongside Arab nationalists without differentiating themselves. What was important, the leadership argued, was what the party and the nationalists had in common, not what set them apart.

By the beginning of the general strike in 1936 the PCP had moved behind the traditional Arab leadership. Figures such as Hajj Amin al-Husseini became the focus of attention. Despite the vacillating, self-seeking role of the Arab Higher Committee, the PCP viewed it as the legitimate leadership of the Revolt. From its stand of unflinching opposition to the national movement, the party had swung to a position of uncritical support for the most reactionary elements in the movement.

But another lurch was coming. When the committee called off the strike in October 1936 the PCP declared that it had retreated and denounced the move as a 'shameful betrayal'.[36] Its shift came too late—the party, at least at leadership level, had collapsed into the official Arab leadership.

During the general strike the party's Arab members were instructed to call for a closing of ranks behind the Arab leaders. Jewish members were instructed to support Arab demands and oppose Zionist efforts to profit from the strike. This was a principled position, but the leadership found difficulty winning over the largely Jewish membership. For years it had struggled unsuccessfully to break from left Zionism, a problem complicated by the lurches over the national question and the popular front.

The pressures exerted by the Revolt proved too much: many Jewish members would not support armed actions directed against the Jewish community and several were expelled. In 1937 the leadership created a separate Jewish section, ostensibly to cope with the different conditions in the settler community. In fact the move was an accommodation to left Zionism and was soon expressed in the section's assertion of the 'progressive' elements of Zionism and its agreement on a policy of 'entrism' in Zionist organisations. The Jewish section became a lobby within Left Zionist organisations which were wholly integrated into the settler community. As part of the Zionist movement their members shared an interest in acquiring Arab land and excluding the indigenous population from economic activity.[37]

Once the PCP began to orient on such a current it was soon absorbed. By 1938 the Jewish section had broken its links with the parent organisation; internationalism was dead. The party never recovered.[38]

The PCP was a small organisation: it never had more than a thousand members, most of them Jews.[39] Nevertheless, it operated during a period of mass activity and might have been expected to play a more influential role. That it did not do so was an indicator of the pressure exerted by Zionism within the settler community and of Jewish members' deep suspicion of the Arab population. However, it was also an expression of the distortions and lurches of Stalinism, which disarmed the PCP at crucial moments when the anti-colonial struggle was at its height.

The abandonment of a Marxist approach to the national question at precisely the moment when this issue dominated Palestinian politics was a disaster. It prevented both Arab and Jewish members supporting legitimate national demands without collapsing into the traditional leadership. The misorientation which resulted meant that the party was unable to offer any lead to the large numbers of radicalised Arab workers, peasants and poor who rejected the collaborationists of the ruling families and the feeble opposition of the Istiqlal. Worse, when the PCP split it entirely discredited Marxist opposition to Zionism and the Arab ruling class. Stalinism failed the movement; it was over 30 years before a radical current re-emerged among the Palestinians.[40]

Towards disaster

The resistance movement did not recover from the final assault launched by Britain and the Zionists in 1938-39. Although the British White Paper of 1939 recognised Palestinian fears of

Zionist domination—a reflection of the energy and determination of the Revolt—its main concern was to prepare the ground for the stabilisation of the Palestinian situation in the light of the threat of war. When Britain then 'froze' Palestinian politics it did so under conditions which favoured the Zionists.

By 1939 Britain and the Zionists had spent almost five years engaged in destroying the anti-colonial movement. The Palestinian economy had been seriously weakened, hundreds of villages and towns attacked, thousands of activists imprisoned.

On the other hand the impact on the settler community had been positive: the *yishuv* had benefited economically; its militias had been strengthened; its political cohesion improved. The Second World War further boosted Zionist economic and military capacity, increasing the gap between the two communities. By 1945, when it had become clear that British power in the Middle

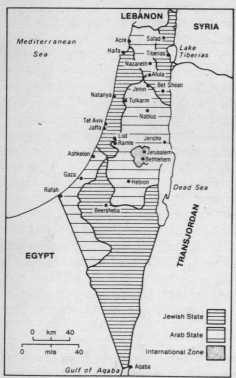

The 1947 United Nations partition plan for Palestine

East was on the wane and that there would be a new battle for possession of Palestine, the Zionists' advantage was immense.

In April 1948 the Zionist militias began to implement a plan of attack designed to drive the Arab population from large areas of Palestine. In 13 carefully prepared phases, Plan Dalet aimed to capture cities and villages allotted to the Arabs in the UN Partition Plan of 1947. It was intended to make unworkable the Palestinian Arab state proposed in the UN plan, to enlarge the proposed Jewish state, and to expel the Arabs from the largest possible area.[41]

The offensive relied for its success on swift attacks on Palestinian communities by well-armed and well-trained Zionist forces. Its architects also anticipated that much of the population could be induced to move by the use of terror. On 10 April 1948 a combined force of the Irgun and Stern groups descended on the village of Deir Yassin near Jerusalem and slaughtered two-thirds

The borders of Israel after the 1948 war

of the 400 inhabitants. Similar attacks by ordinary units of the *haganah* took place at other villages where it was believed that the impact of mass murder would have maximum impact.[42] Under bombardment or direct assault, or in fear of slaughter, hundreds of thousands of Palestinians fled.

The Zionists' strategy of 'cleansing' areas they wished to occupy[43] also owed its success to the lack of any coherent Arab organisation: British repression had ensured that there was no single Palestinian Arab authority, no effective military force and no policy of mass resistance. The only Palestinian military force active in 1948 was the Jaysh al-Jihad al-Muqaddes (Vanguard Army of the Holy War) formed a few months earlier by the Mufti. It had some 5,000 men, about 4 per cent of the number mobilised by Zionist militias, and few modern weapons.[44] A second army formed by Arab nationalists in Damascus, Jaysh al-Inqadh (Arab Liberation Army), included between 3,000 and 4,000 men, of whom 1,500 were Palestinians. Also poorly armed and trained, they remained largely passive in the face of Zionist attacks.[45]

These were the only Arab military forces present during the Zionist offensive. In mid-May 1948, after British withdrawal from Palestine, five Arab states sent some 15,000 men to defend Arab sovereignty.[46] The Arab force was wholly ineffective. Most of the country had already been 'cleansed' of its Palestinian inhabitants—the coastal plain, Eastern and Western Galilee and all the cities except for Jerusalem, Gaza and those of the West Bank were in Zionist hands.

Of a Palestinian Arab population of 1.3 million, almost a million fled their homes. Most sought refuge in the West Bank and Gaza, areas not occupied by the Zionist militias. Others fled to Lebanon, Syria and Transjordan. About 60,000 remained in areas that came under Zionist control.

When the war ended in early 1949 the Zionists, allotted 57 per cent of Palestine under the UN Partition Plan, had occupied 77 per cent of the country.[47] Their triumph was the result of a huge superiority of arms and methods; it also reflected the condition of an indigenous community which had been enfeebled by 30 years of colonial occupation. Israel was established by the territorial gains of 1948—but the Zionist victory had been made possible years before, above all by the destruction of the anti-colonial movement.

Chapter Five

Israel and the US after 1948

THE ZIONIST MOVEMENT in Palestine had always depended on massive capital inflows to sustain the colonisation process; the state of Israel was even more reliant on such support. After 1948 the economy no longer benefited from the presence of a huge British garrison and its manufacturing industry could no longer rely on exporting to British-influenced areas in the region —indeed, Israeli products were boycotted by all Arab states. The new state needed renewed support from abroad—and this it obtained at an unprecedented level.

Between 1949 and 1965 the net savings of the Israeli economy averaged zero; yet the rate of investment over the same period was 20 per cent—vast sums were being received from abroad to sustain economic growth. In 1969 the American economist Oscar Gass, who had been an adviser to the Israeli government, estimated that during the years 1948 to 1968 Israel received $7.5 billion more in imports of goods and services than she exported.[1] This was equivalent to an excess of $2,650 during the 21 years for every person living in Israel.[2] Of the inflow only about 30 per cent went to Israel on conditions which called for a return outflow of dividends, interest or capital. Gass commented that this was 'a circumstance without parallel elsewhere'.[3]

Of the huge Israeli deficit, 70 per cent was covered by 'net unilateral capital transfers'. This consisted of donations raised by the United Jewish Appeal, reparations from the German government for crimes against the Jewish people during the Second World War and grants by the US government. The remaining 30 per cent was made up of long-term capital transfers —Israeli government bonds, loans by other governments and capitalist investment. Of the whole sum, 60 per cent came from world Jewry, 28 per cent from the German government, and 7.4 per cent from from the US government. Of the long-term transfers, 68.7 per cent came from world Jewry, 20.5 per cent from the US government, and 11 per cent from other sources.[4]

The pattern revealed the strong base established by the Zionist movement, particularly in North America—the source of most funds. Zionist organisations' efforts were not matched directly by the US government but were encouraged by tax concessions to contributors. Giving money to Israel was defined as 'charitable'—in effect the US backed the Zionist state by channelling aid from private individuals and organisations. During the 1950s and 1960s, the sums of money raised in this way were sufficient to allow investment in Israel, to integrate hundreds of thousands of new immigrants,[5] and to sustain arms spending at 50 per cent of the Israeli budget—the highest percentage in the world.[6] Israel continued to exist as an outgrowth of imperialism, sustained by funds from the West.

But Zionist leaders were aware that a more formal relationship with the West was necessary if the state was to survive. Israel's rulers understood that in order to develop such a relationship, one that would integrate Israel into Western imperialism's strategic approach to the Middle East, they were required to prove the new state's utility to the US. This was a task that took them almost 20 years to complete.

Israel and the Cold War

In the years after 1948 the US hesitated over its approach to Palestine. Reproducing the debate among British strategists after the First World War it continued to weigh the utility of a reliable ally in the region against the antipathy to the West which might be stimulated among the Arab states—and the damage this might do to US oil interests.

During the Second World War US interest in the Middle East intensified. Its main goal had been to secure its interests in Saudi Arabia: 'to ensure continued access to that country's abundant oil reserves [and] to see that Great Britain did not gain access to them'.[7] It was already clear that the Gulf region contained the bulk of Western oil reserves—the region was a gold mine, one the US dare not let slip into the hands of its rivals, East or West.

In 1945 the State Department declared that there was a political vacuum in the region and that 'unless the United States could fill this vacuum... the Soviet Union would move in and establish hegemony'.[8] Such Soviet control of the Middle East 'would be intolerable to the United States, for the region's mineral resources and transportation and communication routes were vital to the continued economic and social interests of the American people'.[9]

Local and international developments heightened Washington's determination to secure the Gulf. Oil production in the Gulf oilfields increased dramatically: in Kuwait it rose from 0.8 million tonnes in 1946 to 17.2 million tonnes in 1950; over the same period Saudi Arabian production increased from 8.1 million tonnes to 26.1 million tonnes.[10] US oil companies were making huge profits and the oilfields were playing an important role in fuelling the economic boom of the post-war years.

Meanwhile US strategists saw a growing Russian threat. The Soviet Union, they believed, was intent on penetrating the area from the west—through Greece, the Balkans and Turkey—and from the east by extending its influence in Iran, where the workers' movement was strongly influenced by the pro-Moscow Tudeh Party.[11] These twin concerns led to a concerted attempt to make allies of ruling groups throughout the region. Hundreds of millions of dollars were dispensed from a fund which had been established 'for the purpose of furthering the political and strategic interests of the United States in the Middle East'.[12] King Ibn Saud of Saudi Arabia, for example, received $10 million a year.[13]

	Bahrain	Iran	Iraq	Kuwait	Qatar	Saudi Arabia
1938	—	1.1	10.4	4.4	—	—	0.1
1946	1.1	19.5	4.7	0.8	—	8.1
1950	1.5	32.2	6.4	17.2	1.6	26.1
1953	1.5	1.2	27.6	43.0	4.0	40.5
1955	1.5	16.2	33.6	54.8	5.4	47.5

Gulf oil production in millions of tonnes—the 'gold mine' that the United States wanted to secure

In this context Israel was viewed as an ally—but only one among several potential supporters in the region and one with which a pattern of relations had yet to be established. Thus US support began in January 1949 with a US Export-Import Bank loan of $100 million. There was soon more aid—an expression of hardening Cold War attitudes and US fears of intensified threats to its interests, especially in Egypt and Iran. Between 1949 and 1952 Israel received $86.5 million in economic aid—mainly under the Marshall Plan—and $135 million in loans.[14] These were modest amounts by US standards but large sums of money for a country as small as the new state of Israel, which even by 1952 had a population of only 1.4 million.[15]

But Washington was still not ready to gamble on major arms supplies to Israel, which bought most of its arms in the Eastern Bloc, mainly from Czechoslovakia.[16] US-Israeli affairs were therefore friendly but still not close. This was not good enough for Israel's leaders. Their strategy for survival dictated that the state be organically linked with the West, both in order to achieve economic stability and to be militarily dominant in the region.

In the early 1950s the region entered a period of upheaval which gave Israel opportunities to prove its utility to the West.

In 1951 a bourgeois nationalist government under Muhammed Mossadeq came to power in Iran, pledged to nationalise the country's oil resources. When it evicted the Anglo-Iranian Oil Company it dealt 'a shattering blow to British prestige'.[17] For the first time in over 40 years Britain could no longer rely on almost unlimited cheap oil supplies; the Anglo-Iranian Oil Company—'the greatest overseas enterprise in British commerce'[18] had ground to a halt. The US believed it could use British problems to its own advantage; nevertheless, it was appalled at the possible consequences for American oil companies on the other side of the Gulf. There was a sense of panic in Western capitals as the implications of nationalisation sunk in. Israeli leaders were quick to seize their chance. At the height of the Iranian events the newspaper *Ha'aretz*—closely associated with the government—spelt out its hopes for cooperation between Israel and the West:

> The West is none too happy about its relations with states in the Middle East. The feudal regimes there have to make such

concessions to the nationalist movements, which sometimes have a pronounced socialist-leftist colouring, that they become more and more reluctant to supply Britain and the United States with their natural resources and military bases... Therefore, strengthening Israel helps the Western powers maintain equilibrium and stability in the Middle East. Israel is to become the watchdog. There is no fear that Israel will undertake any aggressive policy towards the Arab states when this would explicitly contradict the wishes of the US and Britain. But if for any reason the Western powers should sometimes prefer to close their eyes, Israel could be relied upon to punish one or several neighbouring states whose discourtesy to the West went beyond the bounds of the permissible.[19]

The Zionist movement had seldom spoken out so frankly. The confidence which had come with the establishment of its own state gave the movement a new boldness—a self-assertion that increased when, within months, further upheavals struck the region.

In July 1952 a military coup brought Gamal Abdel Nasser and the Free Officers to power in Egypt. The political complexion of the new regime was at first unclear but soon its commitment to expel Britain's army of occupation and to adopt an 'Arab socialist' reform programme led to fears that the West would lose its key base in the Arab world—and control over the Suez Canal.[20]

Under these circumstances Israel edged closer to the centre of Western concerns. US aid to Israel rose: in 1951 Israel had received a mere $100,000 in grants; the following year, that of the coup in Egypt, this figure rose to $86.4 million.[21]

But still Israel had not convinced the US that it should be 'the watchdog' of the region. Washington favoured the creation of anti-Soviet military pacts which drew in states believed to be strategically placed in relation to Moscow's expansionist intentions. In 1954 the US initiated a treaty linking the states of the 'Northern Tier'—those which shared borders with Russia—and Pakistan and Turkey signed a mutual cooperation agreement. In 1955 Turkey and Iraq were linked in the Baghdad Pact, later joined by Britain, Pakistan and Iran.[22] Israel was not invited to participate.

But Israel was still eager to prove its military credentials and found an opportunity in the Suez conflict of 1956. Egypt's decision to nationalise the canal provoked bitter opposition in Europe, where British prime minister Anthony Eden spoke of his fear that there would be new Arab revolutions which would 'place their united oil resources under the control of a united Arabia led by Egypt and under Russian influence'.[23] Israel was able to persuade Britain and France to engage in joint military action. Its troops quickly invaded Sinai and the Gaza Strip, routing Egyptian forces. British and French planes bombed Egyptian cities and their paratroops took control of the canal itself.

This was too much for the US, which saw the whole affair as a provocation to the Arab states and a potential boost to the nationalist movement. In addition, the US was perturbed by a development which might reduce its own influence in the region. Washington persuaded the three aggressors to withdraw, leaving Britain and France humbled but Israel in a stronger position: it had not achieved all it wanted but had again showed it could defeat an Arab army—it had punished the 'discourtesy' of a state which sought greater independence from the West.

Moshe Dayan, Israel's commander-in-chief, later summed up the outcome of the Suez events: 'Israel's readiness to take to the sword to secure her rights at sea and her safety on land, and the capacity of her army to defeat the Egyptian forces, deterred the Arab rulers in the years that followed...'[24]

The Suez events also illustrated the extent to which Zionism had its own dynamic. Although the movement still depended upon its close relationship with the Western states, it was not simply a tool of US policy; indeed, its 1956 adventure was regarded by Washington as a serious error. As the British had discovered, Zionism was a product of imperialism and flourished under imperial protection. However, the movement had developed a momentum usually associated with colonising states of an earlier imperial age—it sought more territory, greater regional control and a degree of independence which did not always suit its allies.

A bulwark against nationalism

The West, including the US, was now alarmed by the growth of Arab nationalism—which had received a massive boost from the Suez events—and by the increased success of Russia in the region. In 1955 Egypt had concluded an arms agreement with Czechoslovakia, breaking the Western monopoly on arms supplies to Arab states. After Suez Egypt moved closer to Russia and the two made a series of economic and military agreements. The US response was the Eisenhower Doctrine. The US president declared that any Russian intervention in the area would be met by the United States, with force if all else failed. Israel now pressed hard for US arms and though Washington would not agree to supply them directly it did permit Britain and France to start shipments. In 1959 the US made its first military loans to Israel.

America's new strategy in the region was soon under test. In 1958 Egypt and Syria joined in a United Arab Republic, the first move towards Nasser's hoped-for 'pan-Arab union'.[25] A few months later the pro-British monarchy in Iraq was overthrown by a nationalist regime; at the same time, Muslim Arab nationalists in Lebanon led a struggle against the rightist, pro-Western, Christian president, Camille Chamoun.[26] The anticipated wave of nationalism seemed about to engulf the region.

The US now saw Moscow's hand behind every nationalist advance. Fearing above all for its Gulf oilfields, Washington invaded Lebanon with 14,000 marines, declared a nuclear alert and mobilised a massive strike force ready to intervene throughout the region. According to one of its intelligence officers, Joseph Churba:

> Not a few observers saw the lightning-like coup [in Iraq] as an Egyptian-Soviet conspiracy carrying the incipient threat of a comparable coup in Jordan, resulting in Soviet domination of the Middle East. Citing the Eisenhower Doctrine, Lebanon [President Chamoun] issued the call for United States intervention. Accordingly, to preserve the regional balance the first United States Marine units landed unopposed on the shores of Beirut. Simultaneously, a Marine combat unit from Okinawa [in the Pacific] moved into the Persian Gulf. An airborne battle group from Germany and a Composite Air Strike Force (CASF) from the United States arrived at Adana, Turkey. The Strategic Air Command assumed an increased alert status and the Sixth Fleet concentrated in the eastern Mediterranean. In conjunction with these moves, Turkish troops began to concentrate on

Iraq's borders and two days later, on 17 July, British paratroopers landed in Jordan at the invitation of King Hussein.[27]

The intervention succeeded in preventing nationalist advances in Lebanon, and Washington and London considered similar action in Iraq. However, they did not mount another invasion—a reflection of fears that intervention on a far higher level would rebound to the advantage of the nationalists and of Moscow. Churba, one of Washington's Cold War strategists, later declared: 'The American effort to unite the Arabs into an anti-Communist pact came to an end with the downfall of the monarchy in Iraq.'[28]

Washington's strategy now took another turn: superpower competition in the region was to be conducted by means of economic competition backed by use of friendly local states. In Churba's words: 'The rules of engagement were now confined to the indirect strategy of undermining the opponent through the instruments of trade, economic and military aid, limited intervention and war by proxy.'[29]

Israeli ambitions to play a wider role fitted this strategy to perfection. Its leaders anticipated that Israel's presence as a Western proxy eager to demonstrate its growing military power would act as a brake on the Arab nationalist regimes. As an appreciative assessment of the Israeli role later put it:

> In the 1960s Israel reduced the ability of Egypt to pursue President Nasser's expansionist efforts in the Arabian Peninsula and the Persian Gulf. This was understood by some of the threatened Arab states and by the Shah of Iran, who regarded Israel as a reliable, if essentially covert, ally in the effort to curb radical Arab expansion in the region.[30]

During this period Israel also played a little-publicised role on behalf of its Western backers by acting as a conduit for Western, mainly US, influence in the Third World. Its role was precisely defined by Arnold Rivkin:

> A free world state wishing to enlarge its assistance flow to Africa might channel some part of it through Israel because of Israel's special qualifications and demonstrated acceptability to many African nations.[31]

Israel's 'acceptability' was said to lie in its image in the Third World of being a state associated neither with East nor West. As such it offered military and technical training, set up joint industrial projects and, most important, channelled aid to regimes which found it difficult to accept such assistance directly from Western imperialist states. Between 1960 and 1967 Israel developed a close relationship with no fewer than 15 African countries, among them states such as the Congo (now Zaire), Ghana, Nigeria and Kenya, which were judged by the US to be of strategic importance.[32] In addition, it forged a close relationship with South Africa, later to prove useful for the channelling of US arms to the apartheid state.[33]

'Watchdog' at last

By performing such roles Israel won steady increases in economic and military aid from the US. During the 1950s American aid averaged $54.5 million a year.[34] Between 1960 and 1966 this increased to an average of $70 million, with the military component taking a larger and larger share.[35] In 1959 military loans to Israel amounted to $400,000; by 1966 the figure had reached $90 million.[36] Among US sales were the first advanced systems Israel had received—Hawk anti-aircraft missiles, described as 'purely defensive weapons' by officials who maintained that the US took an 'even-handed' approach to the region.[37] These were followed by Patton tanks and a range of standard US equipment. Integrating these with substantial supplies from Britain, France and Canada, Israel had been able to build up a considerable arsenal.

By the mid-1960s Israel's armed forces were superior to the combined power of the neighbouring Arab states. But still such firepower had not been tested in a conflict fully endorsed by the West. The opportunity came in 1967.

During the mid-1960s the anti-colonial movement in Yemen had caused major problems for Britain and in Syria the Baathist government had nationalised oil. The West feared further strategic losses, an anxiety the Israelis deepened by picturing a massive Russian threat throughout the Arab world.[38] US arms supplies to Israel again increased, along with exchange of military intelligence. Israel was now openly challenging Egypt and there was a series of border incidents. In 1967, as Israel and Egypt moved towards war, the US put its intelligence-gathering apparatus at Israel's disposal.

According to US diplomat David Nes:

> During the months before the June 1967 hostilities the military intelligence requirements required by Washington from American embassies, the Central Intelligence Agency and the military intelligence staffs in the Middle East were very largely based on Israeli needs, not on American interests.[39]

Nes believed this situation was 'unprecedented'.[40]

The 'Six-Day War' of 1967 was another crushing victory for the Zionist state. Its triumph over the forces of Egypt, Syria and Jordan was complete. Arab nationalism was humiliated and Nasser even resigned as Egypt's president (he soon withdrew the

Year	Total US aid	US aid to Israel	Year	Total US aid	US aid to Israel
1948	3,017	—	1966	6,989	126.8
1949	8,267	—	1967	6,440	13.1
1950	4,850	—	1968	6,894	76.8
1951	4,380	0.1	1969	6,791	121.7
1952	3,839	86.4	1970	6,787	71.1
1953	6,496	73.6	1971	8,078	600.8
1954	5,793	74.7	1972	9,243	404.2
1955	4,864	52.7	1973	9,875	467.3
1956	5,402	50.8	1974	8,978	2,570.7
1957	4,976	40.9	1975	7,239	693.1
1958	4,832	61.2	1976	6,413	2,229.4
1959	4,954	50.3	1977	7,784	1,757.0
1960	4,804	55.7	1978	9,014	1,811.8
1961	4,737	48.1	1979	13,845	4,815.1
1962	7,034	83.9	1980	9,694	1,811.0
1963	7,314	76.7	1981	10,549	2,189.0
1964	5,215	37.0	1982	12,076	2,219.0
1965	5,310	61.7	1983	12,744	2,497.5

US aid to Israel in millions of dollars

resignation). The West was appreciative: there were no reservations about Israeli action such as those which had followed the Suez events. In Britain, **The Economist** declared: 'It is not only Israel's chestnuts which have been drawn out of the fire; it is those of Britain and America as well...'[41] In the US the mood was captured by the **Los Angeles Times**: in a special publication on the war it applauded Israel for doing what the US could not:

> Unlike Vietnam, it was a short, decisive and brilliantly fought war. Unlike Vietnam it did not rend this country in two and sorely trouble the conscience of so many Americans.[42]

The Vietnam war had limited US effectiveness in the Middle East, argued the **Los Angeles Times**, and other powers such as Britain and France 'had no zest for intervention'.[43] Under these circumstances Israel had acted as if it represented America's best interests, succeeding militarily without involving Washington in a potentially costly confrontation.

The hesistant tone of American pronouncements in the 1950s—when US policy was conducted with one eye on the Arab response—was gone. In 1969 the then minority leader of the House of Representatives (later president) Gerald Ford declared: 'I firmly believe that the fate of Israel is linked to the national security interests of the United States. I cannot therefore conceive of a situation in which the US Administration will sell Israel down the Nile.'[44]

Israel was now identified with US interests—it had succeeded in making itself the 'watchdog'; it was to be richly rewarded.

Israeli occupation of the West Bank, Gaza and the Golan Heights, which had been seized from Jordan, Egypt and Syria respectively in the 1967 war, met with US approval. Its military positions in Sinai and along the Suez Canal were regarded as a useful block on Russian activity, as they prevented Soviet ships using the Suez Canal to pass from the Mediterranean to the Indian Ocean. In addition, Israel provided the US with information on Russian military equipment captured from the Arab states and offered advice on design and tactics to be used against Russian arms.[45]

There was soon another opportunity to test Israel as a US proxy. In 1970 King Hussein of Jordan feared that the Palestinian national movement might topple his regime. Via the US he requested American, British and Israeli help. US forces in Europe were put on alert and the US Mediterranean fleet, boosted from two to five carrier task forces, sailed towards Lebanon. Israel and the US agreed that if, as Syria had promised, its forces intervened to aid the Palestinians in Jordan, Israel 'would intervene militarily to save Hussein's regime'.[46] Israeli defence minister Moshe Dayan later recorded how joint US-Israeli action helped protect the Jordanian regime:

> Hussein asked the United States for help. Washington agreed and promptly put her 82nd Airborne Division on full alert, dispatching at the same time a sharp warning to Syria. An Israeli armoured unit was also moved to the northern border close to the battle area. The move did not go unnoticed by the Syrians—nor was it meant to... The Jordanian army attacked the Syrian invasion force, inflicting heavy casualties, and compelled it to retire to Syria.[47]

Bernard Reich comments:

> Israel was able to take actions that the United States could not because of political and military constraints; it thus acted on behalf of the United States in support of King Hussein... There was close coordination between the Israeli embassy in Washington and the White House, as well as at other levels and in other locations. The possibility of Israeli intervention was a factor in the Syrian withdrawal from Jordanian territory, which permitted Hussein's forces to deal effectively with the threat and to terminate the Palestinian role in his kingdom. Israel served its own interests and those of the United States.[48]

Israel was now being viewed by the West as its agent in the Arab world. For aggressive American strategists such as Churba the Zionist state allowed the West to protect its allies among the Arab regimes without having to resort to direct, large-scale military intervention. He argued: 'Ever since its establishment Israel has served as a 'lightning rod' for the oil-rich countries and pro-Western regimes by diverting the attentions and energies of the Arab radicals away from them.'[49] Ten years earlier this had been the view only of Israeli strategists and of a minority of the US intelligence establishment. Now it had become the orthodoxy in Western capitals.

From the late 1960s Israeli requests for arms were answered by massive US exports. There was a leap in military loans: during the 1960s these had averaged $22 million annually—between 1970 and 1974 the figure rose to $445 million.[50] This was made possible by a Defence Procurement Act which gave the US president power to transfer military equipment to Israel 'without total cost limitation'. A leading American politician commented: 'Great Britain, at the height of its struggle with Hitler, never received such a blank cheque.'[51]

Israel began to receive the most sophisticated US weaponry, including the latest aircraft—weaponry that most US allies, including those in NATO, did not possess.[52] The US also provided Israel with technical and political intelligence on how best to use nuclear weaponry. In December 1970 the US newspaper the **Jewish Post** observed: 'The experts who before the Six Day War felt that India would become the next member of the nuclear club now believe that the next member will be Israel.'[53]

By 1972 Israeli prime minister Golda Meir could assert: 'We have reason to assume that the principle of continuous military supply, especially of planes, is a permanent principle in the relations between our two countries.'[54] By 1973, on the eve of the October War, the US had become almost the sole source of supply for the Israeli forces.

Oil and war

American strategists still regarded the area as perplexingly volatile: Britain had been defeated in Aden, on the Western edge of the Arabian Peninsula, and a nationalist regime under Muammar Qaddafi had come to power in Libya. In addition there was a new destabilising factor: the Palestinians had again emerged onto the scene as a political force.

The main concern was the impact of these developments on oil. Although little Middle East oil was used in the US itself, most of its allies were dependent on supplies from the Gulf, where major American oil companies made enormous profits. In 1970 **Business Week** magazine commented:

Only 3 per cent of the oil consumed in the US is from the Middle East but the American military forces in Europe and the Far East are dependent on Middle East and North African supplies. And the sagging US balance of payments is bolstered by more than $1 billion in profits remitted annually by oil companies from operations in the region. Of the free world's proven crude oil reserves of 480 billion barrels, 333 billion, or 70 per cent, are in the Middle East. Libya has another 35 billion—almost as much as the US... which has 39 billion, including Alaska.[55]

Middle East oil was becoming more important. It was relatively cheap to exploit. In 1971 Middle Eastern wells averaged 4,500 barrels per day (b/d); those in the US averaged just 15b/d. Production costs in the Gulf area averaged six cents a barrel; in the US costs averaged $1.75.[56] The huge difference in costs—and in profits—was partly a function of the accessibility of Middle East oil but also reflected the difference in labour costs. Oil workers' trade unions had been broken up in the 1950s and Arab oil workers were paid a fraction of the wages demanded by workers in Texas or Alaska. The Gulf oil industry was more profitable than any other in the world and was making the largest contribution to US earnings abroad.[57]

The situation was becoming more complex for US strategists. For the first time there was an alliance between a 'radical' oil-producing state (Libya) and the states of the Gulf and by 1970

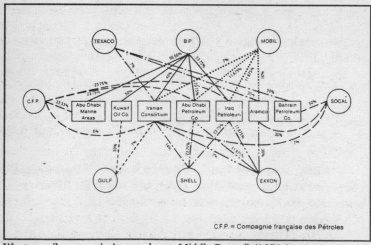

Western oil companies' control over Middle East oil (1970s)

the Libyan regime had led the Organisation of Petroleum-Exporting Countries (OPEC) in a successful effort to raise prices.[58] There was anxiety among some of the oil companies that US support for Israel had become so extensive that it would seriously damage relations with increasingly assertive OPEC members.[59]

Washington's strategists insisted, however, that if oil interests were to be protected it was essential to maintain a strong local ally. The arming of Israel continued and in 1973 reached a new level of intensity. On 6 October 1973 Egyptian troops launched an offensive across the Suez Canal, throwing Israel into a military crisis. Faced with a threat to its closest ally the US reacted speedily. On 13 October President Nixon ordered a massive airlift to assist Israel—all manner of sophisticated weaponry was delivered, enough to resupply Israeli forces and allow a successful counter-attack. It was soon followed by an agreement to supply $2.2 billion of military goods covering every area of Israeli needs.[60]

Israel emerged from the 1973 war shaken but strengthened by Washington's demonstration of support and ready to play a leading part in the US plan for 'peace' in the region. This strategy, masterminded by Henry Kissinger, set out to confirm Israel as the regional superpower, to isolate the Arab states and force them to make peace deals with Tel-Aviv. In the years after the 1973 war US aid to Israel again increased dramatically. In 1973 total American aid was $463 million; the following year it increased over 500 per cent to $2.5 billion, of which $1.5 billion was in military grants—by far the highest sum ever given by the US to an ally.[61] According to Reich:

> The October War inaugurated a period of Israeli dependence on the United States for war material. No other country could provide or was prepared to provide Israel with the vast quantities of modern and sophisticated arms required for war...'[62]

At the same time Israel and the US entered agreements to cooperate in arms production which laid the basis for an Israeli arms industry. Within ten years Israel was able to produce a range of weapons which included jets, tanks, ships and missiles.[63]

US-Israeli deals over this period again changed the status of the Zionist state. It not only became the regional superpower but began to play a global role as a major arms manufacturer in its own right. It channelled arms to US allies in Latin America such as Chile, Argentina, Nicaragua, Honduras and Guatemala, and in the Middle East it forged a closer relationship with Iran and, in Lebanon, with the Christian bloc dominated by the neo-fascist Phalange. Its link with South Africa proved more and more profitable: sales of arms were built up until, by 1980, they accounted to 35 per cent of all Israel arms exports.[64] This much increased Israeli leaders' confidence in their ability to act for the US in a way which benefited both states. As an Israeli minister declared:

> We shall say to the Americans: do not compete with us in Taiwan, South Africa, the Caribbean area... or in other areas where we can sell weapons directly and where you cannot operate in the open. Give us the opportunity to do this and trust us with sales of ammunition and military hardwarae; let Israel act as your agent.[65]

From Tehran to Tel-Aviv

The mid-1970s was a more satisfactory period for US strategists. Despite the threat of upheaval in Lebanon, key areas of concern seemed stable. In Egypt Nasser was dead and Sadat had introduced his pro-Western 'open-door' policy.[66] In the Gulf oil production was rising steadily and even the forcefulness of OPEC, which had increased oil prices many times, had its spin-off— economic development of the Gulf was advancing rapidly, with US companies among the main beneficiaries.

Washington felt more confident about its lesser allies in the region. It was willing to supply arms to its new-found friend in Egypt, to Gulf regimes now awash with petrodollars, and most important, to its old ally Iran under Shah Mohammed Reza Pahlavi. In the mid-1970s arms sales to Iran rose dizzyingly. In 1970 they totalled $113 million. By 1977 this figure had increased to $5.8 billion.[67] The US was backing the Shah as a 'second Israel' in the east of the region, as a guardian of the Gulf who could be relied upon to police the region in the same way that Zionism had patrolled the eastern Mediterranean. But within a few years the Pahlavi regime began to collapse and by 1979 it was gone.

US strategists were horrified; their first reaction was to re-emphasise support for Israel. A few months after the fall of the Shah Ronald Reagan told the **Washington Post:**

> Our own position would be weaker without the political and military assets Israel provides... the fall of Iran [*sic*] has increased Israel's value as perhaps the only true remaining strategic asset in the region on which the United States can truly rely.[68]

Military grants to Israel, which had been running at $500 million in the mid-1970s, rocketed up to $2.7 billion in 1979; total US aid to Israel rose from $1.8 billion in 1978 to $4.8 billion the following year—all was in the form of direct cash transfers, none being tied to specific projects, as was the case for all other countries receiving US backing.[69] And of the $4.8 billion channelled to Israel in 1979 no less than $4 billion consisted of military grants and loans: Israel was being armed to the teeth.[70]

By 1983 the US government's own statistics told a startling story. Since 1948 Washington had dispensed $258 billion of aid worldwide. Of this sum over $25 billion—almost 10 per cent of all US aid—had been directed to Israel.[71] This was reinforced by continued inflows from the international Zionist movement, although direct US aid now dwarfed the sums received from all Zionist organisations.[72] Over 60 per cent of aid had been in military grants and loans, allowing Israel to maintain its forces at a level unmatched anywhere else in the world.[73]

Between 1976 and 1980 Israel's military expenditure *per capita* was an average $1223 each year.[74] This was almost twice that of Russia, more than twice the level of the US, three-and-a-half times that of Britain, and 25 times that of its neighbour Egypt.[75]

Lebanon and after

By the early 1980s US and Israeli policy in the Middle East were scarcely distinguishable. Even the *blitzkreig* invasion of Lebanon in 1982, which caused mass protests in Israel, did not disturb the US administration. According to Ze'ev Schiff and Ehud Ya'ari, Israel's leading reporters on military affairs, news of Israel's intention to enter Lebanon and destroy the Palestinian guerrilla force, risking confrontation with Syria, barely registered in Washington—a reaction taken by the Israeli government to be an endorsement of its proposed course of action.[76] Indeed, the US had much to gain from the defeat of Syria in Lebanon and the further marginalisation of the Palestinian movement.[77]

Only after the massacres of Palestinians in the camps of Sabra and Shatilla did the US voice concern; then its own troops entered Lebanon, ostensibly to 'stabilise' the political situation and help re-establish the Lebanese state apparatus. In fact the US presence helped to legitimise the Israeli occupation of much of the country. In February 1984 Sandro Pertini, the president of Italy—a NATO member and close US ally—demanded US and Israeli withdrawal. He said:

> American Marines have become hostages to Israeli policy. If the United States had the political will to force Israel to withdraw in accordance with UN resolutions 508 and 509 there would be no need for the Marines... Let us speak plainly, the Americans are remaining in Lebanon only to defend Israel, not peace.[78]

When the US eventually withdrew it was a result of casualties suffered in a massive bomb attack by Lebanese guerrillas. The spectre of Vietnam was returning. The Marines were evacuated and Lebanon once more left in the care of Israel.

The Lebanese events illustrated the extent to which Israel was prepared to take its own initiatives. Although the invasion fitted broad US foreign policy needs in the region it had not been planned to serve Washington's interests. After the difficulties encountered during the 1956 Suez invasion Israel had taken care not to abuse its relationship with the US. But by 1982, after 25 years of unhindered aggression in the Middle East, Israel's rulers were brimming with self-confidence. Washington had successfully found a watchdog in the region—but its watchdog was in danger of slipping its chain.

One reaction in the US was the strengthening of the small 'Arabist' lobby, which increasingly saw Israel's conduct as a threat to US economic economic interests in the Arab world, notably in the Gulf.[79]

But financial and military backing for Israel was not affected. In 1983 the General Accounting Office, which supervises US government spending, published a report on American aid to Israel. This spelt out that US aid should be maintained and in particular that non-military support should continue.[80] Accordingly US aid rose again. In 1983 a large part of the Israeli debt to the US, accumulated under the American Foreign Military Sales programme, was retrospectively declared a grant and almost half the year's debt of $1.7 billion was simply 'forgiven'.[81]

By the mid-1980s the figures had taken on an unreal quality. By 1985 Israel was receiving $3.9 billion in grants—30 per cent more than in 1982. The **Christian Science Monitor** calculated that every American family of four was contributing an average of $50 a year, through taxes, to the Zionist state. The population of the US was more than 250 million; that of Israel, including its Arab citizens, was four million.[82]

The export of such massive sums was Washington's guarantee of Israel's survival against external threat; it also guaranteed a massive capacity to strike at those who questioned Israeli rule within the territories under its control. Thus from 1967, when the West Bank and Gaza came under occupation, Israel had new means to impose its will on the Palestinian population. For the next 20 years it was able to suppress opposition in the territories by means of hugely superior force. The US gave Israel the military means to dominate the Arab world—it also provided the mechanism by which over a million people in the Occupied Territories were compelled to accept Zionist rule.

The identity of interests

Since 1967 the US has been an uncritical backer of Israel. Nothing the Zionist state has done—its invasions, occupations, massacres and repeated wars—has brought the relationship into question. Even the invasion of Lebanon in 1982 and the Palestinian *intifada* at its height, met by ferocious Israeli repression, has left US aid unaffected. In January 1988, two months into the Uprising in the West Bank and Gaza, **The Jerusalem Post** could note that the US had not laid down any conditions for its economic aid to Israel and that, as planned, $1.2 billion had been transferred from Washington to the accounts of the Israeli government as part of the year's aid package.[83]

Such an attitude is without parallel in US foreign relations. Despite the warnings of a growing pro-Arab lobby in Washington, the US has refused to use its immense influence over the Zionist state to influence Israeli policy. For 30 years Washington has used aid as a weapon to discipline even its closest allies.[84] Israel has faced no such threats. It remains the keystone of US Middle East policy. Reich summed up Israel's place in this scheme:

> US interests and concerns in the Middle East can be catalogued with substantial agreement, although debate surrounds their priority. Preventing Soviet dominance (and the expansion of Soviet power and influence in the area); assuring the flow of oil at reasonable prices, particularly to US friends and allies; assuring access to regional markets, as a means of recycling the petrodollars earned by the regional states through the sale of oil; and the security and prosperity of Israel are at the core... there is general agreement that Israel is an important interest and that no other state in the Middle East is identified in quite the same way...[85]

According to this view the US does not have to argue the case for each dollar it invests in Israel. The Zionist state plays a role for which no other state in the Middle East is qualified. Among the semi-feudal ruling groups and military dictatorships which make up the majority of Middle East regimes, Israel is a pillar of stability. As long as the Arab regimes remain subject to movements from below which threaten their relations with the

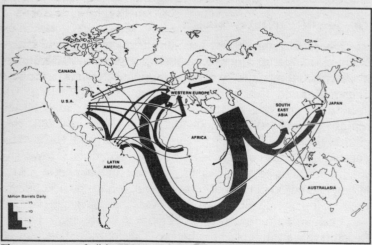

The movement of oil in 1981

West, Israel will remain the centrepiece of US strategy, an ally the US cannot afford to see threatened, for an effective challenge to the Zionist state would bring relations with its other allies into question.

For more strident Cold War analysts Israel has become part of the US, an extension of the West in a distant, hostile region. Churba has argued:

> In this global framework Israel's role is singular. It arises from the unique characteristics of Israeli society and its special link with the United States. The link is viewed as 'organic' regardless of all the imaginable political and economic changes that may intervene. And inasmuch as Israel represents the only secure logistical link in the entire region between Western Europe and Japan, its role as an access point makes it indispensible to any solid Western security structure. From this perspective, American support for a strong Israel can be justified wholly on the grounds of 'national interests'—grounds valid in all circumstances except in the context of a totally isolationist America.[86]

As long as the mineral resources of the Middle East continue to attract the interest of Western imperialism Israel will remain the key element in its strategy for the region and will play a leading role in its global network of alliances. Provided it is still capable of playing a 'watchdog' role, Israel's future is assured.

The Zionist state, a product of imperialism, has been sustained and strengthened by imperialism and integrated into its strategic planning. Any approach to change in the Middle East must confront this fact. To challenge the Israeli state is to confront imperialism.

Chapter Six
The Palestinian diaspora

PALESTINIAN NATIONALISM had been a product of the struggle against Britain and the Zionist movement, the direct confrontation between Palestinian Arab society and imperialism. After 1948 it was shaped by a very different experience—that of life within the Palestinian *diaspora*. The new Palestinian nationalism was a product of the encounter with Arab capital.

The Zionists' military campaigns of 1948 led to the dispersal of the Palestinians. Of a total of approximately 1,300,000 Palestinian Arabs,[1] almost a million were driven from their homes by the Zionist militias, most fleeing to the West Bank and Gaza, and to the neighbouring Arab countries—Lebanon, Syria, Jordan and Egypt. According to figures collected in 1952 the refugees were dispersed as follows:

West Bank (annexed in 1948 by Jordan)	363,689
East Bank (Transjordan)	100,981
Gaza (annexed in 1948 by Egypt)	201,173
Lebanon	100,642
Syria	82,701
Total number of registered refugees	849,186

An unknown number of refugees also fled to Egypt and Iraq; in addition many did not register with the United Nations refugee organisation UNRWA.[2] Some 60,000 Palestinians remained within the area occupied by the Zionists.

By the early 1950s there were some 1.4 million Palestinians, of whom almost a million were displaced persons.[3] The refugees were mainly housed in over 80 camps in the neighbouring 'host' countries, where they became the responsibility of the United Nations Relief and Works Agency (UNRWA), which supplied food and shelter. At this stage the Palestinian issue was viewed, especially in the West, as a question of welfare and the refugees as constituting an undifferentiated poverty-stricken mass.[4] However, while most inhabitants of the camps were desperately poor, the *diaspora* as a whole was composed of Palestinians of all classes—it reflected the class character of pre-1948 Palestine. In addition, the *diaspora* was soon shaped by the class nature of the societies into which the refugees had been driven.

Arab Palestine had been a highly-structured society and its

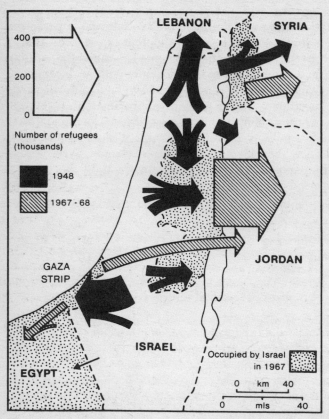

The movement of Palestinian refugees after the wars of 1948 and 1967

classes coped very differently with the experience of expulsion. The landowners had mixed fortunes. Israel paid no compensation for the huge areas of land that had been seized and many families lost all their property, though most had some transferrable assets and few ended up in the camps. Landowners from the West Bank, annexed by Jordan in 1948, retained their land, and many profited from the effects of the expulsion. They benefited from the drop in labour costs which resulted from the influx of dispossessed and from the eagerness of those with capital to invest in property.[5]

The bourgeoisie was insulated from the worst effects of the expulsion. Palestinian merchants, bankers and entrepreneurs had well-established links to neighbouring countries and were quick to transfer movable assets. Some 44.7 million Palestinian pounds, $19 million at 1945 exchange rates—or about 16 per cent of total non-Jewish capital in Palestine—was in the form of assets that could be transferred abroad. So great was the volume of bank transfers to Jordan, for example, that the money supply there doubled during the early 1950s.[6] Their ability to shift capital allowed Palestinian businessmen to leave their homes for nearby Arab capitals before the final Zionist offensives were under way and many were soon in business in the Arab countries, helped by a successful effort to retrieve capital frozen in banks seized by the Zionists.[7]

Pre-1948 Palestine had produced a significant layer of professionals; this new petit bourgeoisie was less well insulated from the effects of expulsion than the bourgeoisie and many of its members ended up in the camps. However, most found employment in the host countries or were soon able to move to other Arab countries where their skills were in demand. Skilled manual workers were also consigned to the camps but many soon found a way out. For some years in the late 1940s and early 1950s they found employment in the Gulf states, mainly in the oil industry.[8]

For the bulk of the population there was no escape. The 80 per cent of registered refugees described by UNRWA as 'former peasants, unskilled workers and their dependents'[9] had little prospect of relief from life in the camps. Their treatment by the rulers of the neighbouring countries reflected the preoccupations of the Arab regimes. All had viewed the conflict in Palestine with complete cynicism; they had offered the Palestinian population no assistance until, following the Zionist offensive, their forces entered Palestine to occupy the territory that remained under Arab control. Avi Plascov accurately describes their attitude and its implications for the mass of Palestinians:

> Regardless of all public or secret resolutions, the Arab countries had no intention of either granting the Palestinians any decisive role in the... war or any say in the political fate of Palestine... The Palestinians were doomed to be crushed beneath the cumulative pressure of the pragmatic interests of particular Arab rulers, British interests, their own disunity and weakness, and the outcome of the war.[10]

The Arab rulers viewed the army of Palestinian poor—almost 800,000 people—as unwelcome visitors. In each of the host countries the regime's main concern was to consolidate its control over a turbulent population stimulated by the anti-colonial movements and by the Palestine issue. The presence of large numbers of impoverished and embittered Palestinians was seen as a dangerous destabilising factor and the camp dwellers were treated accordingly.

There was formal and informal discrimination against Palestinians from the beginning. In Syria, Palestinians were granted equal rights with Syrian citizens, though in practice it was difficult for the poor to find employment and wages and conditions were always worse than for Syrians. In Jordan, where the flood of refugees had created a huge pool of unemployed, Palestinians with education or technical skills were recruited to government service but the poor remained without jobs or income except for UNRWA hand-outs. In Lebanon discrimination was formalised: Palestinians were excluded from all state employment and in practice from most private employment.[11]

The camp populations also suffered political repression. In Lebanon the camps were patrolled by the notorious *Deuxième Bureau*, while in Jordan the police and the army kept the camps under close surveillance and ruthlessly put down demonstrations of discontent.[12]

The effect of the expulsion was to exaggerate class differences among the Palestinians. In 1948 the fate of the capitalist and that of the landless peasant were quite different; in subsequent years these differences were sharpened by the unequal effects of economic discrimination and political repression. While all Palestinians lacked full rights (except, in theory, in Syria), those with capital or with skills to sell were able to escape the camps and sidestep the worst discrimination. The bourgeoisie and petit bourgeoisie were rapidly absorbed into the Arab economies. Meanwhile the majority, the poor, faced unemployment, repression and an apparently hopeless future.

The new bourgeoisie

For the next 20 years the economic development of the Arab world encouraged a process of migration by Palestinians from the host countries—a 'second *diaspora*'. By 1970 almost 200,000 Palestinians were living in the Gulf states and Libya; by 1980 this figure had reached 554,000, with the largest concentrations in Kuwait (278,000) and Saudi Arabia (127,000). Of a total Palestinian population estimated, by 1980, to number 4.5 million, 12.6 per cent were living in the Gulf and North Africa.[13]

Almost without exception this migrant population was bourgeois and petit bourgeois in character. However, for a few years in the early 1950s skilled workers and some labourers found employment in the Gulf states. By 1953 there were 3,000 Palestinians employed by the Arabian-American Oil Company (Aramco) in Saudi Arabia and large numbers worked in the oilfields, construction and transport in Kuwait and Qatar. They played the leading role in establishing trade unions, presenting the Saudis and the US-controlled Aramco with their first taste of working-class power—a reflection of the rapid growth of the working class in the Gulf but also of the highly politicised character of the Palestinian workforce.

In 1953 Palestinians led a major strike against Aramco, demanding union recognition, an improvement in housing conditions and fairer distribution of oil revenues. Thirteen thousand workers went on strike, the government sent in troops and hundreds were arrested. However, the strikers held out for three weeks and the oilfields were paralysed. Although union recognition was not won there were improvements in wages and conditions. In 1954, 160 Palestinian militants were deported from Saudi Arabia, another 100 expelled in 1955 for 'unauthorised political activity' and activists faced repression in Kuwait, Bahrain and Qatar, where there had been smaller-scale disputes.[14]

In 1956 Palestinians also led strikes and demonstrations in Saudi Arabia against the invasion of Suez. The army again intervened, many strikers were arrested and foreign workers were deported. A royal decree was then issued banning all strikes and work stoppages and a ban imposed on the entry of Palestinian workers to the Gulf states.[15] By the late 1950s only those Palestinians with capital or professional qualifications were admitted. It was not until well into the 1970s that Palestinian workers were again accepted in the Gulf, though under strict controls.[16]

The Palestinian communities that developed in the Gulf states from the late 1940s consisted mainly of businessmen who moved in to exploit the rapid growth of the oil-fed economies, and the professionals, technicians and administrators who served the

Country	Total	Percentage Local Population	Percentage Total
Israel and occupied territories	1,834,800	47.0	41.2
Israel	550,800	14.0	—
West Bank	833,000	—	—
Gaza	451,000	—	—
Jordan	1,148,334	53.3	25.8
Lebanon	358,207	11.5	8.0
Syria	222,525	2.5	5.0
Iraq	20,604	0.2	0.5
Egypt	45,605	0.1	1.0
Libya	23,759	0.7	0.5
Saudi Arabia	136,779	1.6	3.0
Kuwait	299,710	22.0	6.7
UAE	36,504	3.5	0.8
Bahrain	2,100	0.6	—
Qatar	24,223	9.7	0.5
Oman	50,706	6.0	1.1
United States	104,856	—	2.3
Other	140,116	—	3.1
Total	4,448,838		

The distribution of Palestinians in 1982

Gulf regimes. The sophistication of the Palestinian bourgeoisie placed it in a prominent position in countries such as Kuwait and Saudi Arabia, where genuine national bourgeois classes, as opposed to networks of trading families, did not begin to emerge until the 1970s. Palestinians were particularly active in trade, construction and finance and many became extremely wealthy as the oil boom began in the 1960s. As one journalist sympathetic to the Palestinians asked:

> Are there 100 or 300 Palestinian millionaires in the Gulf? Estimates vary, but there is no doubt that most electronics companies belong to them, and they include merchants, entrepreneurs, bankers and world-class wheeler-dealers.[17]

At the same time educated Palestinians became almost indispensable to the Gulf regimes. The kingdoms and emirates that were emerging from backwardness and colonial domination lacked a cadre of specialists to run the economy and the apparatus of state. There were few volunteers from the more developed Arab states willing to go to the bleak cities of the Gulf but Palestinians had little alternative and were considered especially appropriate in former British colonies as many spoke English.

In Saudi Arabia Palestinians ran whole government departments and for many years staffed the country's embassies abroad. In Kuwait it was estimated that as recently as 1982, 25 per cent of all state employees and 30 per cent of teachers were Palestinians.[18] Even in the United Arab Emirates (UAE), where the Palestinian community was relatively small, Palestinians dominated the top layers of the legal profession and the media.[19] According to one analysis of employment in the Gulf, even by the mid-1970s, 'were the Palestinians to be forced to leave, the media would cease to function'.[20]

This new petit bourgeoisie accumulated capital in its own right and many Palestinians who had originally moved to the Gulf to exploit their education established businesses there or in the host countries where their families often still lived. In these countries too, the economies had begun to grow, partly as a result of the oil boom and the import of capital from migrants, notably from the Palestinians themselves.

By the 1960s a new layer of Palestinian capitalists had emerged in the Arab countries, playing a role out of all proportion to the Palestinians' numerical significance. Palestinian companies, or companies with large Palestinian holdings, were prominent throughout the region. Some of these were huge organisations which were household names: Intra Bank, owned by Yusif Baidas, became the largest financial institution in Lebanon and had holdings in London, Paris and New York.[21] Arab Bank, founded by Abd al-Halim Shuman in Palestine in the 1930s, managed to transfer its operations to Jordan in 1948 and expanded to become one of the largest financial institutions in the Middle East, with operations in Europe and Africa.

In Kuwait, the Al Hani construction company played a leading role in the building boom of the 1960s and 1970s. The Contracting and Trading Company (CAT) and the Consolidated Contractors Company (CCC) also specialised in Gulf construction and later worked in Africa and Asia. Palestinians also had major holdings in Middle East Airlines and the Arabia Insurance Company.[22] There were hundreds of smaller companies.

The effect of the second *diaspora* had been to further emphasise Palestinian class differences. In the 20 years following the expulsion the Palestinian bourgeoisie had re-organised and extended pre-1948 capital, while sections of the petit bourgeoisie had participated successfully in the general growth of Arab capitalism. For these sections of Palestinian society—perhaps 15 per cent of the whole Palestinian population—there was the possibility of integration into the regional economy—of employment, education, travel and sometimes considerable wealth. While they were seldom granted citizenship of Arab states and lacked the political power to which some had been accustomed in pre-1948 Palestine, they nevertheless enjoyed a lifestyle far beyond the reach of most of their fellow Palestinians.

For the majority of the Palestinian poor there were no escape routes: permanent employment was difficult; education a privilege; travel almost impossible. While the Zionist movement had not discriminated between the Palestinians when it drove them from their country, Arab society did. The Palestinian bourgeoisie and petit bourgeoisie shared much with the Arab ruling classes: the Palestinian poor, in contrast, shared the fate of the regimes' victims—the Arab workers and peasants.

By the 1960s a huge gulf had opened up between the Palestinian bourgeoisie and the masses of the camps. The bourgeoisie was fully integrated into Arab capitalism and closely aligned with the local ruling groups, differing from them in only one major respect: it did not enjoy control over property in its own territory and did not direct its own national political apparatus. It did not operate within the framework created by all rising capitalist classes. In short, it lacked a state of its own.

Al-Fatah

When a Palestinian mass movement re-emerged in the mid-1960s its leadership was not concerned with what had become the major feature of Palestinian life in the years since the expulsion—the huge difference between the wealthy minority and the masses of the camps. The main current of the new movement called itself the Palestinian Liberation Movement, or al-Fatah. (It derived the shorter name by reversing the initials of its full title: al-Harakat al-Tahrir al-Filastini. Al-Fatah also means 'Opening' or 'Conquest', and is the title of the 48th *sura* of the Koran.)

Fatah emphasised the common interests of the Palestinians, whom it saw as a national group seeking 'liberation'—the return of the homeland. Fatah's message was simple: that all Palestinians should join the struggle to regain their rights and that all efforts should be directed against the common enemy, Zionism. Palestinians should thus sink their class differences in a united movement.

The movement's main task, said Fatah, was to launch 'mass revolutionary violence' against Israel. But in doing so it should avoid any threat to the Arab regimes in those countries where Palestinians were active. In accordance with this principle of 'non-interference' it called on Palestinians not only to sink class differences among fellow Palestinians, but also their differences with the Arab rulers. Fatah wanted a national movement capable of securing a liberated Palestine which could then be reintegrated into the Arab world. It wanted a movement which would win for the Palestinians a conventional national state in which Fatah would direct affairs. In this sense Fatah set out to secure the interests of the Palestinian bourgeoisie.

Fatah developed within the privileged layers of the *diaspora* and many of its assumptions reflected the aims and aspirations of a growing class seeking to assert its political independence. The organisation had its origins in the early 1950s among a group of students in Cairo, most of whom were the sons of relatively prosperous Palestinian families. Its most prominent member, Yasser Arafat, was related to the Husseinis, the most powerful landowning family in pre-1948 Palestine.[23] Other early Fatah members were sons of merchants and small businessmen; almost all were from families—'generally solid Sunni Muslim bourgeois'[24]— able to offer their sons university education.

Several of Fatah's founding members had spent the years since 1948 attempting to organise guerrilla resistance to Israel from Egyptian territory with the aim of raising the level of conflict to a point at which Egypt and the Arab states would be drawn into war. In such a confrontation, the students believed, the Arabs would emerge victorious and would restore Palestine to its former inhabitants. The group, which included future PLO leaders such as Arafat, Salah Khalaf (Abu Iyad) and Khalil al-Wazir (Abu Jihad), had some connections with the fundamentalist Muslim Brotherhood—most of its influences were from the right.[25] Its strategy reflected the Palestinians' weakness. The students were the only current among the Palestinians—apart from cells of the Muslim Brotherhood—to attempt to continue the struggle. In the absence of a Palestinian movement they looked towards non-Palestinian forces to secure the return of Palestine—but their assumptions about the character of national struggle caused them to look automatically towards the Arab ruling classes.

The students' approach also revealed a form of doublethink which was to become a serious contradiction in Fatah's strategy: although they were suspicious of the Arab regimes and condemned their role in the 1930s and during the 1948 events,[26] they relied upon the Arab rulers to repossess Palestine on behalf of its people.

From Cairo the group moved to Kuwait where, in 1959, Fatah was founded. Its members' education had allowed them to sell their skills in the Gulf and several became wealthy, and influential within the Palestinian community. Salah Khalaf commented:

It is not a coincidence that Fatah was founded in Kuwait. Many of us had good positions in the country: Yasir Arafat was a respected engineer in the Ministry of Public Works, Faruq al-Qaddumi (Abu Lutuf) headed a department at the Ministry of Public Health, Khalid al-Hassan and Abd al-Muhsin al-Qattan were part of the high government administration, Khalil Ibrahim al-Wazir (Abu Jihad) and I were teachers in secondary schools.[27]

In fact Arafat established his own contracting business and made large sums of money. Another leading member of Fatah, Khalid al-Hassan, has commented that if Arafat had stayed in business he would have become a multi-millionaire.[28] Khalid al-Hassan himself became chief executive of Kuwait municipality, one of the most powerful positions occupied by a Palestinian working for the Gulf regimes. As Salah Khalaf said: 'Compared to Palestinians living in other Arab countries, we were privileged.'[29]

But wealth was not enough to satisfy the young nationalists. Like all Palestinians they were stateless; they had neither a territory of their own nor a political system which gave them even limited participatory rights. Khalaf observed:

> Although we had travel documents delivered by this or that Arab state, we were obliged to obtain exit and entrance visas which were granted sparingly and only after repeated and time-consuming application. No matter that we were Egyptian, Syrian, Jordanian or Lebanese subjects, the authorities of our adopted countries continued to treat us like foreigners, and suspicious ones at that.[30]

Like other young Palestinians in the Gulf states, the Fatah activists were ambitious young professionals, materially well-off but intensely frustrated by their marginal social and political position. The experience of being part of the Arab economy, yet peripheral to the Arab political system, dominated their approach to politics and shaped their attitude to the Palestinian struggle. It was during the group's period of consolidation in Kuwait that it put forward principles which included the assertions that Palestinian liberation would involve a national struggle and the use of 'mass revolutionary violence' but this should be limited by a strict policy of non-interference in the affairs of the Arab states.

The policy of 'non-interference', which remained at the core of the group's ideas, was a product of the experience of the Palestinian bourgeoisie and petit bourgeoisie in the *diaspora*. The community within which Fatah operated owed its existence to the development of the local economy and the growing apparatus of state. Nationalist activity was possible precisely because of the status of the new Palestinian communities, which had their own stake in the local economy. As Yasser Arafat later recorded, the first publication of the new group was financed from his own pocket—his circumstances, he said, had been 'convenient'[31]—a result of the large sums he had been able to accumulate in Kuwait.

Arafat and his friends were not concerned with the fate of the Palestinian worker activists who in the mid-1950s had been expelled for leading strikes; their preoccupation was with a form of Palestinian nationalism compatible with the stability of the states within which they were beginning their activity. Their principles, which were to guide a whole new generation of nationalists, were a reflection of the dependence of the Palestinian bourgeoisie and petit bourgeoisie upon Arab capitalism. A former British diplomat in the Gulf described the situation bluntly:

> The presence of thousands of Palestinians in the Gulf has alarmed some [Western] observers who fear that their commitment to Palestine will unsettle the traditional systems in the Gulf. But like the majority of expatriates they are there for the money so they have an interest in maintaining and supporting the regimes that pay them.[32]

Fatah's determination to initiate a struggle for the liberation of Palestine meant that the group had taken a large step forward from the collaborationist politics of the earlier generation of nationalists. But it had already reproduced an important element of the earlier nationalists' position: like them Fatah pledged not to disrupt the structures of imperialism. It did not seek to threaten the *status quo* but was a Palestinian adaptation to it.

The Arab Left

Fatah's strategy was also a response to the failures of Arab nationalism and to the deficiencies of the Arab left.

The rulers of the Arab states surrounding Palestine had shown only cynicism in using the conflict with the Zionist movement to further their own ambitions. In the years after 1948 they offered nothing to a Palestinian population stunned by *al-nakba*—the disaster—and attempting to come to terms with a new oppression: that of the 'host' states themselves. But from the early 1950s the growth of Arab nationalism brought new hope for the Palestinian masses.

In 1952 Nasser had come to power in Egypt. He rapidly achieved popularity throughout the Arab world by his expulsion of British forces and the defiant approach which had led up to the Suez events of 1956. The nationalist current was further boosted by the 1958 coup in Iraq which brought General Qassem to power and by the nationalist upsurge that same year in Lebanon.

The new ruling groups declared themselves committed to 'revolution', 'Arab unity', 'anti-imperialist' struggle, and to a struggle on behalf of the Palestinians, but in each country they were in fact preoccupied by the effort to develop a new state capitalism, with all its implications for domestic politics, including the establishment of a deeply repressive internal regime. By the early 1960s Palestinian hopes had turned to disillusion. Ten years after he came to power Nasser announced that he had 'no plan' for the liberation of Palestine.

For Palestinians seeking an alternative to the Arab regimes there were, in theory, two options—the Communist parties and the radical nationalists.

The 1950s were a decade of disaster for Communist parties in the Middle East. For more than 20 years they had pursued strategies which did not serve the interests of the workers and peasants of the region but satisfied the needs of Moscow's foreign policy. After the isolation of the Russian revolution in the early 1920s and the emergence of a new ruling bureaucracy in Russia, the Communist International had quickly degenerated. Setting aside the principles which had guided socialists during the 1917 revolution and which had been the founding ideas of the International itself, the Comintern had become an arm of the Stalinist bureaucracy.

Stalinism insisted on the building of 'socialism in one country' —in effect the extension of bureaucratic control throughout Russia and the implementation of forced collectivisation of agriculture and a crash programme of industrialisation. All other concerns, at home and abroad, were subordinated to these priorities. Duncan Hallas observes:

> The Comintern now [1928] existed, for Moscow, as a subsidiary agency for the defence of this process of

industrialisation and of the bureaucracy which directed it. Any external upheaval, any upset in international relations, anything which might have adverse effects on the foreign trade of the USSR... was out.[33]

Comintern strategy went through a series of complex twists and turns but its central concern remained that of serving the Russian ruling class, principally by minimising the possibility of external upheaval. Rather than working to deepen the contradictions in Western imperialism the International was used to ensure that Russia's new rulers were better able to establish working relationships with other ruling classes.

By the mid-1930s the Comintern's approach to the countries of the colonial world was dominated by the related notions of a theory of change by 'stages' and that of the all-class alliance. The Stalinist approach asserted that in countries less developed than the industrialised states of Europe and North America, socialist revolution was impossible. Rather, social change must proceed through 'stages', the first of which, in countries dominated by the imperial powers, would be a 'democratic' stage. Only later would it be possible for the working class to advance towards the possibility of socialist revolution.[34]

In 1935 the Syrian Communist Khalid Bagdash spelt out how such an approach applied in the Arab world. He told the Seventh Congress of the Comintern:

Socialism is our final goal. But before we can lead the masses to the direct struggle for socialism, we must successfully pass through the preceding stages. At present we are at the first stage of the struggle, the stage of the fight against international imperialism...[35]

In order to ensure a successful passage through the 'democratic' stage of change, Communists were to forge alliances with 'progressive' non-proletarian forces, forming a 'popular front' which included 'patriotic' elements of the bourgeoisie and the petit bourgeoisie with the working class and the peasantry. The status of the working class was relegated to that of a mere component in a 'bloc' of classes.

By reducing the role of the working class and of independent Communist leadership the popular front strategy abandoned the central tenets of the Marxist tradition. Nowhere was this more costly than in the revision of the Comintern's approach to the national question. In 1920 the International had adopted Lenin's 'Theses on the National and Colonial Questions'. These anticipated upheavals in those countries dominated by the imperial powers. Here, Lenin had argued, the Communist movement should adopt a precise approach:

> the Communist International should support bourgeois-democratic national movements in colonial and backward countries only on condition that, in these countries, the elements of future proletarian parties, which will be communist not only in name, are brought together and trained to understand their special tasks, i.e. those of the struggle against the bourgeois-democratic movements within their own nations. The Communist International must enter into a temporary alliance with bourgeois democracy in the colonial and backward countries but should not merge with it, and should under all circumstances uphold the independence of the proletarian movement even if it is in its most embryonic form.[36]

From the mid-1920s the Stalinist formula prescribed that Communist parties in the colonial world should not merely support the bourgeois leaderships of nationalist movements but align with them, thus surrendering their independence. The strategy was rehearsed in 1925 in China, with disastrous consequences.[37] Ten years later it was applied in Palestine, with similar results. Here the Palestine Communist Party became an uncritical supporter of the Mufti, who was already wholly compromised by his relationship to the occupying power. The Palestinian party collapsed into the most corrupt elements of the national movement, violating the principles which had lain behind Lenin's approach.

A decade later the Comintern was liquidated by Stalin, for whom it no longer served a purpose. But its strategies remained the orthodoxy of Communist parties worldwide. In 1944, in a guide to policy for Arab Communists, Khalid Bagdash could write:

> Our demand is not nor will be to confiscate national capital and the factories. We promise national capital and the

national factory owner that we will not look with hate or envy at his national factory but on the contrary we desire its progress and flourishing. All that we demand is the amelioration of the lot of the national workers and the realisation of democratic labour legislation which will regulate relations between the employers and workers on the basis of justice and national solidarity.[38]

Guided by this approach throughout the 1940s and 1950s the Communist parties of the Middle East passed up a string of opportunities to advance the workers' movement. Egypt was the most important of the Arab countries: it was the most highly industrialised and had produced a substantial working class with a long tradition of struggle.[39] When the workers' movement re-emerged on a mass scale after the Second World War a new Communist party found itself projected into a position of leadership but, saddled with Stalinist formulas, it was unable to see a way forward. In the words of one of its leading members: 'the masses were ready to follow us. But we no longer knew where to lead them...'[40]

By the early 1950s the Egyptian party had split into a set of warring factions unable even to discern the character of the new Nasserist regime.[41] Reunified under Moscow's direction it eventually moved into a position of uncritical support for Nasser and by 1959 had effectively ceased activity. Such was the disorientation induced by the Stalinist approach that the party could tell its members incarcerated in the Egyptian regime's prison camps that 'We are a party in power.'[42] It liquidated in 1964 on the grounds that with 'the working class' (the Nasserist bureaucracy) in power, independent proletarian organisation was unnecessary.[43]

There was an even more costly experience in Iraq. Here the party was stronger than in Egypt and by the late 1950s was well placed within a rising workers' movement. By 1959, with the nationalists under Qassem in government, most party members were anticipating an attempt to seize power. In the event, in line with Moscow's insistence that it collaborate with 'progressive' sections of the ruling group, the party passed up the opportunity.[44] Within months it was the subject of a campaign of repression and four years later thousands of its members were victims of a massacre organised by the Baathist regime.[45]

In two key Arab countries the left had surrendered to nationalism; elsewhere it pursued strategies likely to produce the same result: in Lebanon, for example, the Stalinist approach led the party to court 'progressive' personalities such as Pierre Gemayel, founder of the extreme right-wing Phalange.[46] Meanwhile on the edge of the Arab world, in Iran, a different disaster had unfolded.

Throughout the 1940s the workers' movement had threatened the Western-backed regime of the Shah. When the nationalists under Muhammed Mossadeq came to power in 1951 the movement surged forward, only to be reined in by its leading political component, the pro-Moscow Tudeh Party. The party failed to exploit revolutionary possibilities and Iran was soon again under full imperialist control, with the workers' movement a victim of the Shah's revenge. The Tudeh adopted a policy of 'inactive survival': in effect it declared that it was not possible to challenge the Pahlavi regime.[47]

By the 1960s the Communist parties of the region were widely mistrusted among young activists for having adopted policies of collaboration with the new ruling groups. In addition they were tainted by Moscow's equivocal position towards the Zionist movement. Moscow had backed the establishment of Israel in 1948, when Stalin's desire to keep Britain on the retreat dominated all other considerations. This had had a devastating impact on many Communists in the Arab countries.[48]

Among Palestinians the Communist tradition also suffered from the reputation of the PCP: those who had been active during the national movement of the 1930s remembered how the Palestinian party had first collapsed into the national movement and later surrendered to Zionism. Stalinism had ensured that the left was not a pole of attraction for those who sought a radical solution to the Palestinian problem.

The radical nationalists

In contrast, the Arab nationalists had a significant impact. Their development reflected the growth of new petit bourgeois layers of professionals, technocrats and military men who had emerged in a series of Arab countries during the 1930s and 1940s and sought to displace the colonial powers and traditional ruling classes. The most influential early formulation of their ideas was that of the Syrian Michel Aflaq, who formed the Baath ('Resurrection') Party in 1940. Aflaq called for the unification of the 'Arab fatherland' and its 'renewal and resurrection'.[49] The Baath's slogans were 'Unity, Freedom and Socialism' and 'One Arab Nation with an Immortal Mission'. Aflaq described himself as a 'patriotic nationalist', maintaining: 'We want socialism to serve our nationalism'.[50]

The Baath attracted mainly students, technocrats and army officers in Syria and Iraq, though it had small groups in other Arab countries. Its essentially elitist politics did not draw in workers and peasants, and its Palestinian recruits, mainly from Damascus and Baghdad, were principally students. But the Baath did have an impact across the Arab world; its main importance for the Palestinians was its contribution to a climate of pan-Arabism that influenced large numbers of young activists throughout the region.

A second current of Arab nationalism that had a more profound effect on the Palestinians was the Arab National Movement (ANM), founded in Lebanon in 1949 by a group in which several Palestinians were prominent. Its main slogan was 'Unity, Freedom, Revenge, Blood, Steel, Fire.'[51] It also emphasised Arab unity, seeing this as the first requirement for any further progress in the region. One of its founders, Palestinian George Habash, recorded the anti-Marxist sentiments of the group:

> We rejected the principle of class struggle. We believed that all classes in the Arab countries could be mobilised in the overall national struggle.[52]

The ANM set up branches throughout the Arab world, most successfully in Lebanon, Yemen, Jordan, Syria, Iraq and Kuwait. It was an enthusiastic supporter of Nasser's Free Officer government in Egypt, with its formal commitment to pan-Arabism and its anti-imperialist, pro-Palestinian rhetoric. The movement saw Egypt as the highest expression of the Arab nationalist ideal and spent most of the 1950s and 1960s raising support for Nasser. It argued that the fate of Palestine depended upon the ability of the Arabs to achieve the sort of unity advocated by the Egyptian regime. Its impact among Palestinian students and professionals, especially in Lebanon, was considerable, though like the Baath, the ANM rarely penetrated beyond petit-bourgeois circles.

The combined impact of the radical nationalists was substantial. They formed an important pole of attraction on the Arab left, in relation to which Fatah defined aspects of its own politics—among the group's key ideas were principles that challenged the pan-Arabism of Nasser, the ANM and the Baath. By the late 1950s Fatah had decided that the main weakness of Palestinian nationalism in the 1930s had been its dependence upon the Arab rulers and that now it was necessary for Palestinians to initiate their own struggle for liberation. It argued that Arab unity could only come about after the liberation of Palestine and that Palestinians should establish a movement that would not maintain links—like the ANM's tie with Egypt—with any regime.

The group regarded this as a vital development in Palestinian strategy. Khalid al-Hassan later commented: 'We reversed the slogan [of Arab unity] and this is how we reversed the tide of thinking.'[53] In fact nothing in Fatah's strategy had changed: it had not freed itself of dependence upon the regimes. Rather it had deepened the contradiction evident in its approach from the beginning: the idea that Palestinian struggle could both be independent and capable of forcing the Arab rulers to act on its behalf.

Chapter Seven
Fatah and the left

FIFTEEN YEARS after the expulsion of 1948 the mass of Palestinians felt increasingly bitter at the conduct of the Arab regimes. UNRWA observed:

> what is not in doubt is that their longing to return home is intense and widespread... [they] express their feeling of embitterment at their long exile and at the failure of the international community, year after year, to implement the resolution so often affirmed.[1]

Under these circumstances Fatah began to make headway. Its main appeal was to young businessmen and professionals from the Gulf but it also began to attract activists from the camps. Its attraction lay in the simplicity of its slogans—for a Palestinian struggle, for a return to the homeland—which struck a chord with the exiled masses. Unlike Nasser and the radical nationalists, with their promises of 'revolution' to be achieved through an abstract 'Arab unity', Fatah spoke plainly: it called for 'the Return'.

In 1962 Fatah made a breakthrough. Nasser's admission that he had 'no plan' for Palestine, and the dramatic success of the Algerians in expelling the French after nine years of guerrilla war, appeared a vindication of the group's ideas. Activists flocked to Fatah, which began to take on the appearance of a genuine movement. This development caused great anxiety among the Arab leaders, who recognised the Palestinians' potential for destabilisation in the region and, led by Nasser, took the initiative. In 1964 the regimes founded a Palestine Liberation Organisation (PLO) under the leadership of Ahmad Shuqeiry, a 'safe' Palestinian lawyer charged with the task of heading off the new movement.

The regimes hoped the PLO would help them pass responsibility for the liberation of Palestine to the Palestinians themselves and at the same time allow them to control the new movement.

Nasser's move backfired. It projected the Palestinian question to the centre of Arab politics, giving Fatah a huge audience. Fatah debated whether to enter the PLO and even attempted to do a deal with Shuqeiry, but eventually decided to act alone.[2] In January 1965 it launched its first guerrilla raid against Israel, beginning what it called the Palestinian 'revolution'.[3] As its attacks, launched mainly from Jordan, stepped up over the next two years, more and more young Palestinians were drawn in.

The atmosphere in the camps began to change—for the first time in 20 years Palestinians were again politically active. A generalised political movement developed with tremendous speed, in which the masses of the camps were deeply involved. Fatah had helped to release tremendous energies—yet the narrow nationalism of its strategy was to misdirect and waste them.

National struggle and 'non-interference'

Between 1966 and 1970 Fatah led a movement that galvanised the *diaspora*. It did so on the basis of a strategy based on two principles—those of national struggle and guerrilla warfare. But both these principles were quite inappropriate solutions to the problems faced by the majority of Palestinians.

The students who in the early 1950s had attempted to continue the armed struggle from Cairo had assumed that their task was to reinvigorate the national movement. According to Salah Khalaf, even then they were deeply suspicious of the Arab rulers:

> We were convinced, for example, that the Palestinians could expect nothing from the Arab regimes, for the most part corrupt or tied to imperialism, and that they were wrong to bank on any of the political parties in the region. We believed that the Palestinians could rely only on themselves.[4]

Nevertheless the students turned to the Egyptian government of King Faruq for help. When Faruq fell, they lobbied the new Nasser government. They were acting far from independently —indeed they were acting through the very political forces they claimed to dismiss.

'Revolutionary violence'

The second principle that guided Fatah was that of 'mass revolutionary violence'. The Palestinian model to which the organisation looked was that of the Qassemists—rural guerrilla warfare carried out by small bands of fighters—the pattern that had developed during the most successful period of struggle against the British in the 1930s. In the early 1950s founding members of Fatah had tried to initiate similar attacks as part of the effort to drag the Arab states into war; it was several years before Fatah developed the idea of 'mass' armed struggle.

This emerged in the idea of 'people's war', stimulated by the success of the Vietnamese and of the Algerians. Khalil al-Wazir has explained the impact of the Algerian struggle:

> When the Algerians started their revolution in 1954, there were only some few hundred Arabs against 20,000 French troops and well-armed settlers with much combat experience. The revolution in Algeria was to us proof that a people can organise themselves and build their military power during the fighting.[9]

This idea appears to have been grafted on to the notion that armed action could help in the general mobilisation of the Palestinians and to 'provoke' the Arab masses and thus press the Arab states into action against Israel.[10]

In 1964 a Fatah delegation visited China in an effort to obtain arms. According to Arafat, the Palestinians were told that they were wasting their time attempting to start guerrilla warfare:

> They told us: 'What you are proposing is unbelievable. You can't do it. You have no bases in the territory to be liberated and no prospect of creating them. From where will you start? There are no conditions for guerrilla warfare.'[11]

On the basis of their own experience and that of the wars in Algeria, Cuba and Vietnam, the Chinese were right. Guerrilla warfare required large areas in which to operate, terrain suitable for hit-and-run attacks and which provided safe areas in which guerrillas could hide, and above all a population willing to support and protect the fighters. None of these conditions was satisfied in the case of the Palestinians, where the home territory was occupied by the hostile Zionist population. (Attempts to conduct warfare elsewhere, in Arab states in which there were large Palestinian populations and where conditions were more favourable, would, of course fall outside Fatah's principle of 'non-interference'.) The same points were made when a group visited North Vietnam for talks with military leader General Giap in 1970. Palestinians do not seem to have been able to answer the criticisms that were raised.[12]

When Fatah launched attacks against Israel in 1965 they were isolated attacks against installations carried out by small groups of activists. For two years the pattern was maintained; then, in 1967, Fatah made its only attempt to launch a wider armed struggle on Palestinian territory. Following the Arab defeat by Israel in the 1967 war, over a million Palestinians in the West Bank and Gaza came under Israeli occupation. In an attempt to assert the Palestinian identity in the wake of the defeat and to try to initiate 'popular war', Fatah sent several hundred guerrillas into the West Bank.

The Fatah leaders appear to have been divided about what they should expect. According to Salah Khalaf:

> Our objectives were modest, and at no time were we naive enough to think that we could endanger the security of the Israeli state. We wanted to raise the morale of the Arab masses, harass the enemy and oblige it to remain constantly on the alert and to perturb the Israeli economy. It was the Arab and sometimes international mass media which blew our operations way out of proportion, thereby giving rise to the dangerous illusion that we would be able to liberate Palestine.[13]

However other Fatah leaders believed they were initiating prolonged guerrilla warfare on the Chinese model:

> The fact that there were now nearly one million Palestinians under Israeli occupation suggested that conditions were right for a popular war of liberation. Those who entertained this idea believed they could now apply Mao Tse-Tung's thoughts about revolutionary armed struggle. The one million Palestinians under Israeli occupation would be the revolutionary sea in which Mao's fish—in this case

Palestinian guerrillas—would swim. On the West Bank and Gaza the oppressed Palestinian masses would give aid and shelter to their fighters in the short term, and in the long term they would rise up against the Israelis.[14]

One indication that Fatah had high hopes for the 'long war' strategy was the fact that a number of its leading figures, including Arafat (who was almost captured by the Israelis) were participants in the initial operation. But the strategy was a terrible failure, Fatah losing hundreds of fighters to the Israeli occupation forces, who easily isolated them from the Palestinian population. Fatah beat a hasty retreat and returned to the practice of attacking Israel from neighbouring countries; however, it did not abandon its talk of mass armed struggle.

From this point the movement was operating with a strategy flawed in both its major principles: on the one hand its 'revolutionary violence' was ineffective against the Zionist enemy, on the other hand its strategy of mass mobilisation was bringing it closer and closer to confrontation with the Arab regimes.

The radical critics

The first clear criticisms of Fatah from within the new Palestinian movement began to emerge in the late 1960s. They came mainly from former members of the ANM who in 1967 had left to form the Popular Front for the Liberation of Palestine (PFLP).[15] The Front reflected the process of radicalisation which had been under way in the Arab nationalist movement for some years, partly as a result of Fatah's success. In 1967 it underwent a sudden conversion to 'Marxism-Leninism'.[16]

In fact the Front and the series of splits it produced during the late 1960s had absorbed a form of radical nationalism common among national liberation movements worldwide at this period. It incorporated many of the ideas to be found in the politics of the Communist parties—particularly the Arab world's highly-Stalinised organisations—a generalised commitment to 'the masses'; the theory of class blocs; the 'stages' theory; and the need for close links with the 'socialist' countries.[17]

The Popular Front and the current that emerged from it in 1968, the Democratic Popular Front for the Liberation of Palestine (PDFLP—later simply the Democratic Front—DFLP)[18], argued that

Fatah was under a petit-bourgeois leadership indistinguishable from that which controlled many of the Arab states. The Democratic Front criticised Fatah's willingness to accept arms and finance from Arab states—it had had various sources of supply since the early 1960s—maintaining that the organisation had become 'a tactical weapon in in the hands of the regimes'.[19] It also rejected Fatah's principle of non-interference in the affairs of the Arab states. Both the Popular Front and the Democratic Front called for the redirection of the Palestinian struggle in the interests of the mass of Palestinians.

Despite the shallowness of the Fronts' political theory they were able to point up the enormous contradictions in Fatah's strategy. But their audience was small—at this point Fatah seemed unstoppable, appearing to most Palestinians and to much of the population in the region as a whole as the only self-reliant Arab force. Recovering from the defeat on the West Bank in 1967, Fatah scored an important success when 300 of its guerrillas fought off an Israeli assault by 15,000 troops and tanks at the Fatah base near Karameh in Jordan.[20]

This was the first Arab victory against Israel since 1948—and it had been achieved by irregular Palestinian forces. There was jubilation throughout the Arab world: even King Hussein was compelled to comment: 'The time may come..when we will all be *fedayeen*.'[21] Karameh was the signal for more Palestinians to flock to recruiting centres in the camps, while in Egypt, where Nasser had been humiliated by the crushing defeat of the 1967 war, thousands rushed to Fatah offices to enrol as guerrilla fighters.[22]

Critics like those in the Fronts were marginal: Fatah had control of the movement, confirmed by its assumption of the PLO leadership in 1969 at the expense of Shuqeiry's successor, Yahya Hammuda, and the arms and finance that were now flooding from Arab states. The PLO had ceased to operate on the periphery of Arab politics; under Fatah's leadership it had taken centre stage.

A double contradiction

Fatah's achievement had been to combine Palestinian capital with the energies of the Palestinian masses; it had seemed to reconcile the aspirations of the new bourgeoisie with those of the camps. But the approach was flawed: the interests of Palestinian capital were tied to those Arab capital in general—and Arab capital had its own relationship with the system that dominated the region, that of Western imperialism. Meanwhile, the interests of the mass of Palestinians could only be satisfied by entering into conflict with the ruling classes of the region—by extension, with imperialism itself.

This put the Palestinian movement at an enormous disadvantage in relation to its Zionist enemies. On Herzl's principle, Zionism had set out to orient itself on the imperialist system and had been successfully integrated into it, with the result that a settler state had been established at the expense of the Palestinians. This dictated that the mass of Palestinians challenge imperialism. But the Palestinian leadership did not seek to challenge the political structures of the region, they sought merely to modify them and therefore worked for an accommodation with the system. Israel was at one with imperialism; the PLO both against it and for it. Saddled with such contradictions the Palestinian movement was never able to mount an effective challenge to Zionism.

Black September

In 1970 the PLO's rise came to an abrupt halt as the central contradiction in Fatah's strategy was exposed. By 1970 the movement had developed a 'state within a state' in Jordan. Here 70 per cent of the population was of Palestinian origin. The PLO had overwhelming support among Palestinians and the backing of many of the people of the East Bank—Jordanians proper. It operated its own army (having taken over the PLO's Palestine Liberation Army),[23] guerrilla groups, civilian administration, welfare and educational organisations. It ran affairs in the camps, in large areas along the border with Israel, in the northern towns and in the capital.

The ruling class in Jordan was weak. King Hussein's support was limited to the landowners, some sections of the bourgeoisie and petit bourgeoisie, and nomadic tribal leaders. His power rested almost exclusively on the state apparatus, in particular on the British-trained army. By 1970 the PLO had the support of many government officials and even sections of the army. John Cooley, a journalist who observed the 1970 events in Jordan, quoted Fatah claims that: 'there are entire [Jordanian] army units which are not at all "sure" [of their loyalty to the Hussein regime]. And not all of them are led by Palestinian officers either—we have plenty of sympathisers among the non-Palestinians.'[24]

Many Palestinian activists, including leading cadres of Fatah, argued that the movement should take power. Abu Daoud, who was commander of guerrilla operations, recalls:

> I was of the opinion that we not only could but should have knocked off Hussein... this was the feeling not only of the leftists and the so-called radicals in the other guerrilla organisations, it was also the feeling and the wish of the majority of us in Fatah—the fighters and the young officers. Among ourselves—and I am talking now about Fatah's young officers—we discussed the question of overthrowing Hussein very seriously and very frequently... Arafat always said 'No'. He told us that making war against Hussein or on any Arab regimes was not the way to liberation.[25]

The Fatah leadership was adamant: it was not prepared to confront Hussein—indeed it spent months trying to reassure him that it would respect the integrity of the Jordanian state. Salah Khalaf recalls 'our tireless reiteration that one of Fatah's principles from the very beginning had been non-interference in the internal affairs of host countries'.[26] All through 1970 Fatah allowed time to drift by, convinced that 'King Hussein wouldn't dare'.[27] Meanwhile the king and his supporters prepared to crush the movement.

Such was the extent of Palestinian strength in Jordan that the Democratic Front was able to raise the slogan 'All power to the resistance'. It called for a 'broad front' of the guerrilla groups and an effort to seize power on the basis that 'the victory of the Palestine liberation movement over the Zionist enemy depends on victory over imperialism in the Arab region'.[28] The Front received widespread if passive support from Palestinians and even some Jordanians.[29]

Eventually, under pressure from Hussein's frequent attacks, its own members, the demands of the Fronts and a final crisis precipitated by a spate of hijackings,[30] Fatah at last endorsed a general strike, demanding that the Jordanians convoke a 'people's assembly' to choose a new government that would include Palestinian representatives. Hussein now loosed his troops on the PLO, with Arafat belatedly declaring that 'the Palestinian revolution will fight to defend itself to the end until the fascist military government is overthrown'.[31]

Arafat now desperately called for help from Iraq's Baathist government, which only a month before had promised to intervene if the Palestinians found themselves in difficulty. The 12,000-strong Iraqi expeditionary force in Jordan did not move. He called on Egypt, and on Syria, which sent tanks towards Jordan but then ordered their retreat.[32] Meanwhile Israel secretly supplied Jordan with ammunition and other supplies.[33] Three thousand Palestinians were killed and much of the PLO infrastructure broken up. The *fedayeen* were forced back to the camps and were then attacked in further savage assaults. Within months the movement in Jordan had been entirely destroyed.

Lessons of the disaster

For most of 1970 Hussein had been unable to assert his control in Jordan. After years of repression Palestinians had begun to enjoy a taste of their own freedom and there was a widespread desire to bring down the king and place the resistance movement in power. But Fatah was committed not to disturb rulers like Hussein. As the leadership of a movement that had extended well beyond the expected limits, it was paralysed. It could not break out of the political structures within which it had developed: it could not lead what Khalid al-Hassan called 'a real revolution'.

The fall of Hussein would have had a destabilising effect throughout the region. The PLO would have found itself in power at a time when the movement had a genuine mass base and was operating in a highly radicalised atmosphere. It would immediately have found itself in confrontation with Israel and the US, both of which had prepared for just such an eventuality. The Arab regimes would have faced the problem of whether to back the Palestinians or line up with Hussein's Western supporters and risk problems with their own populations. In short, the Palestinians found themselves in a position to challenge imperialism and all its Arab allies.

But Fatah could not act—and its inaction kept Hussein in power. The implications of the subsequent defeat were bleak. The movement had been crushed by one of the weakest regimes in the region, in a country in which the majority of the population was Palestinian and the state apparatus was in disarray. The principle of non-interference in the affairs of Arab states had been exposed —the Palestinian movement had produced its first clash with a local ruling class and had been ruthlessly suppressed. It was unlikely that the movement would fare better elsewhere, unless a radically different strategy was adopted.

But Fatah drew the most negative conclusions. It attacked the Fronts for 'political extremism' and 'provocations'.[34] Salah Khalaf later commented:

> The proliferation of leftist slogans—such as the one inviting the masses to 'give all power to the Resistance'—the distribution of Lenin's portraits in the streets of Amman and even in the mosques, the calls for revolution and the establishment of a socialist regime—all this attested to a criminal obliviousness.[35]

Tellingly, he added: 'The extremists jumbled together the fight for national liberation (which Fatah advocated exclusively) with the class struggle.'[36] Khalaf was right, the Fronts had attempted to pursue the only course the movement could take if it was not to be destroyed: recognising the threat posed by a ruling class at bay, they demanded that it be tackled before it turned on the movement and devoured it. The Fronts, even if their own political perspectives were far from clear, correctly linked Palestinian national liberation with class struggle. Confrontation between the Palestinian masses and the Arab rulers was at the heart of the struggle for Palestinian self-determination.

But for Fatah, which believed Hussein was devious and self-serving but essentially a legitimate ruler, any hint of class confrontation was a deviation from the narrow politics of nationalism.[37] Even the fact that on the eve of the attack on the PLO, King Hussein had appointed a new military government under a Palestinian, General Muhammad Daoud, did not cause Fatah to ask whether national loyalty was not sometimes subsumed by that of class.

There were other ominous signs. When it seemed that Hussein might fall, Israel and the US had agreed to back him and during the September fighting Israel had gone on to threaten the Syrian gesture of support to the PLO and to supply the Jordanian forces with arms. The shared interests of the Jordanian ruling class and the Zionists were plain; their cooperation had been organised through Washington and expressed American determination to halt the rise of the Palestinian movement.

The situation dictated that the PLO should confront an Arab-Israeli alliance which served imperialism; this, of course, the Fatah leadership could not do. Instead it hoped for support from other Arab regimes, which it believed would intervene to save the movement. In the event Syrian and Iraqi forces stood aside and the whole Arab world looked on while an Arab ruler savaged the PLO. If the regimes would not defend the PLO against attacks within an Arab country, despite widespread support for the PLO among the Arab populations, how could they be expected to take any initiative against the immensely strong Israeli state?

Fatah preferred not to contemplate these difficulties. When the PLO left Jordan to establish a new base in the camps of Lebanon, it was even more rigid in its insistence that the movement must respect the Arab rulers. It was determined that the movement should never again threaten an Arab state and suffer a defeat like that of 1970. As a result more tragedies were to follow.

Chapter Eight
A state without a territory

THE PLO that moved its operations to Lebanon in 1971 was much weakened militarily but was soon able to recover. This was a result of two processes that had been taking place in the years before the Jordan debacle. First, Fatah had been able to establish even closer links with the Palestinian bourgeoisie. The defeat of the Arab states in the 1967 war had convinced many bourgeois who had been sceptical about the prospects for the movement that Fatah offered the only way forward. Constantly reassured by Fatah that it would not threaten their privileged positions in the Arab economies a series of wealthy individuals swung behind the national movement.

This was especially true in Lebanon, where the growing strength of the Palestinian movement had produced a backlash among the local ruling class, especially the Maronite Christians who dominated the country's thriving banking sector, and who determined to reduce Palestinian influence. The problem came to a head in the mid-1960s when the Palestinian-owned Intra Bank, the largest in Lebanon, was put under sudden pressure by withdrawals from members of the ruling families in Kuwait and Saudi Arabia in what seemed to be action coordinated by Lebanese bankers. The Lebanese Central Bank refused to provide a loan to Intra, even though its assets outweighed its liabilities, and the bank collapsed, depriving thousands of depositors of their savings and removing a source of finance for Palestinian businesses throughout the region.

The Intra Bank affair changed the attitudes of many Palestinians. Faced with what they saw as an attempt to squeeze them out of Lebanese capitalism, some of the *diaspora*'s most successful bankers and industrialists concluded that their only alternative was to back the project for an independent Palestinian capitalism. Smith comments:

> Henceforth, they argued, Palestinians would either have to share their profits with their Arab rivals... or invest their funds in an area where Palestinians had a say in the government and in the way affairs were handled... the only answer to many Palestinian businessmen in the *diaspora* after the collapse of Intra seemed to be the creation of a state where economic influence could be secured and maintained through political power, namely through the establishment of a state of their own.[1]

If, until the mid-1960s, the organisation had been a representative of the more vigorous and adventurous sections of the Palestinian bourgeoisie and petit bourgeoisie, by the end of the decade it had been given the seal of approval as the whole bourgeoisie's 'official' representative. As a result large sums of money began to find their way from Palestinian business into Fatah's coffers.[2]

The second development which massively assisted Fatah was the establishment of closer links with some of the most important Arab regimes. In 1969 Fatah persuaded King Faisal of Saudi Arabia that it represented an organisation led by trustworthy Muslims fighting for a religiously acceptable cause. Khalid al-Hassan was able to convince the king that the allegation Fatah consisted of communists was 'a dirty lie' and Faisal agreed to impose a 5 per cent 'liberation tax' on the wages of all Palestinians working in Saudi Arabia. The money collected would be made over to the PLO. The king also ordered that Fatah should be supplied with finance and weapons.[3]

The organisation was now being underwritten by the wealthiest state in the region—but at a price. Arafat's biographer has commented:

> The significance of Saudi Arabia's support for Fatah cannot be exaggerated. As time proved, with Saudi Arabia on its side, Fatah was indestructible—as long as it was pursuing policies the Saudis could endorse.[4]

The Saudi ruling class was among the most reactionary in the region. It controlled a country that was overwhelmingly backward but contained pockets of industry that brought huge sums of money to the royal family. Hundreds of thousands of migrant workers laboured in the oilfields and cities but were denied all political rights. Only a ruthlessly administered police state kept the ruling group in power. Saudi support for the PLO was therefore not the result of assurances that Fatah members were believers. The PLO had another role to fulfil. As Tabitha Petran pointed out:

> Arab regimes quickly embraced al-Fatah, whose professed lack of ideology they found reassuring. Oil states, in particular Saudi Arabia, saw in aid to al-Fatah a means of preserving social peace at home. Palestinians made up much of the Saudi workforce and had been largely responsible for the great strikes that paralysed Aramco's operations in 1953 and 1954. A by-product of al-Fatah's organisation of Palestinians in the Gulf could be a 'well-behaved' labour force.[5]

The PLO was now recognised as an agent of social control. Its weight among the Palestinians made it a credible force; its conduct in Jordan soon proved it posed no threat to the Arab regimes. For regimes such as that in Saudi Arabia the PLO had the potential to act as a policeman among a radicalised and therefore subversive population. Support for Fatah could be a political investment.

Other sections of the movement also received backing from the regimes. This process had begun in the mid-1960s, when the Baath Party, which had come to power in Syria in 1963, had established Saiqa ('The Thunderbolt'),[6] in an effort to keep pace with Fatah. In Iraq, the rival section of the Baathist movement, which had come to power in 1968, had established the Arab Liberation Front (ALF).[7] Each organisation acted as a lever for its sponsoring regime within the PLO, of which, like the two Fronts, both Saiqa and the ALF were members.

In the light of Iraq's rivalry with Syria, and the animosity between Syria and the ANM and its offspring the Popular Front, the Iraqis also supported the Popular Front—an example of the cynicism with which the Arab regimes used the Palestinian movement and the tangled alliances which resulted. Meanwhile the Democratic Front received support from various sources, including Syria.[8]

With such backing the PLO was soon able to rebuild its apparatus on an even grander scale. Military and civilian organisations were extended, press agencies, research institutes and radio stations were established and offices opened abroad. The PLO was beginning to take on the attributes of the state that Fatah had long aimed to establish.

The 'ministate'

Direct Arab influence was now playing an important role in moulding the movement's strategy. This became clear following the 1973 war between the Arab states and Israel, when American allies among the Arab states joined a US initiative aimed at preventing a threat to Israel such as that which had emerged during the war and at minimising the possibility of disruption to oil supplies.[9] Washington offered the bait of a Palestinian 'ministate' in the West Bank and Gaza, under Israeli and Arab supervision, in return for Palestinian recognition of Israel within the borders it had established in 1948.

Fatah accepted, dropping its principal aim—the liberation of the whole of Palestine—in favour of the prospect of the ministate, which was to be pressed on Israel by the US. Although the Fatah leadership had long debated the character of the Palestinian 'entity' for which it struggled—the extent of its territory, whether it should co-exist with Israel, and whether it should give citizenship to Israeli Jews—it had never publicly conceded the Zionist movement's right to control any area of Palestine.[10] Now it seemed prepared to accept Zionist domination of most of historic Palestine.[11] The Democratic Front—the 'Marxist-Leninists' of earlier years—declared that the struggle for such a state was a 'transitional demand' and backed the project.[12] The Popular Front led a 'Rejection Front' which opposed the scheme.

When the Fatah leadership accepted the proposal it finally abandoned even a rhetorical commitment to its 'revolutionary' attempt to replace Israel with a 'democratic secular state' of Palestine. For the emphasis on Palestinian self-activity it substituted the notion of striking a bargain with the US and the local ruling classes.

Fatah's position was not popular—most Palestinians recognised that they would not benefit from such a state. The majority of Palestinians came from areas of Palestine not within the proposed territory and discussions about the project were an admission they would never see their homes again. In addition, many were repelled by the idea of a ministate policed by Israel and the Arab regimes, and most believed that the PLO leadership was being drawn into a long process of diplomatic manoeuvring designed to further weaken the Palestinian movement. Few believed that Israel—busy with its project of integrating the West Bank and Gaza into the national economy—had any intention of surrendering territory.

Alan Hart, Arafat's biographer and a strong supporter of Fatah, points out that the leadership's position was one 'which would require the Palestinians to accept the loss, perhaps for all time, of 70 per cent of their original homeland'.[13] He observed:

> If in 1974 Arafat and his senior colleagues had openly admitted the true extent of the compromise they were prepared to make, it and they would have been repudiated and rejected by an easy majority of the Palestinians who were actually engaged in the liberation struggle.[14]

On this vital question the leadership was at odds with thousands of activists who had been radicalised by ten years of struggle and sought liberation from both the squalor of the camps and repression of the Arab regimes. In the most militant camps the ministate plan received an especially hostile reception. Salah Khalaf recalled that in Tal al-Zaatar camp, in Beirut, he found, 'to my amazement the walls of this desperately poor shanty town plastered with slogans denouncing the Palestinian ministate!'[15] But Fatah, with its grip on the PLO leadership and control of the movement's finance and administration, won provisional support for the proposal at the Palestine National Congress (PNC)—the movement's assembly.[16]

Two important events now occurred which pushed the PLO even closer to the regimes. First, the Arab governments appeared to rally behind the Palestinians. At an Arab summit in October 1974 they affirmed:

> the right of the Palestinian people to establish an independent national authority under the command of the Palestine Liberation Organisation, the sole legitimate

representative of the Palestinian people, in any territory that is liberated.[17]

Fatah was delighted: it appeared to be receiving just the recognition it had long craved. The PLO was being acclaimed, in effect, as the Palestinian state, and recognition was coming from the very forces to which Fatah had allocated the key role in Palestinian liberation. Arafat described the Rabat summit as 'a Palestinian wedding feast'.[18]

Fatah and the Arab states were working hand-in-hand when Arafat appeared to pull off a second coup. A month after the summit he appeared at the United Nations to make a speech 'with olive branch and freedom fighter's gun'[19] and the PLO was admitted to the organisation with observer status—a further confirmation in the eyes of its leadership that it was achieving the status they had long desired. For Salah Khalaf, with this recognition, 'All our objectives on the international scene had thus been reached.'[20] This seal of approval encouraged a host of states to grant full diplomatic status to the PLO. The organisation soon had wider diplomatic recognition—from a hundred states—than did Israel.[21]

But the PLO was trapped. Its relations with the Arab states had involved the leadership in a web of diplomacy from which it was never to escape. Arafat jetted from capital to capital collecting large cheques and handsome promises; but the Arab rulers balked at using the oil weapon which, as shown by their capacity to control oil production during the 1973 war, alone could bring US pressure on Israel to move towards concessions.[22] Meanwhile another confrontation was looming.

War in Lebanon

The PLO's second major conflict with an Arab state occurred under circumstances very different from those of the confrontation in Jordan. The Lebanese civil war of 1975-76 found the Palestinians fighting a long defensive struggle against the militias of the Lebanese right and the armies of Syria.

There were ominous signs long before the war began. In the mid-1970s Lebanon was in turmoil. The growth of the Gulf oil economy had had a dramatic impact in Lebanon, where Beirut operated as a clearing house for huge volumes of 'petrodollars'.

Rapid, uneven development brought industrialisation and the commercialisation of agriculture accompanied by rural depopulation and an increase in the numbers of urban poor. By 1970 there was rising social tension and by 1973 repeated mass strikes. The left grew rapidly, leading some Lebanese leftists to believe that a situation with revolutionary possibilities was emerging. The country was sliding towards a crisis in which the control of the state by the Maronite-dominated ruling class was certain to come into question and in which the Palestinian population was bound to be affected.[23]

The PLO now had its main base in Lebanon among 200,000 Palestinians living mainly in 15 camps—some 8 per cent of the country's population.[24] The Palestinian presence was a major factor in Lebanese politics; the development of the resistance movement in the mid-1960s had already had a radicalising impact and Lebanese affairs could hardly be distinguished from those of the Palestinians. Nonetheless, as in Jordan, the Fatah leadership scrupulously avoided 'domestic' Lebanese issues. Although the Popular Front and Democratic Front established relationships with the Lebanese Left, Fatah remained aloof. Even as the country moved towards civil war, Fatah leaders quoted the principle of non-interference and the negative lessons of Jordan, and instructed Palestinian forces to abstain from all activity in the 'Lebanese' arena.

In 1975 the civil war began with attacks by Lebanese rightists on Palestinians in the Beirut camps. Still quoting the principle of non-interference, Fatah refused to intervene. In the early phases of the war only the Popular and Democratic Fronts joined the militias of the mainly Muslim Lebanese National Movement against the rightists' Lebanese armed forces.[25] Fatah continued to make strenuous efforts to keep the Palestinians out of the conflict, and when Syria threatened invasion, to come to an agreement with the country's leader, President Assad. When the Syrians sent in 40,000 troops to aid the Lebanese forces, Fatah was finally forced to engage in desperate fighting to save the camps.[26]

The PLO was badly mauled but survived—but now Lebanon was under the control of a Syrian army of occupation which confined the PLO to small areas of the country. The Palestinians were trapped, physically and politically. For the next six years they remained active only in pockets of Lebanese territory, while the

Arab states developed ever closer ties with the PLO factions, using them quite cynically in inter-Arab disputes.[27]

The movement had lost direction; it became, in the Palestinians' own jargon, 'Lebanised': bogged down in disputes over the allocation of resources and activists' loyalties to factions within the leadership.[28] Political debate was largely replaced by rhetorical position-taking—so-called 'outbidding' became a substitute for discussion between the major currents. The Fatah leadership, which only 15 years earlier had initiated the fightback, was often viewed sceptically. The leadership seemed a world away from the concerns of the masses in the camps: according to more than one young activist the leadership in Beirut was massively top-heavy—it 'had more cars than drivers'.[29] Bureaucracy was stifling the movement.

This was the situation when Israel launched its third invasion of Lebanon in 1982. Despite courageous opposition from Palestinian forces, the Israelis' *blitzkreig* attack allowed them to smash a way through southern Lebanon and lay siege to Beirut. For over two months PLO fighters held out in the Lebanese capital, but, utterly isolated—not one Arab country offered tangible assistance—they eventually left by sea.[30] The Israeli army remained, to supervise the massacres of Sabra and Shatilla in which the Lebanese Phalange murdered between 3,000 and 3,500 camp dwellers in cold blood.[31]

The Arab states passively received shiploads of guerrillas who they consigned to camps safely isolated from the Arab capitals.[32] The PLO was almost back where it had begun in 1964—under the control of the Arab leaders. But there was still more conflict to come—in 1983 Fatah split, with a pro-Syrian faction under Abu Musa declaring the majority Arafat group to have sold out the cause. With the backing of Syrian forces the Fatah 'rebels' drove the remaining Arafat loyalists out of Lebanon as another convoy of ships left bearing guerrillas for the Arab states. The events reflected the fact that the PLO had been almost completely colonised by the Arab regimes—Syria using the Fatah 'rebels' as if they were part of its own armed forces. The Popular and Democratic Fronts remained formally neutral but soon they, like the Abu Musa section of Fatah, were based in Damascus and under strong Syrian influence.

By 1984 Fatah's diplomatic manoeuvrings were exhausted.

The long-running ministate saga came to an end with the US admitting it had no intention of pressing Israel into concessions. The Palestinians were still victims, both of Israel and its backers and of the Arab regimes—but now they were more vulnerable than ever.

Isolation

Following the exodus from Beirut the PLO established its headquarters in Tunis. Armed operations were now at an end—for the first time in 20 years Palestinian forces were unable to attack Israel directly; all the organisation's concerns were defensive. Guerrillas began to infiltrate back into Lebanon but here they were forced to concentrate in the camps, where their main task was to try to defend a Palestinian population which was coming under pressure on all sides.

The camps were no more than islands in a sea of hostility. Israel controlled the centre and south of Lebanon, Syria the east and much of the north of the country. Even when in early 1985 Israel carried out a partial withdrawal pressure did not decrease. Instead an increasingly aggressive Lebanese Shiite militia, Amal, launched a murderous attack on the Beirut camps. Its months-long siege was another index of the isolation of the Palestinians and the ingrained hostility of Arab rulers. Amal had been armed and trained by Fatah in the 1970s but had come under Syrian influence and following the Israeli invasion in 1982 had been converted into an instrument of Syrian policy.[33]

President Assad of Syria now seemed intent on complete destruction of the Palestinian camps; he was supported by Israel, which maintained close relations with the Maronite militias. These assisted bombardment of the camps and helped supply sections of the Lebanese army which joined the fighting alongside Amal.[34] Only determined resistance by the few Palestinian guerrillas who remained within the camps prevented further massacres.[35]

By the mid-1980s the Palestinians' enemies in the West and in the Middle East believed the PLO to be finished. Its Lebanese bases had been all but eliminated; it seemed that only the shell of the guerrilla movement remained.[36] Arab regimes which had backed the movement since the 1960s began to distance themselves and there were repeated complaints from the PLO that states pledged to back the movement financially had refused to pay. In November 1987, for the first time in the history of the Arab League, member states made the Palestinian issue a minor item on their summit agenda, then dominated by the Gulf war between Iran and Iraq. The PLO seemed to be fading into insignificance.

A few months later everything changed. In December 1987 the *intifada* opened a new chapter in Palestinian history.

Chapter Nine
The Occupied Territories

THE UPRISING reinvigorated the PLO. Since its re-establishment in the early 1950s the Palestinian national movement had developed almost exclusively within the *diaspora*. Although the West Bank and Gaza had been under Israeli occupation since 1967 the centre of gravity in the national movement had remained outside Palestine. From 1987, for the first time since the 1930s, a mass Palestinian movement engaged directly with Zionism.

The West Bank (including Jerusalem), Gaza and the Golan Heights had been seized by Israel during the 1967 war. For Israelis in the Revisionist tradition—so-called 'maximalists'— this marked a triumph which took the Zionist state a step nearer to creation of a true *Eretz Israel*—a state which occupied all historic Palestine and even wider areas of the Levant.[1] For others—the 'minimalists' —it allowed the extension of Israeli borders in a way which at least strengthened the state.

In practice, the difference between the two currents was more tactical than strategic, for they shared the philosophy of colonisation which was at the heart of the Zionist idea. Successive Israeli governments formed by Labour (containing 'minimalists') and Likud ('maximalists') viewed the territories as a legitimate extension of the state within which land and natural resources —and the 1.3 million Palestinian Arabs who had come under Israeli control—were to be systematically exploited.

The first principle of Israeli occupation was that of settlement: the 'Judaisation' of the land. Under the Labour governments of the late 1960s and the 1970s settlement of Jews in the West Bank was concentrated around Jerusalem and in the Jordan Valley. Eighteen settlements were established in these two

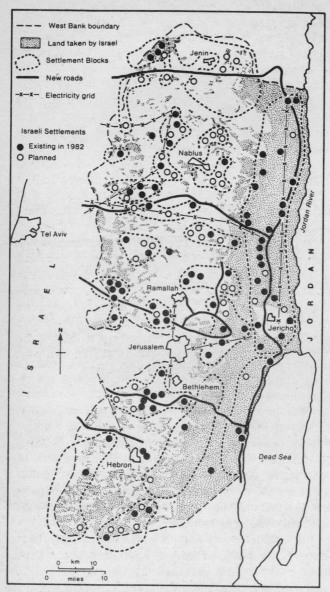

Legend:
- – – – West Bank boundary
- Land taken by Israel
- Settlement Blocks
- —— New roads
- —x—x— Electricity grid

Israeli Settlements
- ● Existing in 1982
- ○ Planned

Jenin

Nablus

Tel Aviv

Ramallah

Jericho

Jerusalem

Bethlehem

Hebron

Jordan River

J O R D A N

I S R A E L

Dead Sea

N

0   km   10
0   miles   10

Jewish settlements and land acquisition in the West Bank, up to 1982

140 *Intifada*

areas.[2] In 1977 the Likud bloc came to power. Its Revisionist background dictated a more ambitious approach: it was determined to integrate the whole area into Israel 'proper'. The Palestinian population of the area was to be fragmented by the establishment of scores of Jewish colonies around and between Arab villages and towns.

The combined effect of Israeli policy was that by 1982, 198,000 *dunam* (200 square kilometres) had been seized from Palestinian owners for civilian colonies alone.[3] Other figures suggest that between 200,000 and 300,000 *dunam* of state land had been 'reclaimed' for additional civilian and military uses;[4] 110 settlements had been established, populated by some 50,000 people.[5] In Gaza 115,000 *dunam* had been appropriated and 17 small settlements with a combined population of about 2,500 established.[6] By 1988, 55 per cent of land in the West Bank and 30 per cent of land in Gaza was in Israeli hands.[7]

The settlements were not merely housing complexes—some were fortresses and all were guarded by both the Israeli army and settler militias. According to Likud prime minister Menachem Begin, the settlements were 'facts'; they represented Israel's determination to absorb the territories and to banish forever the idea of a Palestinian state—even the most modest ministate—on any land controlled by Israel. They were also seen as part of the historic progress of the Zionist movement. In 1982 Likud minister Mordechai Zippori spelt out the government's view:

> The continuation of settlement is the backbone of the Zionist movement in the West Bank and it is the only means to defeat any peace initiative which is intended to bring foreign [Palestinian] rule to Judea and Samaria [the West Bank]... The presence of an Arab majority in the West Bank should not prevent the Israeli authorities from accelerating the settlement process in the occupied territories... I was born in Petah Tikva [one of the earliest Jewish colonies established in Palestine] which was surrounded by many Arab villages such as Kufr Anna, Abu Kishesh, and Khayriyeh—and no trace has been left of those villages today, but Petah Tikvah remains.[8]

This approach was endorsed by the Zionist movement. In 1981 the World Zionist Organisation (WZO) approved a plan for the territories which would settle 120,000 Jews in the West Bank (not including 70,000 Jews living around Jerusalem) by 1985. The WZO expressed the approach bluntly:

> The best and most effective way of removing every shadow of doubt about our intentions to hold on to Judea and Samaria is by speeding up the settlement momentum in these territories... The purpose of settling the areas between and around the centres occupied by the minorities [the Palestinians] is to reduce to a minimum the danger of an additional Arab state being established in these territories. Being cut off by Jewish settlements, the minority population will find it difficult to form a territorial and political continuity.[9]

If land was Israel's first concern, water was a close second. Between 1948 and 1967 Israel's hydraulic engineers had devoted much effort to diverting the water of Jordan and Lebanon into the Israeli system—in effect they stole huge volumes of water from neighbouring states, raising water production to 1.3 billion cubic metres a year. The capture of the West Bank brought Jordanian waters fully under control and gave a cover for far more systematic theft: by the mid-1970s water production had risen to 1.7 billion cubic metres annually.[10]

Israel seized the water resources of the West Bank with fanatical determination. Between 1967 and 1983 not one Palestinian village or individual received permission to drill a well; although Israeli settlements were permitted to drill up to 27 new wells.[11] At the same time hundreds of water pumps in areas still held by Palestinians were shut off and at least one irrigation canal bulldozed.[12] A similar policy was imposed in Gaza. In a region in which water was the most-prized natural resource the effect was the destruction of whole communities.[13]

The workers

The combined effect of land and water seizures was to change the character of rural life in the occupied territories. Although agriculture did not decline in all areas, for improved methods sometimes resulted in much-increased productivity, there was a sharp fall in the proportion of the population working the land (the process was speeded by the attraction of urban employment).[14] In 1968, 45 per cent of the West Bank labour force was engaged in agriculture; by 1980 the figure had fallen to 26 per cent.[15] In Gaza in 1966 agriculture employed 33 per cent of the labour force; by 1985 the figure had fallen to 18 per cent.[16] The overall effect was much to reduce Palestinian self-sufficiency and to leave many without work.

Rural unemployment and under-employment added to a pool of unemployed labour that had always been high in the territories, for a large part of the population was composed of refugee camp-dwellers. These numbers were also increased after 1967 as a result of loss of jobs in the previous local Jordanian and Egyptian administrations and the general dislocation which resulted from occupation. Israel was not slow to take advantage. By 1968 Israeli employment agencies had been established in Gaza[17] and were soon supplying the needs of an Israeli economy which had entered a period of rapid growth. There was little tradition of industrial employment in the West Bank and Gaza[18] but Israel was not seeking skilled labour—rather it required large numbers of workers who were prepared to do unskilled labour for a fraction of the wages being paid to Jews. Recruitment of Palestinians went ahead apace. Just six years after the occupation, the Bank of Israel could report: 'things have reached such a pass that unskilled jobs have come to be considered the preserve of workers from the administered areas [the West Bank and Gaza]'.[19]

During the 1970s the Israeli economy went through a series of slumps and small booms but the Palestinian workforce continued to grow. By 1981, 37 per cent of the labour force in the West Bank was employed in Israel; the figure for Gaza reached 43 per cent: a total for the two areas of some 110,000 workers.[20] But these figures did not tell the whole story. Many workers were not registered with labour offices and by the early 1980s an estimated 20,000 workers from the territories were employed 'unofficially' in Israel. All these workers were employed under conditions far less favourable than those of Jewish workers. In 1984 Sarah Graham-Brown commented:

> From the Israeli point of view, these workers formed a convenient and controllable source of unskilled and semi-skilled labour to do jobs which Israelis, even the least privileged, were less and less willing to do. The territories'

workers were, and still are, largely unorganised—they cannot belong to the Histadrut (the Israel trade unions federation), and unions in the territories are not recognised in Israel. Hence they will take wages that are unacceptably low for Israeli unionised labour...[21]

Workers from the Occupied Territories have been discriminated against systematically. By 1977 Israeli figures showed that 86 per cent of workers were in unskilled jobs; less than 0.1 per cent of Palestinians registered with labour offices went to clerical or professional jobs—despite the fact that large numbers of Palestinians had passed through secondary education.[22] Meanwhile only 25 per cent of Israelis were sent to unskilled work; 18 per cent went to professional jobs.Israel ensured that this large pool of cheap Palestinian labour remained under strict control. Workers were forbidden to remain in Israel overnight without a special pass for night or shift work. Each morning tens of thousands of workers passed through Israeli control points where their identity cards and permits could be checked; many then travelled for hours to reach their place of work, repeating the long journey at night. The West Bank and Gaza had become Arab 'bantustans' on the South African model, serving a society from which their populations were excluded for all purposes except that of work.

There were additional benefits for Israel. In 1970 the Israeli government imposed a social benefits tax averaging 30 per cent of workers' income. This was the same level as that imposed on Israeli workers but, as Israeli law did not extend over the Occupied Territories, workers from these areas received limited benefits: for example they received no pensions, unemployment insurance, injury compensation or extended child benefit. The balance in taxes raised in the territories but not spent on Palestinian workers was retained by the Israeli state.[23]

Israel's labour organisations made no attempt to correct the situation. After the 1967 occupation of the territories the Histadrut expressed fears that the flow of cheap labour might affect Jewish workers' wages and conditions but when it became clear that Palestinians were taking jobs Jews would rather not do the organisation dropped its criticisms. In addition, the Histadrut was a major employer—a key part of the structure of Israeli capitalism—and related organisations such as the *kibbutz* movement were eager employers of labour from Gaza and the West Bank. The racism which had emerged in the 1920s with the Histadrut's campaign for 'Jewish Labour' and the 'Jewish product', and which had discriminated against Israel's Arab citizens, was not challenged. There was no attempt to extend Israeli law to workers from the territories or to offer them trade union membership. As a result they remained in the most menial occupations. Graham-Brown observed:

> The majority of jobs [filled by workers from the territories]—unskilled building labour, agricultural work and service jobs such as cleaning, working in restaurants, garbage disposal and so on—do not present any real threat to the wage structure of organised [Israeli] labour. In the Israeli economic and social pecking order, the workers from the territories are in all respects at the bottom of the heap.[24]

Even after ten years of integration into the Israeli economy the wages of workers from the West Bank and Gaza were, on average, only 40 per cent of those paid to Israelis.[25]

A new market

Israel's policy towards industry in the Occupied Territories was pursued on two fronts. On the one hand tariff barriers were manipulated in favour of Israeli goods: barriers were erected to discourage an already weak industrial sector 'exporting' to Israel, while Israeli goods were given open access to the territories.

On the other hand Israeli government policy actively discouraged the local bourgeoisie by effectively cutting off finance. Immediately after the occupation in 1967 all banks were closed; later only Israeli banks were allowed to open.[26] As a result Palestinian industry—and much of agriculture—remained small scale and backward. After ten years of occupation industry contributed only 4.7 per cent of Gross Domestic Product in the West Bank and 7.5 per cent in Gaza.[27] In 1981, 90 per cent of all 'industrial establishments' in the West Bank were still based on family capital; only 37 out of 2,207 employed more than 20 workers—585 were single-person operations.[28]

As the population in the West Bank and Gaza grew—to some 1.5 million by the mid-1980s—the territories became immensely valuable markets for Israeli goods. By 1986 the occupied territories had become Israel's largest export market after the US, absorbing $780 million worth of goods.[29] Their trade with the Arab states (such as that of the West Bank with Jordan) had been reduced to a trickle.[30]

The territories functioned as a colonial extension of the Israeli economy; they were a source of labour and a controlled market which operated at almost no cost to the Israeli state. This was an important consideration for a system which had always been wholly dependent on outside support. Israel's rulers faced only one problem—that of continued Palestinian resistance.

In 1967 the PLO's attempt to begin a campaign of guerrilla warfare in the West Bank had been crushed using methods of mass arrest and detention borrowed from the British approach of the 1930s. In Gaza guerrilla activity continued fitfully until 1971 when student demonstrators were shot, 12,000 Palestinians were arrested, and thousands deported to Jordan. Israeli troops then entered the Gaza camps, killed scores of guerrillas, and put the area under close military control.[31]

After 1967 a series of strategies was tried in the West Bank. Israel first attempted to decapitate the opposition movement by expelling leading activists to Jordan. In 1969 it expelled 223 Palestinians, plus one entire *bedouin* tribe. In 1970 it expelled 406 Palestinians.[32] But control of the area still proved difficult and in the mid-1970s the Israeli government opted for a strategy of co-option. In 1976 it allowed municipal elections which it hoped would bring 'moderate' local officials into office. It anticipated that such officials would not back the PLO and would provide an alternative leadership which could take over some political responsibilities.

The results shocked Israel: the voters rejected traditional leaders and elected nationalists, most of whom refused to co-operate with the Israeli authorities. Many were jailed, expelled or otherwise punished. In the late 1970s Israel tried another strategy of co-option. This drew on an earlier Zionist experience, that of the 1920s, when in an attempt to draw Palestinian Arabs away from the growing nationalist movement, the settler leadership established the Hizb al-Zurra—the Farmers Party. This soon failed but 50 years later the Israeli government re-ran the project by setting up the Movement of Palestinian Leagues, known as the Village Leagues.

The Leagues were intended to organise a layer of rural collaborators which would mediate Israeli control of the Arab population. First presented as a system of cooperatives 'which will work for the benefit of all villagers',[33] the Leagues soon had their own budget, armed militias with interrogation centres and prisons, and even a bi-weekly newspaper. One of the Leagues' leading figures, Jawdat Sawalha, made the purpose of the project plain; they were intended, he said, to fight against the influence of the PLO and to negotiate on behalf of Palestinians with the Israeli state.[34] Israel declared that those who cooperated with the Leagues could expect to benefit; all those who refused to participate would be punished.

The Leagues were a failure. They succeeded in drawing in only small numbers of socially marginal and politically ostracised elements, mainly itinerant labourers and former members of the Jordanian secret police regarded with contempt by the mass of Palestinians. In 1982 the Israelis attempted to convert the Leagues into a new political party, the Democratic Movement for Peace. The initiative collapsed amid allegations of assault, murder and corruption against the Leagues' leading members.

However in the course of its efforts to use the carrot of collaboration, Israel had also used its customary stick. Most elected municipal councils which would not cooperate with the Leagues had been dismissed, local finance had been cut off and all independent institutions paralysed. When locally elected leaders provided a focus of opposition there were attempts to assassinate them. By the early 1980s Israel had succeeded in alienating every section of West Bank society.

The level of Palestinian resistance did not decline. Under the slogan of 'steadfastness', the population of the West Bank and Gaza mobilised around every local institution that remained intact: schools, universities, mosques and cultural associations became part of the framework of political opposition. Now Israel resorted to traditional methods of repression. By 1985 'elite' Israeli troops were being used in both Gaza and the West Bank, 'indiscriminately rounding up, questioning, beating and shooting live bullets at Palestinian civilians'.[35] The territories were 'punished' more and more severely for acts of resistance: the infrastructure allowed to decay, health and education to reach the point of collapse. According to an Israeli academic, conditions in Gaza were 'beyond disgrace'.[36]

In 1986 an Israeli organisation—the West Bank Data Base Project—published a report on Gaza. It declared that Gaza was 'the labour camp of Tel-Aviv' and fast becoming the 'Soweto of the state of Israel'.[37] The situation was said to be 'potentially explosive'.[38]

Chapter Ten
The Uprising

THOSE who had believed Palestinian nationalism to be dead had not understood the history of imperialism in the Middle East. When Britain and then the US had undertaken to be guarantors of the Zionist movement they had built a contradiction into the heart of their own strategy for the region. Their efforts had not simply led to the establishment of a new state, Israel, but had dispossessed an entire people. Despite the combined efforts of Israel and the Arab leaders the mass of Palestinians could neither be fully integrated into the structures of capitalism nor physically eliminated. When the *intifada* erupted on the West Bank and Gaza it was a reminder that imperialism had created a political contradiction which the system could not resolve.

The Uprising expressed two key aspects of this problem.

First, Israel had continued to operate as an aggressive colonial state. Its occupation of the West Bank and Gaza had resulted in systematic exploition of the Palestinian population, combined with intense political repression.

Second, the Palestinian response had remained a nationalist one. Though Israeli capitalism had changed the character of the Occupied Territories, producing a new Palestinian working class, the exclusivist character of Zionism—its racist division of Arab from Jew—meant that the Palestinian response continued to be expressed in strictly nationalist terms. The Uprising showed that it was impossible to separate the Palestinian response to exploitation from the national question. But it also showed the limits of nationalism—the fact that Palestinian nationalism, itself an adaptation to Arab capitalism, was not capable of expressing the interests of the mass of Palestinians.

The revolution of stones

All through 1987 Israel increased pressure on the population of Gaza, punishing opposition to its policy of repression by increasingly violent methods. There was a series of attacks on protesters by the Israeli armed forces, each followed by strikes and demonstrations, but the spark which finally produced an explosion of anger was the killing of four Gazan workers on 8 December. Their funerals a few days later marked the beginning of mass defiance.

The scale of the movement was soon evident and Israel drafted in reinforcements for the army—within days there were more soldiers in Gaza alone than had been used to occupy the West Bank and Gaza in 1967.[1] But the protests could not be contained and soon spread to the West Bank. By 21 December Palestinians in Israel had participated in a strike in support of the Occupied Territories; the whole Arab population living on Palestinian territory had been drawn into the movement.

The most notable feature of the Uprising was the ability of the Palestinian participants to sustain their activity against hugely superior Israeli forces. Demonstrators armed with no more than stones fought an army equipped with every modern means of destruction. Behind the rhetoric of the 'iron fist', Israeli leaders were both astonished and impressed by the level of resistance.

Former foreign minister Abba Eban observed that Israel's armed forces were 'one of the wonders of the world'. He declared: 'Never in history has so small a community [Israel] been able —and ready—to wield such vast capacity of defence, deterrence and reprisal.' Comparing the strengths of the combatants Eban noted that Israel could field '540,000 men, some 3,800 tanks, 682 aircraft with awesome bomb capacity and thousands of artillery pieces and missiles and an imposing electronic capacity'. On the other hand the PLO had '8,000 men in scattered places, zero tanks and aircraft, a few guns and no missiles but a variety of hand grenades, stones and bottles'.[2]

In fact the Uprising made no use of Palestinian guerrilla forces; its activists were unarmed youths. Despite Israel's determination to crush the movement with 'force, power and blows' they continued the protests throughout 1988 with scarcely a pause. The movement brought a sense of hope to the people of the Occupied Territories and there was a rapid increase in morale which recalled other periods of mass struggle. In the late 1960s Palestinians in the camps of Jordan and Lebanon had flocked to join the *fedayeen* and the civilian organisations of the PLO. Then, participants had described the impact of this 'revolution':

> The Palestinian felt after the Revolution that he's living like a normal person again after a life of humiliation...
> Before the Revolution meetings in the camps were limited to social problems; after it discussion became political—the land, the nation, the Revolution...
> I feel proud to be a Palestinian, one of a people that is revoltutionary, struggling and suffering. We were lied to many times, others tried to bury our existence as Palestinians. But with the Revolution we broke our handcuffs...[3]

Such sentiments were heard again as the people of the Occupied Territories joined in collective struggle. In Gaza there was a surge of confidence; journalists were told:

> Do not feel sorry for us. We are not starving people. We do not want your food. And we are not afraid. No one is afraid of their guns any more.[4]

Six months into the Uprising, Israel's West Bank commander acknowledged that there had been an 'irreversible' rise in Palestinian self-confidence.[5] This found its expression in the revitalisation of local organisations such as trade unions and women's organisations. Meanwhile a new network of committees sprang up in every village, town and camp. These emerged spontaneously but within a few months had been formalised through the Unified Command of the Uprising. Based on leading PLO figures within the territories—mainly well-established members of Fatah—they were in close communication with Tunis and the Arafat leadership.

The Command distributed regular leaflets—*bayanat* (appeals)—which called for strikes, demonstrations, boycotts of Israeli goods and the development of 'self-help' initiatives. Almost all were successful. Israeli troops failed to drive protesters from the streets. They attempted to break 'commercial strikes' by forcing shopkeepers to open their stores and merchants to continue trading. But where they opened one shop, another closed. Where markets were compelled to trade, others remained shut. And the army was powerless to discipline the tens of thousands of Palestinian workers who responded to strike calls by refusing to travel to work in Israel.

Israel's elimination of local Palestinian leaderships now left it without any means of mediating the conflict. Its only response was to increase the level of repression: scores of villages were placed under curfew, hundreds of 'collective punishments' imposed, and thousands detained. According to the Palestine Human Rights Information Centre, by the end of 1988 at least 30,000 Palestinians had been detained.[6] According to Amnesty International, by May 1989, 5,000 Palestinians had been placed in administrative detention and at least 1,100 were being held in extremely harsh conditions at Ketziot in the Negev Desert.[7]

By July 1989 more than 600 Palestinians had been killed. Still the protests did not subside.

Problems of the Uprising

For many Palestinians the Uprising seemed to have brought an almost miraculous change. New forces had come into action which had revitalised the nationalist movement and there was talk of 'rebirth' accomplished through 'revolution'. The reality was more complex—but in the heat of the struggle few activists seemed able to assess the real strengths of the movement, or its weaknesses.

Even the Western media, long a friend of Israel, had been forced to recognise the achievements of the movement. In December 1988, reflecting on a year of *intifada*, **The Guardian** commented: 'The Uprising has succeeded brilliantly in many ways —most of all in putting the Palestinian cause back on top of the international agenda and creating unprecedented unity in Palestinian ranks.'[8]

This summarised the major achievement of the Uprising. It had proved the Palestinians could not be physically eliminated, as some Zionists hoped, or wholly marginalised, as the Arab rulers intended. It had also succeeded in compelling the rulers of the Western states, including Israel's closest backers, to view the Palestine question with new seriousness.

In addition, the Uprising had had an effect on some sections of Israeli society. Although many Israelis still maintained that the

Occupied Territories should be integrated into the Zionist state, others had concluded that the Palestinians had erected an immoveable obstacle. There was the first full realisation that Israel's colonising adventures had to come to an end. Liberal and left-wing Zionists began to organise opposition to policies in the Occupied Territories, although protests in Israel were on a small scale. More worrying for the country's rulers was a growing mood of disquiet within the Zionist movement abroad.[9]

These developments represented a huge step forward for the nationalist movement, which had been on the retreat since Black September in 1970. However, they did not indicate that the Palestinians had altered their relationship with Israel and imperialism: troops still occupied the West Bank and Gaza; workers still laboured for Israeli employers; discrimination was still a fact of daily life; and huge sums of money still arrived from the US to guarantee the existence of the Zionist state. In short, despite Palestinian claims, there had been no 'revolution'.

This stark fact was not addressed by the PLO leadership, which maintained that the *intifada* was 'our revolution'[10] and an 'irreversible revolutionary impulse'.[11] Such an approach was consistent with the Fatah tradition, which had viewed opposition to Zionism, under its own control, as the highest level of political activity: in 1965 Fatah had declared the first guerrilla attack on Israel was the beginning of *al-thawra*—the revolution.

The unprecedented level of general collective activity led others in the PLO and sympathisers in the West to misjudge the impact of the Uprising. According to Joe Stork, of the US-based, pro-Palestinian **Middle East Report**—the most widely-read radical publication on the region produced in the West—a situation of 'dual power' had emerged in the Occupied Territories:

> It is precisely this protracted condition of dual power which constitutes the uprising's main achievement, and the main target of the Israeli military regime. This dual power is manifest everywhere—the merchants' strikes, the tax resistance, the local organising.[12]

But there was no 'dual power'—no section of Palestinian society had been able to threaten the integrity of the Israeli state. Although Palestinians' collective organisation had reached an unprecedented level, and some parts of the Occupied Territories had for a while been turned into 'no-go' areas for Israeli troops, social relations were not on the brink of transformation.[13]

It was the sheer scale of Palestinian resistance that led the PLO leadership to claim a new 'revolution'. Palestinian radicals were more specific: for the Popular Front the most important aspect of the Uprising was the involvement for the first time of Palestinian workers. For the Front, the 'proletarianisation' of the West Bank and Gaza had produced a potent new force—a working class capable of playing a 'vanguard role in confronting the occupation'.[14] After six months of industrial action the Popular Front declared that the action of the Palestinian working class —'the class most exploited by the occupation and its repressive policies'—had revealed Israel's 'dependence' on labour recruited from the territories. The Palestinian working class, it asserted, had at last become conscious of its power and was 'compelled to assume its historic role in the struggle for freedom and liberation'.[15]

But even the working class of the territories did not have the power to bring fundamental change. Although Israeli colonisation had indeed created a new proletariat, the underlying exclusivism of the Zionist approach had strictly limited its development. The same racist approach which created the Zionists' 'parallel economy' of the 1920s ensured that in the 1960s and 1970s workers from the West Bank and Gaza were excluded from mainstream economic activity.

Israel's core industries were exclusively Jewish. Even by the 1980s labour from the territories did not fill skilled jobs in Israeli manufacturing, in telecommunications, or in the transport network; there were no West Bankers or Gazans working in government service or in finance. Instead, the 11 per cent of the Israeli workforce composed of Palestinians from the territories occupied 'dirty' jobs and took seasonal employment on the land.[16]

Even when Palestinian strikes affected particularly vulnerable Israeli employers they caused only temporary difficulties. This was a result of the fact that some unskilled labour could be replaced quickly, that some strikers were absent from work only for short periods, and that much of the labour force lived at subsistence level and in the end was forced back to work.

In the textile industry, where large numbers of Palestinians worked in small factories and sweatshops, production in the larger units was not paralysed but fell by up to 20 per cent.[17] In construction, with a labour force in some sectors more than 60 per cent Palestinian, productivity fell by between 20 and 25 per cent.[18] In hotels and catering the impact was also limited. The president of the Israeli Hotels Association commented: 'The truth is that it hasn't affected us... Today we cancelled leave for our Jewish staff to cover for absentees.'[19] In agriculture, where Palestinians made up the bulk of the seasonal workforce, Lebanese and Portuguese workers were brought in on special visas and students worked to bring in the fruit and vegetables.[20] Many private producers and *kibbutzim* were able to save part of the crop.

The overall impact of the Uprising on Israel's economic life was considerable—but it was not decisive. The Bank of Israel reported that the *intifada* had cost $650 million in export earnings, including $280 million in tourist dollars that the Uprising kept out of the country.[21] The greatest impact of the movement had been in relation to the Occupied Territories: Israel's 'trade surplus' with the territories had decreased by 76 per cent over the year. However Israeli business activity as a whole had decreased by only 15 per cent, according to the Bank of Israel. This was a result of the fact that over the year Palestinian strikes had caused only a 25 per cent decrease in total labour from the Occupied Territories—a shortfall that employers had made up by increasing the productivity of Israeli workers and importing foreign labour.[22]

The impact of the *intifada* on the Israeli state was considerable but was also less than most Palestinians had expected. According to Israeli officials, by July 1989 military costs during the year were expected to rise to $526 million.[23] In an economy with extremely limited domestic resources this constituted a large sum. However it amounted to less than 20 per cent of total US aid for the year—aid which Washington showed no sign of withholding. Despite the demonstrations, the strikes and the Palestinian boycott of Israeli goods, after 20 months of the Uprising the Israeli economy had been disturbed rather than threatened.

Israeli workers and the Uprising

The racist division of labour in Israel meant that the Uprising did not threaten the country's economy. A second, complementary factor was the remarkably unified response of Jewish society.

At no point during the Uprising did any significant section of the Jewish population of Israel offer practical solidarity to the people of the West Bank and Gaza. On the contrary, the most important section of Israel society, the Jewish working class, proved that its loyalty lay with the Zionist state.

During the highest point of Palestinian activity, the strikes of early 1988, the Israeli government and Israeli employers were assisted by the leadership of the Israeli labour movement. In January Yisrael Kessar, the general secretary of the Histadrut, told his members that he was leaving his office to spend several days, unpaid, working on the harvest.[24] His gesture left the Histadrut membership in no doubt as to where its responsibility lay. There was no dissent: the Histadrut continued to play its role as an integral part of Israeli capitalism, part of the apparatus keeping Arab and Jew apart. Israeli workers were not mere observers of the *intifada* but participants in the effort to destroy it.

The conduct of Israeli workers was further confirmation that Zionism had incorporated the entire Jewish working class. The impact of Jewish nationalism on workers had been clear from the earliest years of the settlement process, when Jewish immigrants found that their future in Palestine depended upon the exclusion of the Arab population from the land and from economic activity—*that they had a specific material interest in the subjugation of the Palestinians*.

The pattern had been continued after the establishment of the Israeli state. Despite the high level of struggle of Israeli workers for improved wages and conditions—a feature of Jewish life in Israel—there had been no hint of political solidarity with the Palestinians.[25] In the 1960s Israeli socialists had observed:

The experience of 50 years does not contain a single example of Israeli workers being mobilised on material or trade-union issues to challenge the Israeli regime itself; it is imposssible to mobilise even a minority of the proletariat in this way. On the contrary, Israeli workers nearly always put their national loyalties before their class loyalties.[26]

The *intifada* furnished further confirmation of the hold of Zionism. Just as Jewish workers had laboured to gain advantage from the Palestinian general strike of 1936, so in 1988 they rallied behind the effort to minimise the impact of the Uprising. Israeli workers put their national loyalties before their class loyalties.

This conduct was echoed throughout Israeli society. Although some Israelis opposed their government's policy of repression in the Occupied Territories their numbers were small. Demonstrations called by the Peace Now movement, which in 1982 had attracted tens of thousands in mobilisations against the invasion of Lebanon, attracted far smaller numbers when the issue was that of the defence of Palestinian rights. Yesh Gvul organised for opposition to military service in the West Bank and Gaza—but only a tiny minority of reservists responded. Peace Now, Yesh Gvul and those other campaigns that questioned Israeli government policy in the territories did not question Israel's right to decide the fate of the Palestinian people. They were a liberal critique of a specific strategy of the Zionist state but they did not question the basis of the Zionist venture. They were not anti-Zionist campaigns—they could not express practical solidarity with the Palestinian people. They could not surmount the obstacle which Zionism has long presented to the Jewish people of Israel—their material interest in the exclusion of the Palestinians and in the subjugation of the anti-imperialist movement in the Arab states. Indeed for some Israeli workers the *intifada*—a movement which raised the question of economic, political and territorial rights—stimulated a heightened sense of nationalist feeling.

A phantom state

The Guardian's observation that the Uprising had 'succeeded brilliantly in many ways' carried a rider. It added,

> On balance... the *intifada* has failed to create a workable alternative to occupation: self-help and digging vegetable patches for victory have been encouraged by the general turndown in economic activity: they have not ended two decades of dependence on the Israelis... The PLO's [independent] state is still a phantom one.[27]

This was correct: despite having brought new forces into play, despite its energy, the movement had not been able to throw off Israeli control.

The relation between the apparent effect of the Uprising and its real impact had important implications for the strategy adopted by the PLO leadership. Arafat had not initiated the Uprising; its spontaneity was alien to his political tradition and a potential threat to Fatah's dominance. But the new social forces involved in the Uprising had not proved powerful enough to rupture traditional Palestinian nationalism. The weight of the Palestinian working class was insufficient to raise the level of struggle against Zionism to a point at which a new political direction was demanded. The Uprising was therefore contained within the structures of nationalism and the PLO leadership was able to play the leading role in directing the movement.

Fatah on top

The unanimity with which the people of the West Bank and Gaza backed the *intifada* had partly been a product of Israeli policy. During the 1970s and 1980s the stick-and-carrot approach to political leadership on the West Bank and Gaza had been a disastrous failure. The Village Leagues had collapsed, taking with them the layer of collaborators Israel had hoped would mediate control of the mass of the population. Repression had removed other community figures such as mayors and religious leaders, many of whom had been expelled or placed under house or town arrest. Newspapers and magazines had been censored and banned, and universities and cultural organisations closed. By the mid-1980s Israel had removed almost all those it might have hoped to use as a means of deflecting Palestinian opposition to occupation.

The national movement itself had also created a political vacuum. The PLO's policy of 'steadfastness' was successful in maintaining daily resistance to the occupation but it did not offer a way forward for the people of the territories. The conduct of the PLO leadership seemed increasingly futile: Arafat's frenetic diplomatic activity was leading nowhere—indeed, the PLO was being marginalised by the Arab states. Meanwhile in the West Bank and Gaza repression was increasing and the leadership of the national movement was unable to provide a channel for the accumulated anger and political energy of a new generation of activists.

The population of the territories was youthful; it was unmarked by the political traditions of those who had lived there under Egyptian or Jordanian rule and relatively free of the constraining influence of Fatah's nationalism. When the *intifada* erupted leadership fell initially to the youth, often those who earned the right to lead by virtue of their energy, courage and imagination in confronting Israeli troops. But the Uprising needed coordination and direction, and within days the organisations of the PLO were playing the leading role.

Since its expulsion from Lebanon Fatah had paid increasing attention to its network of support in the territories, channelling large sums of money through Jordan to back its activities. When the organisation grasped the significance of the events, it was able to exercise its customary influence, especially through elected leaders such as mayors and through leading businessmen and professionals. In Gaza the Popular Front had a following in the camps, and in the West Bank the Democratic Front and the Communist Party had support among professionals and some poorer Palestinians, but Fatah's hold was undisputed.[28]

Together, Fatah and the radicals supplied most of the formal organisation of the Uprising. Khalidi comments:

> The Uprising... shows that by expelling many traditional leaders, and intimidating others, Israel created the conditions for a secret, underground, loose but apparently unified leadership structure to arise. By and large, these new leaders are graduates of Israel's prison system—a major training ground for Palestinian revolutionary cadres. They are, as well, members and cadres in the major Palestinian political organisations. They mean it when they say that the PLO represents them.[29]

In addition, religious organisations made their appearance. Since the 1950s Palestinian nationalism had been essentially secular in character. This reflected the secular nature of Arab nationalism as a whole and the particular structure of Palestinian society, 10 per cent of which was Christian. From the early 1970s Islamic 'activism' had increased its influence throughout the Middle East; the current grew more modestly in Palestinian communities, but the revolution in Iran and the marginalisation of the PLO after 1982 gave it greater prominence.[30] By 1988 the number of mosques in the West Bank had doubled in 20 years; in Gaza, with its almost exclusively Muslim population, the number of mosques had also doubled, to 160, over the same period.[31]

From the mid-1980s Islamic Jihad became influential among young activists, especially in Gaza. It argued for *jihad* (holy war) against Israel and for the liberation of the whole of Palestine, criticising the PLO for its compromises and lack of dynamism. However it did not challenge the principles of Palestinian nationalism: it was a militant religious current within the nationalist movement. In 1987 members of the Islamic Jihad faced particularly intense repression from Israel and several were killed shortly before the Uprising. When the *intifada* began Jihad members were active in organising demonstrations and strikes and when the PLO formed permanent local committees the organisation was included.

The movement was therefore coordinated by Fatah, the Popular Front, the Democratic Front, the Communist Party and Islamic Jihad acting jointly in the interests of 'national unity'.

The Muslim Brotherhood, which had been active in Palestine since the 1940s, now feared marginalisation and made a major effort to establish an alternative current within the *intifada*.[32] With Saudi support it created the Islamic Resistance Movement, known as Hamas ('Zeal'), which declared itself part of the Palestinian national movement but argued for a 'Palestinian Islamic state'.[33] For several months it attempted to organise independently but within a few months it too had coordinated its activities with the Unified Command of the Uprising. Thus though there were diverse currents within the leadership, none challenged the premises of Palestinian nationalism and none was able effectively to contest Fatah's domination.

The ministate again

These developments both challenged and strengthened the PLO leadership. For the first time in almost 20 years the Palestinian movement was in direct conflict with Israel rather than an Arab state. If Fatah proved capable of moving at the pace of the mass movement, so resisting the challenge of the nationalist radicals and the Islamic current, it would again have leadership of a movement of enormous symbolic importance in the Arab world—that of a struggle against Israel and imperialism. Fatah did indeed adjust to take leadership of the movement—and was able to exert a new influence in its main field of political activity,

Arab diplomacy. As the Uprising continued, Arafat used his new-found strength once again to rally the Arab states behind the ministate strategy.

Thus Fatah directed the movement in characteristic fashion: although the Uprising had given the PLO greater freedom from the influence of the Arab states, Arafat used his room for manoeuvre to orient the organisation back towards the Arab regimes.

Chapter Eleven
The impact of the intifada

THE UPRISING gave a massive boost to the PLO, placing the organisation back at the centre of Arab politics. The PLO leadership's reaction was to take an initiative it had long planned but had been unable to implement. After 12 months of *intifada* it declared a Palestinian state in the Occupied Territories and recognised the state of Israel.

Western governments lauded Arafat and, after 25 years of violent opposition to the PLO, the US Administration began talks with the movement's representatives in Tunis. The almost unthinkable had happened: the PLO had achieved international respectability and had taken the issue of a Palestinian state onto the agenda of discussions with the most powerful Western governments.

But why was the US at last prepared to recognise the PLO and to open talks about the future of the Occupied Territories? The Palestinian leadership saw an explanation in the pressure of the *intifada* on Israel and the wave of international sympathy for the people of the Occupied Territories.[1] The real reason lay elsewhere; it could be traced to America's most enduring concern in the Middle East—its economic interests.

Even after a year of the Uprising it was clear that the Zionist state was not under threat. There was therefore no question that its Western backers should seek a new arrangement to secure their interests in the Middle East. Neither were Western governments swung towards the PLO as a protest against Israeli policy. Worldwide television coverage of Israeli conduct in the West Bank and Gaza stimulated a wave of sympathy for the people of the territories, but sympathy did not force the hand of Western governments. The apparent change in Palestinian fortunes at the international level lay in the least obvious success of the Uprising: its impact *outside* Israel and the Occupied Territories.

Imperialist strategy in the Middle East many years earlier had made the Palestinians a potentially destabilising factor in the region. When the PLO emerged in the 1950s this potential soon became a reality: across the Arab world it acted as a radicalising force. In Jordan and Lebanon the presence of the armed Palestinian movement pushed the regimes into crisis. Elsewhere the symbol of Palestinian resistance was a potent one. Following the collapse of the Arab armies in the 1967 war the Palestinians seemed a model of self-confident anti-imperialist struggle and the *kufiyya*—the headscarf—became a badge of resistance.

Despite the PLO leadership's accommodation with Arab capitalism the mass of Palestinians were still subject to relentless pressure exerted by both Israel and the Arab regimes. Although the regimes hoped for the PLO's demise, large sections of the population in the Arab states continued to back the Palestinians.

This was never more clear than at the moment of the organisation's most serious defeat. In 1982, following Israel's invasion of Lebanon, PLO fighters left Beirut by sea. One ship passed through the Suez Canal, en route to Yemen. *A million* Egyptians assembled on the banks of the canal to show their solidarity.[2] When, five years later, the Uprising displayed a new energy in the movement there was an immediate response throughout the Arab world.

The first reaction came in those countries with the largest Palestinian populations. In mid-December 1987, with the Uprising less than two weeks old, 10,000 demonstrated in Sidon, Lebanon. Many were Palestinians, others Lebanese Muslims long allied with the PLO.[3] In Jordan a solidarity demonstration was pre-empted by the arrest of Palestinian activists.[4] On 29 December police made arrests in Bahrain to stop solidarity activity: already the Palestinian issue was affecting the Gulf states.[5]

The most alert of the Arab regimes sensed the danger. On 29 December the Syrian regime was the first to act, organising a mass solidarity rally in Damascus. **Middle East Report** observed:

The government here, as throughout the Arab world, has been left to play catch-up or clampdown to stem the tide of anti-government sentiment spurred by its [the Uprisi success... As self-styled leader of Arab forces of 'progres confrontation' [with Israel] Syria is playing catch-u co-opt as hard as anyone.[6]

As pressure in the Occupied Territories continued to rise the Syrian regime sponsored solidarity meetings and rushed leaders of favoured Palestinian organisations onto public platforms and television screens alongside government spokesmen; 12 February was declared a 'voluntary work day' to benefit the Uprising.[7] A similar approach was adopted in Algeria where in February a government-sponsored rally was attended by Arafat, Habash and Nayef Hawatmeh.[8]

In several countries formal statements from the regimes in support of the Uprising were not enough. In early January a pro-- Palestinian demonstration was organised in Tunisia; participants were clubbed by police.[9] Later in the month leaflets calling for demonstrations in support of the Uprising appeared in Baghdad; a number of Palestinians were abducted from their homes by security forces.[10] On 20 January students organised a march in support of the Uprising at Fez University in Morocco; troops attacked the march killing several participants. On 24 January an illegal solidarity demonstration in Amman, Jordan, was broken up by police. Student activists at Yarmouk University were arrested and hundreds of Palestinians elsewhere in Jordan were detained.[11]

Kuwait was the first Arab state to give financial support to the *intifada*. In mid-January it donated $5 million to what Kuwaiti ruler Shaikh Jaber al-Ahmad al-Sabah called 'the blessed resistance'.[12] But on 8 February Palestinian youth—part of a 300,000-strong Palestinian community—joined a solidarity march in Kuwait City; police broke up the demonstration with tear gas and batons. The next day the newspaper **Al-Ra'i al-Am**, expressed the regime's feelings: 'Such demonstrations could be exploited by those who fish in troubled water to create disturbances,' it argued.[13]

The Arab regimes' approach was neatly summed up by **Mideast Mirror**:

Official expressions of support throughout the Arab world for the Palestinians and the current Uprising are legion but private enterprise demonstrations bring a chill to ruling bones and are actively discouraged.[14]

A solidarity movement, small in scale but of immense political significance, was affecting almost every Arab country. It had highly subversive potential—the Palestinians were again a symbol of resistance, not merely to Israel, but to the misery and degradation which was the lot of millions throughout the Middle East. The *intifada* threatened to be a catalyst for mass resistance to regimes which owed their own existence to imperialism. Once the idea of such resistance spread outside the Occupied Territories it brought 'a chill to ruling bones'.

Solidarity continued to spread. On 14 February police broke up a thousand-strong solidarity demonstration in Istanbul, Turkey.[15] On 17 March thousands demonstrated outside the US embassy in Khartoum, Sudan, during a general strike in support of the Uprising.[16]

Almost inevitably the solidarity movement had its greatest impact in Egypt. Here imperialism had produced a society of stark extremes. The pro-Western regime was backed by an increasingly confident and wealthy bourgeoisie and a layer of voracious middlemen and commission agents; the mass of a huge population lived at subsistence level.[17] In hock to the International Monetary Fund (IMF) and the US government, and desperate for more funds, President Mubarak was intent on cutting the food subsidies which sustained the masses. Only systematic repression held back a potentially explosive opposition movement, which was also deeply resentful of the regime's record on Palestine: under President Sadat, Egypt had been the first Arab country to recognise Israel.

Early in the Uprising there was extensive media coverage of events in Palestine, accompanied by reports of Mubarak's efforts in Europe and the US to push for an international peace conference on the Middle East. (The real reason for his trip was to appeal for aid and to keep the IMF at bay.) But as the Uprising spread to the West Bank and Israel 'proper' the regime changed its approach. Scenes of Palestinian demonstrations disappeared from Egypt's television scenes and solidarity demonstrations were broken up: 'keeping the lid on popular reaction seems to have been the main concern'.[18] On 23 December leaders of the opposition parties issued a call for Egypt to break relations with Israel and expel the Israeli ambassador. Six days later a call for a two-minute work stoppage was widely supported.[19] On 30 December lawyers took part in a day's solidarity strike.[20]

Now students and Islamic activists came onto the scene. This was too much for the regime, which was engaged in a war of attrition with fundamentalist groups—the *gama'at*[21]—and security forces attacked a demonstration outside the country's most important mosque, al-Azhar in Cairo.

On the same day there was a development of the greatest importance, when for the first time workers joined the solidarity movement. In the northern city of Mehalla al-Kubra workers from a giant textile mill—the largest workplace in the Middle East—fought the riot police after a solidarity march several hundred strong. Here, slogans against Israeli repression of the Palestinians soon became demands for Egypt to break links with Israel, and against the IMF and the US. The government was declared a servant of the West and there were calls to bring down President Mubarak.[22]

The next day interior minister Zaki Badr announced that the government would not allow solidarity demonstrations being used 'to provoke domestic unrest'.[23] He declared: 'Egypt, with all its institutions, supports the Palestinian people but the government will not permit this situation to be used in sabotage and incitement.'[24] Over the following weeks the government found itself in a running battle with the solidarity movement. The Egyptian lawyers' Bar Association—in which the left had strong influence—announced a further demonstration. Badr declared: 'Leftists and Muslim fundamentalists are plotting to subvert the government,'[25] and warned there would be a crackdown on further demonstrations. On 6 January students fought police at Ain Shams University in Cairo and riot police surrounded the lawyers' headquarters in the centre of the city, where a meeting established a Popular National Committee for Solidarity with the Palestinian People.[26]

The solidarity movement had now developed a momentum of its own and political generalisation was accelerating with every demonstration. Egypt showed what every Arab regime feared —that the Palestine question was among the most subversive in the Middle East. In the act of resisting Zionism the Palestinians confronted imperialist control of the region; in the act of solidarity with the Palestinians, Arab students and workers confronted class relations within their own society, and the relations which bound their rulers to the world system.

On 11 January meetings at Ain Shams University drew a parallel between 'the regime's capitulationist policies' *vis-à-vis* Israel and the US and its repression of the solidarity movement. They also pointed to the connection between this repression and the government's 'submission to the US and IMF demands to starve the Egyptian people'.[27] The next day 200 students were arrested at the University of Alexandria.[28]

The student protests gave the left its biggest opportunity for years to win young activists. Meanwhile Islamic fundamentalist groups were organising at the mosques; leading fundamentalist preacher Shaikh Hafez Salama asserted: 'We demand our borders with Israel be opened for *jihad*.' Islamic Jihad leader Omar Abderrahman criticised the government for supporting the proposed Middle East peace conference. 'How can we hand over the problem of Palestine to the East and the West when they are the ones responsible for creating Israel?' he asked.[29]

The government's reply was a statement from Badr: 'I will sever any foot that attempts to march in demonstrations... demonstrations are impermissible even if peaceful in support of the Palestinians in the occupied lands and we will meet this with all our firmness.'[30]

Further conflict at Ain Shams led to 250 students being held in administrative detention and a police presence around major mosques. The protests slowly subsided, largely due to the timorousness of official opposition parties, but erupted again in February, with students demanding the release of imprisoned comrades. Protests continued intermittently throughout the spring as the government gradually regained control. The Egyptian regime had experienced the most serious opposition since the early 1980s.

Only in Egypt did a solidarity movement emerge on a national level. This reflected the level of repression in all the Arab states and the bankruptcy of the Stalinist-dominated left, which in some countries was hardly capable of expressing politics independent of the regime. But it was also a function of the approach taken by the PLO. The organisation could not call unambiguously for solidarity throughout the Arab world: its tangle of alliances with the Arab regimes prevented its identification with a solidarity movement that also targeted the Arab rulers.

Thus in February Arafat visited Kuwait to smooth relations following the solidarity demonstrations. He praised official Kuwaiti support for the Palestinians, in effect condemning the solidarity activists and strengthening the position of Palestinians in Kuwait who had declared the mobilisation 'a tactical mistake'.[31]

Once again Fatah displayed the 'doublethink' which had characterised the organisation since the early 1950s. Khalil al-Wazir, who had responsibility in Fatah for activity in the Occupied Territories, declared in February 1988 that the *intifada* had stimulated unprecedented solidarity worldwide. He added:

> As far as the Arab countries are concerned, a wave of solidarity had emerged, but it has not yet reached a level commensurate with the events in occupied Palestine...
> Of course the interaction between what is happening in the occupied homeland and what is happening in the Arab world could have evolved. But some Arab regimes are more afraid than Israel of what is happening in the occupied homeland, and that is why there are many restrictions on any manifestation of popular solidarity with the Palestinian people.[32]

Some Arab regimes were indeed 'more afraid than Israel' of the *intifada*. They feared that their own populations might follow the Palestinian example, to the regimes' cost. But the PLO believed this development might rebound against *them*—thus Arafat had hurried to Kuwait to discipline Palestinian youth and secure the flow of funds he needed to finance PLO activities.

By mid-1988 the solidarity movement had been crushed by the regimes and Fatah had proved itself in control of the Uprising. At an Arab summit in Algiers the regimes gave Arafat full backing and pledged $1 million a week to help maintain the impetus of the movement.[33] Fatah was caught in the same old contradiction.

The oil factor

Despite the deadening influence of the PLO leadership the *intifada* had proved a destabilising factor in regional politics. The regimes now knew that Israel could not easily put an end to the movement; they must therefore minimise its impact in the Arab world. As the months passed they put increasing pressure on the US to make a gesture to the Palestinians—a move which might slow the Uprising and help stabilise the region. The alternative, they feared, was further generalisation of solidarity into an anti-imperialist movement which threatened their own control.

The Arab rulers knew that the US was always likely to be most responsive when its economic interests, principally oil, were in question. The need to secure the Gulf oilfields had already produced direct US intervention during the Gulf war: in 1986 the Gulf states had insisted that unless the US played a bigger role in the conflict Iran would defeat the Iraqi army. The countries of the southern Gulf, with their immense oilfields, would be vulnerable. When the US swung behind Iraq and sent its fleet into Gulf waters, the war was all but over.[34] The Arab alliance against Iran had been strongly supported by the PLO.

The outcome of the Gulf war had created a new pro-Western alliance between Iraq, Jordan and Egypt. These states were the main movers in pressing the US for action. They demanded US recognition of the PLO and US pressure on Israel to agree to talks on independence for the Occupied Territories. This, they argued, was in the West's own best interests. A continuing *intifada* threatened greater political instability, it could lead to more solidarity action or, worse, stimulate movements with the potential to subvert pro-Western regimes. In the end the West's interests in the Gulf, only recently secured, might be at risk.

In the early 1980s the world recession, particularly severe in the US, had led to a sharp fall in US energy use and a rapid decline in imports of oil.[35] US companies took advantage of the collapse in oil prices to reorganise the pattern of imports, reducing the volume of Middle East supplies and taking more European and Latin American oil.[36] In 1980 the US had imported 2.6 million barrels of oil per day (b/d) from Arab states; by 1983 this had fallen to some 750,000 b/d.[37]

But the minor economic boom of the mid-1980s increased US energy consumption.[38] At the same time domestic production had declined: in 1985 the US produced 10.6 million b/d; by 1988 the figure was down to 9.8 million b/d. Accordingly, imports rose.[39] Such changes led inevitably to renewed interest in the Middle East. In 1986, in a survey on the oil industry, **Time** magazine had

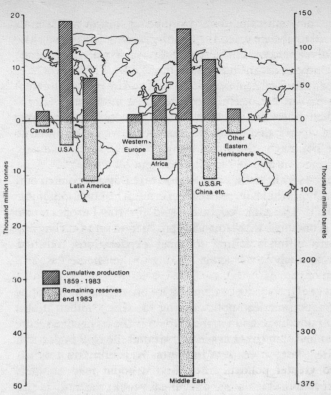

World oil reserves in 1983 compared with total production since 1859

Region/country	Reserves	Percentage
Middle East and North Africa	433,739	62.1
of which: Saudi Arabia	169,000	
Kuwait	90,000	
North America	34,375	4.9
Central and South America	83,315	11.9
Western Europe	24,131	3.4
Sub-Saharan Africa	20,726	2.9
Asia/Pacific	18,530	2.6
Eastern bloc	84,100	12.0
Total	698,667	

Reserves in millions of barrels, 1985

The impact of the intifada 171

lamented that small US oil wells were being shut down: 'The US can ill afford to give up reserves,' the magazine pointed out, 'since it holds only 4 per cent of the world's known supply, in contrast to about 55 per cent in the Middle East.'[40] By 1988 imports of Arab oil had reached 2 million b/d—almost three times the total five years earlier.[41] Projections by the US Department of Energy suggested that between 1989 and 1992 US consumption would remain steady but that domestic production would continue to fall. Correspondingly, the proportion of imported oil would rise: from 44.4 per cent in 1989 to 52.8 per cent by 1992.[42]

In April 1989 **Middle East Economic Digest** pointed out: 'Middle East oil will be increasingly crucial to the US economy in the 1990s.'[43] The same could be said for the European and Japanese economies: with North Sea production set to decline and Far Eastern oilfields failing to meet expectations, Western capitalism as a whole was again looking to the Middle East as a key source of supply.[44]

The fact of increasing US dependence on oil imports had done much to shape American policy during the Gulf conflict; it also influenced policy in relation to the Uprising. The US needed secure oil supplies and stable regimes in and around the Gulf region and North Africa. For 40 years Washington had seen Israel as the keystone of its regional policy. Despite a string of major conflicts the Zionist state had remained a secure ally—but the *intifada* had introduced a new factor. Hitherto America's allies had been both disciplined by Israel, which 'punished' recalcitrant states, and protected by Israel—as when the Zionists attacked the subversive Palestinian presence in Lebanon. But the Uprising had shown a new Palestinian resilience to which Israel seemed not to have an answer and which was especially dangerous for the Arab regimes.

Solidarity action across the Arab world had already shown that the Palestinian issue was still a highly destabilising factor. The longer the movement continued the more likely that the demonstrations and strikes of the West Bank and Gaza could spread like a contagion. The newly-formed alliance of US-supported states—Egypt, Iraq and Jordan—strongly backed by Saudi Arabia, pressed Washington for concessions. The US Administration prevaricated, still hoping to back Israel all the way. Then, in October 1988, Algeria erupted in a 'North African *intifada*'.

'Follow the Palestinians'

For several weeks Algeria had witnessed strikes for increased wages in its largest factories. On 4 October, Algiers was paralysed by huge demonstrations against the government of President Chadli Benjedid. For several days troops fought thousands of people, mainly youths armed only with stones in the manner of the Palestinian *intifada*. Hundreds were killed but riots still spread to every part of the country and there were further widespread strikes.[45] The government declared a state of siege but it was a week before the army regained control.

The events were a response to the collapse of Algerian state capitalism. For 20 years after the war of liberation which had expelled the French, Algeria followed the state capitalist path: industry and agriculture were nationalised, power concentrated in the hands of a ruling bureaucracy, the FLN, and a foreign policy adopted which aligned the country with Moscow.[46] But by the early 1980s inefficiency, indebtedness and growing pressure from the West for 'liberalisation' led to a sharp change in direction. Chadli announced a programme of privatisation, sought foreign capital and moved sharply towards the West, striking trade and arms deals with the US.[47] The West began to view Algeria as a model of Arab pragmatism.

But change had widened class differences. The ruling bureaucracy was now identified with a growing bourgeoisie and a layer of commission agents who had been quick to profit from the economic 'opening'—a pattern seen ten years earlier when Egypt 'liberalised' under Sadat. A rapid rise in the cost of living had been accompanied by shortages of basic goods and in September 1988[48] the government announced austerity measures, ostensibly to offset declining oil revenue.[49] The result had been increased working-class militancy and a rash of strikes. Young workers and unemployed youth then took the initiative with demonstrations against prices rises and shortages. According to **Mideast Mirror**:

> Thousands of young Algerians rampaged through the city centre, looting shops, hijacking buses and setting fire to buildings. Government and wealth symbols were their main targets and they caused millions of dollars worth of damage... Most of those taking part are either unemployed or secondary

school students, some as young as 14.[50]

Chadli's response was to send in thousands of troops but also to concede most of the demonstrators' demands. Wages were increased overnight and shops which had remained largely empty were stocked with goods at the old prices. The regime succeeded in bringing both strikes and demonstrations to an end—but at a cost.

The events were immediately characterised as 'an Algerian *intifada*' by supporters and opponents. For months Algerian television had shown scenes of Palestinian youth defying Israeli troops with no more than stones—conduct it endorsed as a legitimate struggle against oppression. When riots erupted in Algiers the methods were the same: some young Algerians even covered their faces with headscarves, Palestinian-style. Former Algerian president Ahmad Ben Bella, an FLN veteran long exiled to France, called on the Algerian people to 'unite and take matters into [your] own hands like the Palestinians did in their *intifada*'. Since President Chadli could only speak 'the language of tanks', the people should resist, 'even with stones like the Palestinians', he said.[51]

The Arab regimes hurried to support President Chadli. Within 48 hours of the start of rioting, Chadli receiving backing from neighbours King Hassan of Morocco and President Zine al-Abidine Ben Ali of Tunisia, both of whom had crushed massive demonstrations four years earlier.[52] Others also reacted quickly. Although 2,000 miles away, the rulers of the Gulf states understood the danger that a generalisation of the *intifada* could pose. From Saudi Arabia King Fahd sent a message to Chadli. This expressed:

> Saudi Arabia's support for Algeria in the wake of the disturbances and acts of sabotage to which the Algerian capital was subjected by irresponsible elements aiming to destabilise Algeria and undermine its achievements.[53]

The Saudi newspaper **Al-Sharq al-Awsat**—a mouthpiece for the Saudi regime—wrote:

> We would be heartened to see Algeria stable, as we have known it for many years. Its stability means the stability of its neighbours. Instability, God forbid, is contagious.[54]

'Contagion' had produced 'an attempt to strike against legitimacy', the paper maintained. 'Such doings bring the spectre of terrorism.' Using its usual 'code' to spell out that Arab rulers had communicated and agreed to back Chadli's brutal attack on the demonstrators, the paper went on:

It has become obvious over the past few days that all the Arab countries realise the importance of continuity in beloved Algeria. Hence the eagerness of their leaderships, without exception, to see demagogy contained and peace and stability restored.[55]

This view was echoed in Egypt, where President Mubarak declared: 'We are as keen on Algeria's stability and security as we are on Egypt's.'[56] The opposition Tagammu' alliance warned him: 'What took place in Algeria can easily happen in Egypt'.[57]

Mideast Mirror, monitoring Arab press reaction to the Algerian events, observed: 'Arab leaders don't want an Algerian *intifada*'. It went on:

With the likely spread of Palestinian-like *intifadas* into their own territories a major concern, Arab kings and presidents have been prompt in sending messages of sympathy and support to beleaguered President Chadli Benjedid.[58]

The worst fears of Arab rulers were becoming a reality. Now there was a danger that solidarity with the Palestinians had become imitation of the Palestinians.

In the US officials were distressed at the threat to their new-found Algerian ally. They were also aware of the possibility that other, more strategically important friends among the Arab regimes might not survive a similar upsurge from below. In North Africa, King Hassan of Morocco, President Ben Ali of Tunisia and above all President Mubarak of Egypt were vulnerable. Eager not to see a repeat of the Iranian events of 1977-79, which led to the fall of the Shah, the US listened more carefully to its friends in Arab capitals. These argued that although the Algerian explosion had its roots in that country's economic difficulties, the Palestinian Uprising had played a further destabilising role. Washington was urged to make a gesture to the PLO; Arafat was told that the time had come publicly to accept Israel. A month later Arafat recognised the Zionist state and the US agreed to talks.

The final step had not been a result of Fatah's strategy of 'pressuring' the Arab regimes. It was a response to a spontaneous movement of the Palestinian masses; one which had far more potential to destabilise the region than the PLO leadership wished for. The *intifada* had had its effect despite the formal politics of Palestinian nationalism, not because of it.

Chapter Twelve
The 'pseudo-entity'

THE UNITED STATES' agreement to talk to the PLO was accompanied by a hint that it was time to solve the Palestine problem on the basis of a territorial agreement. There was jubilation among many Palestinians, who at last saw the prospect of their own state. But what sort of a state was it to be?

The PLO had already made enormous concessions. First, Arafat had recognised Israel. Since 1948 Palestinian nationalists had avoided even the use of the word 'Israel' or the expression 'Israeli state'; rather, they spoke of 'the Zionist entity'. By accepting the legal existence of Israel, Arafat was acknowledging not only the legitimacy of the Zionist presence itself but its role as the bulwark of Western imperialism. He had publicly recognised what had long been implicit in Fatah's politics: that the organisation accepted Israel as the key link in a chain of alliances which included the majority of Arab regimes, themselves the Palestinians' bitter enemies. Recognition of Israel was a final step to accommodation with the structures of imperialism.

Since the 1950s the national movement had retained the right to wage 'armed struggle' against Israel—indeed this had been its founding principle. By renouncing 'terrorism'—albeit that Arafat retained the right to conduct 'armed actions' in 'occupied Palestine'— Fatah conceded the Israeli and Western characterisations of the Palestinian national movement, equating the violence of the oppressed, an entire dispossessed people, with that of the oppressor, imperialism and its regional representatives.

In tying recognition of Israel to acceptance of the ministate formula Arafat also finally abandoned a principle which had guided the national movement since the 1950s—the understanding that all of Palestine should be liberated and that all Palestinians had a right to return to the homes which had been taken from them by the settler movement. Even during the contorted debates of the 1970s, when Fatah had opted for the ministate, it had maintained that the struggle for the whole of Palestine should be continued. Now even this pretence was gone. Arafat was content with a fraction of historic Palestine.

The ministate debate

Discussion over the character of a possible Palestinian state had been going on for 20 years. Fatah had always been prepared to compromise but at least rhetorically had maintained that in the end it sought a single, 'democratic secular' state.

In 1968 the Palestine National Council had agreed that the first principle of the movement was 'To liberate the Palestinian homeland in its entirety and to exercise Arab sovereignty over it.'[1] The movement was clear that territorial compromise was unacceptable. In 1969 a statement of PLO strategy posed the question, 'Why do the Palestinians refuse to create a Palestinian state in the Western bank of the River Jordan?' It went on:

The Palestinian state in question is one proposed by Israel.
1. This pseudo-entity will become, in effect, a colony exploited by Israel.
2. The formation of this state involves the creation of an Arab Administration designed to act as a pawn in the hands of the Israeli authorities to suppress any revolutionary trends that will appear in this so-called state.
3. Any guarantees given by the Great Powers or the World Organisation [UN] to safeguard the sovereignty of this pseudo-state will be worthless. In the past, guarantors have been unwilling to condemn Israeli aggression except verbally.[2]

The population of the Occupied Territories was also adamantly opposed to a 'ministate'. In 1967, four months after the occupation of the West Bank and Gaza, the National Charter of the Arabs of the West Bank rejected:

the pernicious proposal for the establishment of a Palestinian state intended to form a buffer between the Arabs and Israel, but to be closely linked with the alien Zionist presence. This proposal is an attempt to remove the Palestinian problem from its Arab context and divest it of its national significance, and to isolate the Palestinian Arab people from the Arab nation. The establishment of such a state could only result in the final liquidation of the Palestine problem, the dissolution of the Palestinian people and the dealing of the death-blow to the Arab liberation movement.[3]

The idea of the ministate was fully developed only after the defeat of 1970 in Jordan. The Democratic Front, which had argued for the overthrow of King Hussein in the months preceding Black September, maintained that it was necessary to struggle for the 'unity of the two banks [of the Jordan]': to save the two halves of Jordanian territory before they were lost to Arab sovereignty for good.[4] However, as this apparently meant accepting Jordanian legitimacy in the West Bank, the Front added that if Israeli occupation of this territory could be ended, 'our people will not allow its reconquest by the terrorist government of national treason [Jordan]; it will form [on the West Bank] a liberated zone which will serve as a basis of revolutionary support to the struggle for the downfall of the traitor regime'.[5] Later, the Front argued, there could be an effort 'to liberate the whole of the national territory'.[6]

This contorted formulation was rejected by the rest of the movement, including Fatah, as a retreat from the aim of liberating all of Palestine (and in the case of Fatah because it challenged the principle of non-interference in the affairs of the Arab states). However, it succeeded in introducing the notion of a 'liberated zone' as a step towards freeing all Palestinian territory. A theory of 'stages' was beginning to emerge which soon became the policy of the mainstream of the PLO.

After the October war of 1973 the national movement reassessed the balance of forces *vis-à-vis* Israel. The Democratic Front, which had purged its most insistent 'Marxist-Leninist' elements,[7] argued for a new strategy which would establish a 'national authority' in any part of Palestinian territory that could be liberated. In effect, the Front was calling for a Palestinian state in the West Bank and Gaza. According to the Front's leading figure, Nayef Hawatmeh, the Palestinian people could be won to the project of liberating part of the territory by 'intermediate' or 'transitional' slogans, the most important of which was the call to mobilise the population of the territories. These 'transitional demands' would help direct the aspirations of all Palestinians towards the 'ultimate' task of liberating the whole of Palestine.[8]

But the ministate idea was soon transformed by the diplomatic manoeuvrings which followed the October war. The US was anxious to break up the alliance of Arab states which for a short time had imposed a highly effective oil boycott on the West. US secretary of state Henry Kissinger proposed that the Palestine question should be discussed at a conference where the ministate would be an item on the agenda.

The Geneva conference was in the Kissinger tradition—a Machiavellian effort to entangle the PLO in talks about talks, while Israel was given time to re-arm, and the Arab states to restore political equilibrium at home. Most important, the peace conference would give Egypt's president Sadat time to introduce the policies which would take him fully into the Western camp and allow a separate deal with Israel: this later emerged as the Camp David agreement. The PLO, all too susceptible to the idea of participation at an international conference with the status of a 'state', moved quickly towards the ministate formula. By 1974 it was Fatah policy—effectively PLO policy.

A host of arguments was now advanced for the ministate. Most prominent was the idea that the Palestinians must be willing to accept any part of their territory 'liberated' from Israel as the basis for a state—that to pass up the opportunity of creating a state on part of Palestinian territory was to 'betray' the population of that area. The establishment of such a state was also said to be an exercise in self-determination which the Palestinians must accept if they were to secure the whole of their land. If they did not accept this challenge, it was argued, others—such as King Hussein—would again claim both territory and the right to represent the Palestinian people. The PLO's claim to be the 'sole legitimate representative' of the Palestinian people would be forfeited.

These arguments were rejected by many activists, most forcefully by the Popular Front. The Front maintained that it did not oppose 'the establishment of a revolutionary authority on the soil of Palestine, or part of it, liberated by force of arms'.[9]

However, it declared:

> There is a great difference between that and the establishment of a Palestinian state through negotiations whose basic point, speaking historically, will be the recognition of the Zionist entity and its acceptance in the heart of the Arab nation.[10]

The Front's leading figure, George Habash, insisted that any 'ministate' sponsored by the imperialist powers and the Arab regimes would be one designed to destroy the Palestinian resistance. He asked:

> Have we realised that this state will be squeezed between Israel on the one side and the reactionary Jordanian regime on the other? Have we realised that this state would be the result of an Arab and international gift? This solution will be the 'final solution' to the Middle East problem.[11]

Habash also pointed to the dangers of dividing the Palestinian population and to the feebleness of the 'statelet' which Fatah and the Democratic Front now canvassed:

> Have we thought about the area of this state, and the contradictions that will arise between it and the Palestinian masses whose vital problems will not be solved through this way? This state will be 6,000 sq km, 22.5 per cent of the surface of Palestine. And the rest of our people? An essential contradiction will exist between the state and the Palestinian masses from the 1948 areas whose vital questions will not be solved by this state. Have we thought about the economic resources of such a state?[12]

These criticisms received widespread support. As Salah Khalaf later recalled, many inhabitants of the camps, especially those expelled from parts of Palestine not to be included in the ministate plan, were adamantly opposed to it. 'Coming from the part of Palestine that became Israel in 1948 they considered themselves foreigners in the West Bank,' he recalled. 'They didn't feel they were even concerned with the ministate proposal.'[13] Most Palestinians shared their view.

By the mid-1970s the leadership of Fatah had already conceded far more than most Palestinians supposed. They had entered unofficial talks with the US and with Israel and were secretly bargaining over the extent of a ministate.[14] The negotiations came to nothing and the Geneva peace conference proved an illusion. Israel, the US and Arab regimes got what they wanted—time to reorganise—while the PLO became further entangled in talks about talks. Meanwhile, Arafat had privately accepted that the liberation of the whole of Palestine was out of the question and the attempt to secure a 'ministate' had become Fatah's strategic aim.

The *intifada* and the ministate

The PLO's entanglement in talks about the ministate was one reason for the movement's decline during the late 1970s and early 1980s. It had become less an activist mass movement, more and more a factor in Arab diplomacy. The world of negotiations and talks about deals and double-deals made the PLO leadership distant from the masses; it also made them more dependent upon Arab regimes which sought to use the PLO for domestic reasons and which had no more than a rhetorical commitment to seeing even a ministate established.

The *intifada* changed the situation dramatically. Its destabilising influence led the Arab states to dust off the ministate formula and present it anew to the US, accompanied by the warning that unless there was progress Washington might find that its friends in the region were in deep trouble. They were assisted by a PLO leadership now prepared to discuss the ministate in terms they believed the US could hardly refuse. Leading supporters of Fatah were at pains to show that a Palestinian state would not disturb Israel or the Arab states. Welcoming the declaration of the Palestinian state in December 1988 one Gaza lawyer described the prospect of the state as 'the fulfilment of a dream, a moderate dream'.[15]

Recognition of Israel meant that the ministate was now an end in itself. There was no talk of a 'base' from which to liberate the whole of Palestine, thereby satisfying the aspirations of all Palestinians; instead, a state in the West Bank and Gaza was seen as a means of controlling Palestinian energies. After just three months of the Uprising, Arafat's spokesman, Bassam Abu-Sharif, spelt out how the PLO wished to see the case for a ministate presented to the Americans:

The United States must be made to feel that it is in her interests that an independent Palestinian state be created. This will not happen until the US Administration realises that a Palestinian state in the Middle East will be the safety valve in the region.[16]

A state would contain the Palestinian masses, removing their destabilising influence and allowing the US and its allies to pursue their economic interests undisturbed. Such a state would be integral to the regional system, a guarantor of imperialist hegemony. In case the message had been lost on the US, Abu Sharif repeated it in even blunter terms. The purpose of talks with the US, he said, was to persuade Washington, and indirectly Israel, that a Palestinian state could be fitted into the existing structures of the region.

We want the United States to realise that a Palestinian state will be a factor of stability, not instability. This is the only point we want to establish and we have all the logical and factual information to support that.[17]

Such a view received support from the whole of the PLO. Even the Popular Front, the 'rejectionists' of earlier years, endorsed the declaration of a Palestinian state and talks with the US.[18] The Popular Front's agreement showed how far the radical elements in the movement had accommodated. In 1977, when Bassam Abu-Sharif had been the Popular Front's own spokesman, he had told the **Socialist Workers Party International Discussion Bulletin** that the Front insisted on a programme which was 'clearly progressive and prevents any drifting to the right.' He had added:

For example, a programme which does not allow the leadership to accept a ministate in return for an armed struggle and the recognition of Israel. The PFLP [Popular Front] leads the Left in the Palestinian revolution. Fatah leads the Right.[19]

Not even the PLO radicals were now capable of recognising publicly that the ministate formula was riddled with contradictions. In 1974 US proposals for a peace based on just such a state had drawn the PLO into years of meaningless negotiations. Was the PLO now to enter a similar process, hoping to prolong the Uprising long enough to keep pressure on the US?

If the movement in the Occupied Territories should falter —as, over years, it must—the Arab states might again feel secure and the US confident of its economic interests in the region. What would then be left for the PLO? Even in the best case, one in which the US compelled Israel to concede territory, what could a ministate offer the mass of Palestinians?

'A state without might'

The rulers of Israel's Likud bloc insisted that they would not concede territory to the Palestinians. Israeli prime minister Yitzak Shamir declared that not 'a single centimetre' of the West Bank and Gaza would be made over to a Palestinian state.[20] Jewish settlement of 'Judea and Samaria' (the West Bank) would continue, he maintained. There was no question of talks with the PLO; international recognition of the Palestinian movement was merely a 'bizarre Arafat festival'.[21]

Shamir, as a 'maximalist' on the territorial question, reflected the views of many Israelis but was also under pressure from growing right-wing groups, notably Gush Emunim,[22] which were determined that the process of settling the West Bank should be stepped up. Based mainly in the settler communities, these groups had already established independent militias and promised civil war if their rights to West Bank land came into question. Their champion in the government was Ariel Sharon, former defence minister and architect of the 1982 Lebanon invasion. In April 1989 he declared, 'There will be no second Palestinian state West of the Jordan River.'[23] As far as Sharon and the right were concerned the Palestinians already possessed a state of their own —Jordan. If necessary, he argued, the Palestinians should be 'transferred' there.[24]

Israel's Labour opposition, on the other hand, was publicly committed to some accommodation with the Palestinians. Various schemes were put forward by Labour politicians: each envisaged lengthy talks about the nature of Palestinian representation—a formula no different from that which failed in the mid-1970s. And Labour visions of a territorial agreement were extremely limited. First, all agreed that the Palestinian ministate would occupy only a fragment of Palestine. Israel would not abandon all the land it had colonised in the West Bank and Gaza, large areas of which would be retained for 'security purposes'. Indeed, in early 1988 Labour agreed to a $20 million increase in the Israeli government's settlements budget.[25]

Second, the ministate would be policed by Israel and the neighbouring Arab states. Most proposals favoured a Palestinian state federated with Jordan under the military supervision of Israel, Jordan and perhaps the United Nations. Such a state would have no independent existence. Even those most favourable to the idea of a ministate 'proper'—one not federated with Jordan—saw it as a state in the most minimal sense. Some members of the Labour Party had already sketched out their vision:

> Palestine would, of course, be the Luxembourg; Jordan would be the Belgium; Israel would be the Netherlands... You would end up with the sovereign state of Israel, with its might, and the sovereign state of Jordan, with its might, and the sovereign state of Palestine, without might—but with all the other elements of sovereignty, with a flag and a legislature and stamps and what-not.[26]

Palestine would be the Luxembourg, the Lichtenstein or the San Marino of the Middle East—no more than a sliver of land between neighbouring states.

Third, the ministate would be without the apparatus which defines national states: it would have no army. Arab, Israeli and Western supporters of the ministate had long insisted that a state capable of mobilising independent Palestinian forces was out of the question. Even the most 'radical' Israelis saw Palestinian 'security forces' only as a means of controlling the Palestinian population. According to one Israeli strategist whose ideas were representative of the Labour Party's left wing, means of legal violence in a Palestinian state would exist only to 'protect the regime, contain rejectionist and other sources of domestic disorder, and enforce the state's obligation not to permit acts of violence against neighbouring states to originate from within its territory'.[27]

The PLO agreed. Faisal Husseini, a leading nationalist figure on the West Bank, declared that in lieu of an army he would accept international guarantees for the integrity of a Palestinian state.[28]

A 'state' created on such a basis could not put up even token resistance to its neighbours' armed forces. It could have no foreign policy, no independent identity.

Fourth, the Palestinian ministate would remain under Israeli economic domination. The population of the West Bank and Gaza would continue to provide cheap labour for Israeli employers; the territories would continue to act as profitable markets for Israeli manufacturers. The Palestinian state would have come closer to being a true bantustan: independent in name but in fact a territory operated from a foreign capital.

Little or nothing would change in the lives of the majority of Palestinians. The main task of a Palestinian government would be to provide assurances that neighbouring states would be free of the 'Palestine factor': the 'contagion' the Arab regimes so feared. The new state would guarantee the existence of Israel: in exchange for the name 'Palestine' on a portion of Palestinian land the new state would promise Israel's security. As a result the Palestinian challenge to the Zionist state, to imperialism and to its local allies, would be much diminished.

In January 1989, as talks between the US and the PLO got under way, a former British diplomat summed up the prospects for such a 'state'. Sir Anthony Parsons had been Britain's permanent representative at the UN and was well aware of the intentions of those who canvassed the ministate solution. He observed:

> I find it hard to credit that a Palestinian micro-state (even if ruled by the devil himself), almost certainly demilitarised, roped down by a binding peace treaty and probably by international guarantees, as well as being confederated with Hashemite Jordan, could threaten the existence of the strongest military power in the Middle East. An outsider with a knowledge of past history might think that the boot would be on the other foot.[29]

This comment had much in common with the PLO's own early assessment of the prospects for a ministate. In 1968 the organisation had described such as state as a 'pseudo-entity' which would become 'a colony exploited by Israel'.[30] West Bankers had endorsed this view. The proposal for a ministate was 'pernicious', they said; 'the establishment of such a state could only result in the liquidation of the Palestinian problem'.[31]

Then, Palestinians had feared an attempt to reimpose Jordanian rule; 20 years later a combination of Jordanian, Israeli and Palestinian authority was being proposed—but under circumstances far less favourable to the indigenous population. In the late 1960s the colonisation of the Occupied Territories was just beginning; the Israeli military presence was restricted and few Zionist settlements had been established. By the late 1980s the West Bank and Gaza had indeed become 'a colony exploited by Israel'. The PLO leadership now proposed to formalise that arrangement by declaring the 'pseudo-entity' a state.

The Uprising had seemed to demonstrate a new strength and energy among the Palestinians yet it had produced no more than discussion about a 'micro-state'. This outcome reflected the Palestinians' real predicament—the inherent weakness of Palestinian society *vis-à-vis* imperialism and the deeply conservative nature of the PLO leadership.

Talks about talks

By early 1989, after a series of meetings between American and PLO officials, the prospect of a ministate agreement looked slim. Discussions were conducted on Washington's terms: the main subject on the agenda was 'terrorism' and the Palestinians' responsibility to halt 'terrorist' acts.[32] Meanwhile Israel refused all territorial concessions, agreeing only to elections in the Occupied Territories as a step to discussions with Palestinian representatives.[33]

As frustration began to grow among Palestinian activists Arab leaders called for 'patience'. Egypt's president Mubarak argued that the new US Administration should be given time. US president George Bush, he said,

> well understands the issues and we on the Arab side should not be hasty in any subject or exert pressure around it... we should not pressure him in any way that might lead to adverse reactions in the peace process.[34]

The 'peace process' was beginning to take on the character of the abortive negotiations of 1974. The talks seemed more and more to be a gesture aimed at neutralising the *intifada*. But the *intifada* had not ceased. Israeli pressure in the Occupied Territories increased, Palestinian resistance stiffened and yet again the Uprising proved its destabilising potential.

In mid-April 1989 the towns of southern Jordan erupted in mass protests against food price rises. In the biggest threat to the Hussein regime since Black September in 1970 thousands of youth battled with police and troops for five days. In Ma'an 4,000 protestors seized the city centre; here police joined demonstrators in chanting slogans against the government. In nearby Tafileh youths swathed in the *kefiyyah* hurled stones and declared: 'This is the *intifada* of the East Bank.'[35]

Southern Jordan had been regarded as 'loyalist' territory. The south provided most of the army to which Hussein had turned to destroy the Palestinian movement in 1970. Suddenly this region had become the vanguard of what one Jordanian journalist called 'a nationwide struggle for wider popular participation and a fairer distribution of wealth'.[36] Even where fighting did not take place meetings endorsed calls from the southern cities for the withdrawal of price increases and austerity measures, the resignation of prime minister Zaid Rifai and his government, the punishment of corrupt officials, the lifting of martial law (which had been in operation since 1976), electoral reform, and—in some areas—for practical backing for the Palestinian *intifada*.[37]

The eruption of this movement in a country regarded as among the most stable of Western allies in the Arab world revealed the pressure on local regimes at a time of recession and the fragility of the police state. The US hurried to reassure all its allies in the region by increasing aid to Jordan by over 200 per cent.[38] The regimes were horrified at a movement which bore such similarity to the Algerian events barely six months earlier and which again seemed to have drawn inspiration from the Palestinian Uprising. In Israel the protests were seen to be directly stimulated by the Uprising. Israeli energy minister Moshe Shahal argued that the *intifada* was becoming 'a model for imitation' in the region 'any time there is a need to change reality'.[39]

The Jordanian events also prodded a reluctant Israeli government to agree to 'peace proposals' which the US could present as a major initiative. Prime minister Shamir announced plans for elections in the Occupied Territories; provided those elected rejected the PLO, he declared, Israel would discuss a plan for limited self-rule. *Ha'aretz* summed up the Israeli viewpoint:

...the *intifada* might, if it gets out of control, bring the Soviet Union into the region and embroil the entire Middle East in a war which will wipe out all the trumps currently held by the Americans, from Saudi Arabia to Jordan and Egypt.

This is why the Americans have begun to seriously intervene by pressing the Israeli government to formulate a positive solution. Our prime minister understands that he must present the Americans with a way that will calm the situation, for unless this happens they might well lose. Being so dependent on the United States we must deliver these goods.[40]

This frank assessment—that a 'dependent' Israel must deliver talks that would 'calm' the situation in the region—testified to the destablising power of the *intifada*.

But the PLO leadership interpreted the Jordanian events as a threat. Precisely because these events showed that the *intifada* might help to wipe out all the Americans 'trumps' in the region, the PLO was quick to distance itself from any hint of direct involvement. Anxious to avoid allegations that Palestinians had played a role in the protests, Fatah instructed its members not to join demonstrations and successfully brought pressure on the Popular Front and Democratic Front not to issue leaflets against the Jordanian regime.[41] Even when members of the Muslim Brotherhood and of the Jordanian Communist Party were arrested the PLO in Jordan was silent. For the second time in 20 years Fatah helped to rescue the Hashemite regime.[42]

Fatah feared that Palestinian intervention might jeopardise talks with the US and the prospect of moves towards the ministate. At the same time it wanted to prove it was capable of defining how far Palestinian activity could go. Fatah therefore suppressed Palestinian opposition to Hussein; it placed the PLO in the camp of Hussein, the regimes and the US. But this move did not advance 'peace talks'; rather it reassured the US that Fatah was willing to move at Washington's pace—indeed that the PLO now had no alternative but to do so.

In Washington the Algerian protests and 'the *intifada* of the East Bank' had had a double impact. On the one hand they proved the fragility of local regimes, the destabilising effect of the *intifada* and the need to engage the PLO in discussions which might neutralise the Uprising. On the other hand they proved again the US' need for a strong ally in a volatile region and that there was no substitute for America's trusted Zionist ally. In effect they proved that 'talks about talks' which satisfied the Arab regimes and gave Israel some room for manouevre was still the best strategy.

In November 1988, as Arafat was preparing to recognise Israel, Palestinian journalist Muhammad Hallaj had warned of the dangers in the Fatah strategy:

> Pleasing America is important for reasons known to all. But it is not important enough to become an end in itself. To make pleasing Washington a paramount Palestinian objective is self-defeating. It may take the Palestinians from point 'A' to point 'B' but they risk finding nothing when they get there.[43]

Fatah had proved its willingness to please the US; it had got nothing in return.

Chapter Thirteen
Palestine and the Arab revolution

PALESTINIAN NATIONALISM has failed to achieve the aims it set 30 years ago. Israel's determination to destroy all forms of Palestinian self-organisation has been an enormous obstacle for the movement but of equal significance has been the inadequacy of the nationalist strategy.

The movement which in the 1960s took on the task of liberating Palestine was no longer confronting an aggressive settler movement but a state that had found its place in the imperialist system. This dictated that the Palestinians should be implacably opposed to the whole structure of imperialism—to the imperialist states, to Israel and to imperialism's Arab allies. But Fatah sought an accommodation with imperialism. It set out to persuade the Arab rulers to accept an independent Palestinian state—a partner on whose behalf they should take up the battle against Israel. In short, Fatah sought an accommodation with Arab capitalism.

The strategy foundered on Fatah's inability to resolve the contradiction between the interests of the mass of Palestinians and those of the Arab ruling classes. It could not mobilise a mass movement which expressed the Palestinians' aspirations *and* contain that movement within the political systems controlled by the regimes.

It is significant that the PLO's greatest opportunity arose precisely at the point when the movement extended beyond the limits imposed by Fatah. In Jordan in 1970 the energies released by the national movement caused a rise in self-confidence that allowed Palestinians and some Jordanians to pose an alternative to the Hussein dictatorship. It was Fatah's fear of threatening

Hussein's power that caused it to rein in the movement, leading to the inevitable catastrophe. From 1970 until the eruption of the *intifada* it was downhill all the way.

At the core of the problem was Fatah's insistence on Palestinian unity. It saw the call for unity as a dramatic reversal of the Arab nationalists' appeal for Arab unity: in fact Fatah merely repeated the nationalists' slogan in Palestinian terms. The subsequent tragedy of the Palestinian movement has been its inability to seek a different sort of unity—that between the mass of Palestinians and the other victims of the regimes: the Arab working class and peasantry.

From the moment of expulsion in 1948 the Palestinians found themselves dependent upon other forces in the region. The allies that the leaders of the new movement sought were not among the Arab working class but among their class antagonists—the kings, *shaikhs* and presidents. The Fatah leaders' narrow nationalism has been a key reason for this misorientation but the absence of an effective Arab socialist tradition has also been of great importance. This has meant that the Arab workers' movement has not offered obvious points of contact with the Palestinians, who have conducted their struggle with a strategy which sealed them off from the region's most potent political force.

During the 1950s, as Fatah was putting down its roots, the Communist parties were revealing the bankruptcy of Arab Stalinism. From North Africa to the Gulf the parties pursued 'popular front' strategies of class collaboration which led them to liquidate (as in Egypt), to dissolve into the nationalist regimes (as in Syria), or face butchery at the hands of their allies (as in Iraq).

This had a profoundly negative effect on the Palestinians. For the founders of Fatah, who drew their inspiration from the nationalists of the 1930s, the Communists were anyway marginal. But for the many Palestinians who looked for a radical alternative, the absence of socialist politics was disastrous. The Communist tradition was already mistrusted because of the failure of the Palestine Communist Party in the 1930s and Moscow's support for the Zionist movement in 1948. When Palestinian activists began casting around for a new political strategy they saw Communist parties incapable even of expressing the interests of those suffering under the regimes. This was one important reason why Fatah, which began as an exclusively petit-bourgeois grouping, was able to attract members with far more radical expectations.

When a leftward-looking current finally emerged in the early 1960s its only model was still that of the local Stalinist parties. The 'radicals' of the Popular and Democratic fronts absorbed all the ideas of mainstream Stalinism, from 'socialism in one country' to the alliance with the 'socialist' states of the Eastern bloc. In the absence of a Palestinian Communist Party, the fronts expressed Palestinian Stalinism.[1]

On the basis of such ideas the Fronts criticised Fatah's strategy, especially its policy of non-interference in the affairs of the Arab states and the close link with regimes they deemed 'reactionary', such as those of the Gulf. But they found no contradiction in supporting the local state capitalisms, which they identified as 'progressive' on the basis of their rulers' rhetoric about 'Arab socialism', 'popular power' and ties with Moscow. Syria, Algeria, Libya, South Yemen and sometimes Iraq were embraced as allies, despite their repression of all domestic opposition and their cynical use of factions within the PLO.

The absorption of Stalinism into the nationalist movement also helped to isolate Palestinians from the struggles of Arab workers. The presence of Israel and the expansionary policy that led it into a series of wars allowed the Arab rulers an alibi—they were able to direct domestic discontent into nationalism, with Zionism the main enemy.[2] By the 1960s, with the re-emergence of the Palestinian movement, the regimes were able to identify with Palestinian leaders who were themselves willing to endorse the Arab rulers' anti-Zionist credentials in exchange for diplomatic support, cash and arms.

This gave a whole generation of *shaikhs* and presidents legitimacy and weakened the basis for unity between the Palestinian masses and Arab workers. This has been true whether it was Arafat who appeared alongside the Gulf rulers, or George Habash of the Popular Front and Nayef Hawatmeh of the Democratic Front who shared a platform with the 'progressives' —Syria's Assad, Libya's Qaddafi, Algeria's Boumedienne or Chadli. There has been no part of the Palestinian movement not identified with a section of Arab capital.[3]

The regimes have long understood that although Palestinian nationalism is a potentially subversive movement, its leaders can be induced to play a role which serves the regimes' interests. Thus after the 1967 war, when for the first time in 15 years Egyptians were organising against the Nasser regime, Egyptian government officials met PLO leaders to plead for their help. The Egyptian foreign minister begged the Palestinians to 'make some military operations' in the newly occupied West Bank and Gaza, with the intention of distracting the attention of the mass of the population in states such as Egypt from the military and political failings of their rulers. Otherwise, predicted the minister, 'the masses would turn against their regimes'.[4]

Fatah encouraged such attitudes. Khalid al-Hassan coolly related that he told Saudi Arabia's King Faisal 'to give us the opportunity to direct the anger and bitterness on our side [after Black September] away from violence and into support for positive political action'.[5] He added: 'We didn't need to tell Faisal that if we lost control there would be an escalation of violence... which would lead in time to the collapse and defeat of Arab moderation and, eventually, the downfall of the pro-Western Arab regimes.'[6] A strategy which served the interests of the mass of Palestinians required just such a defeat of 'Arab moderation', but for Fatah it was an idle threat.

The 'radicals' of the Fronts were less crude but tacitly played the same game. Whenever a leading radical appeared in Tripoli, Damascus, Baghdad, Algiers or Aden it was to hail the local 'revolutionary leadership'. The existence of police states which repressed all domestic opposition was simply ignored.

For 30 years the PLO leaders believed they were using the Arab ruling classes—and were used by them. At no point did the major PLO organisations openly criticise regimes with which they had a formal link. Never was this clearer than during the *intifada*. Fatah hurried to place itself at the head of the movement in the Occupied Territories and then to accept the support and financial backing of the regimes; the Popular Front and Democratic Front were not far behind. Soon PLO leaders were appearing with Arab presidents and *emirs*: despite the attack on Palestinian demonstrators in Kuwait City, Arafat visited Kuwait to hail the royal family's backing for the Palestinian cause. Only days later Habash and Hawatmeh joined him to stand alongside president Chadli in Algeria.

But when Algeria's own *intifada* erupted, the PLO leaders

were silent—and only a month later they again appeared alongside the Algerian president as the Palestine National Council met in Algiers. In October 1988 Chadli was the butcher of the Algerian workers; in November he could present himself as friend of the Uprising and of the anti-imperialist struggle. The PLO leaders were his alibi.

The Palestinian leadership could not identify with Algerian workers and the youth who battled with Chadli's army. Nor dare they raise solidarity with Jordanians during the 'intifada of the East Bank'. The interests of the mass of Palestinians required the development of a strong, independent workers' movement capable of *challenging* the Arab allies of imperialism. This the PLO leaders could not countenance; they dared not bite the hand that fed them.

The Stalinist heritage

Nationalism and Stalinism have proved enormous obstacles to the development of the working-class movement in the Arab countries. They have induced passivity among the rank and file and imposed bureaucratic, class-collaborationist leaderships. They have also produced a climate in which expectations of working-class struggle have been low and in which the achievements of workers' struggle have been minimalised or even dismissed.

According to the Stalinist view the working class has a marginal role to play in social change; its interests are subordinated to those of other classes. As a result, Stalinist organisations have minimised or even ridiculed the level of activity that can be anticipated within the proletariat. In fact such an approach was discredited long before the emergence of Stalinism.

At the turn of the century Leon Trotsky pointed out that a process of 'permanent revolution' was at work in countries outside the imperialist heartland. Development was following a pattern which dictated that the capitalist class was not capable of bringing fundamental change, as it had done in Europe. Nor was the peasantry, often numerically dominant in such countries, able to play an independent role. Only the working class could transform such societies, Trotsky argued. This approach was confirmed by a series of revolutionary upheavals, notably that in Russia in

1917, in which the proletariat, even if small in absolute terms, played the decisive role.[7]

The theory of permanent revolution was subversive of the whole outlook of the state capitalist bureaucracy which ruled Russia from the late 1920s. Stalin and his ideologists therefore dismissed the idea, replacing it with the discredited theory of 'stages' and the notion of the need for a 'bloc of classes' in which the proletariat had a modest role to play in an anti-imperialist alliance which included 'progressive' sections of the bourgeoisie, the petit bourgeoisie and the peasantry.[8]

These notions were imposed on the Communist International at terrible cost to the world's Communist parties.[9] Nowhere was the effect more damaging than in the Arab world where, with the exception of the first Egyptian Communist Party, all Communist organisations were formed after the period of degeneration of the Comintern.[10] Arab Communist parties thus began life as the nuclei of cross-class alliances. Their main aim was to win the confidence of the local bourgeoisie and to establish anti-imperialist movements in which the place of capital would be assured. Lenin's injunction that under all circumstances the working class and the Communist parties should retain independence of bourgeois and petit-bourgeois currents was set aside.[11]

This approach led to paralysis on the Arab left. It meant that anti-imperialist movements were influenced overwhelmingly by bourgeois ideas—that in most countries of the region the working class ceased to be a point of reference for struggle. When in the 1960s Fatah declared the working class marginal to anti-imperialist struggle, there was no Marxist alternative to counter its argument. According to Faruq al-Qaddumi (Abu Lutf): 'Workers, especially in the underdeveloped countries, form a simple and ineffective class which cannot be relied on.'[12] There was no independent Communist current capable of a response.

The Arab working class

In fact the working class in the Arab world has long had the potential to act decisively against the ruling classes of the region. In the period following the First World War it was the Egyptian working class which set the pace in the struggle against imperialism. More recently, as development has accelerated, workers have played a leading role in a series of political conflicts which have pitched mass movements against imperialism and against the local ruling classes.

The pattern of change has sometimes disguised the much increased weight of the working class. Thus although for the past 40 years industrial growth in most of the Middle East has been rapid, many Arab societies have apparently still been dominated by relations in the countryside. Where urban growth has been swift, city life has seemed to be dominated economically by traditional craft relations and politically by the urban poor. This picture is a superficial expression of the impact of combined and uneven development.

Modern industry has penetrated all the major Arab states. New industrial complexes have been established, among them those producing steel (Egypt, Algeria, Libya, Syria, Saudi Arabia); aluminium (Egypt, Libya, the UAE, Bahrain), chemicals (Algeria, Morocco, Libya, Tunisia, Saudi Arabia, Kuwait, Qatar), vehicles (Egypt, Morocco, Algeria, Saudi Arabia), and a mass of import-substitutes including plastics, electronic and domestic goods. But their introduction has not been uniform; often the new plants, factories and mills have been established as islands of advanced industry in essentially backward economies.

The new complexes have often operated alongside established industries using outdated methods. There has also been a sharp contrast with traditional craft sectors which still employ a substantial part of the urban population. Thus new manufacturing complexes have been established alongside tiny workshops; advanced sectors have co-existed with those using methods that have not changed for generations.

The sharpest contrast has been between the industrial and agricultural sectors. In most areas of the region, except the Gulf, the rural population has largely used traditional methods of cultivation: in some cases, notably in Egypt, these have hardly changed for thousands of years. Yet agriculture too may be highly advanced, especially where, as in parts of North Africa, it has been developed to serve the European market. The modern co-exists with the traditional; the most advanced technology with the most ancient.

Statistical evidence shows the pattern of development. During the 1970s the average annual growth rate of industry in most Arab countries much exceeded that of the rate of increase in the traditional economy, based on agriculture. For example, in four countries formerly dominated by the rural economy:[13]

Average Annual Growth Rates

Country/years	Agriculture	Manufacturing
Algeria (1974-77)	-0.5	9.1
Egypt (1974-77)	-2.0	5.8
Iraq (1968-78)	0.3	12.2
Syria (1971-77)	5.3	10.0

Such developments have had their demographic impact. Millions of peasants and agricultural labourers have been drawn into the cities. Some have found employment in the new industries; others have remained unemployed or semi-employed, part of the sea of urban poor which has produced phenomenal population growth rates for cities such as Cairo, Alexandria, Beirut and Tunis. Today the old core of such cities is surrounded by a mass of slum and shanty housing inhabited by millions of rural migrants living on the edge of starvation.

Percentage of people in urban areas[14]

Country	1960	1981
Algeria	31	44
Egypt	38	44
Iraq	43	72
Jordan	43	57
Lebanon	35	77
Syria	37	49
Tunisia	32	53

Numerous sociologies of development record such changes —but the corresponding change in class structures has been largely passed over. In particular the growth of the working class has effectively been ignored and the political weight which such a class can exercise within Arab society has been minimised. Those who have approached the question have chosen to emphasise problems of definition and to warn that there is no necessary relationship between the numerical strength of the proletariat and its political potential. In one of the few attempts to analyse class structures in the Middle East, Elisabeth Longuenesse has taken just such an approach. She has maintained:

It is not sufficient to count the number of people working in the industrial sector, even when introducing subtle definitions on the delineation of this sector, and then to conclude that the working class includes a certain percentage of the society and that objective conditions—still less subjective—exist for this class to play a leading role in the socialist transformation of society.[15]

It is true that statistics must be interpreted carefully. For example, World Bank figures showed that by 1980 some 25 per cent of the workforce in the major Arab countries was engaged in industry.

Percentage of workforce in industry[16]

	1960	1980
Algeria	12	25
Egypt	12	30
Iraq	18	26
Jordan	26	20
Kuwait	34	34
Lebanon	23	27
Libya	17	28
Morocco	14	21
Saudi Arabia	10	14
Syria	19	31
Tunisia	18	32

Such figures can be misinterpreted. First, the existence of a large artisan sector throughout the region, sections of which are sometimes counted into 'industry', can be a distorting factor.

Second, the figures cover a wide range of economies with huge differences in population size and types of industry, and comparisions must be made with care. For example, Kuwait's industrial workforce, perhaps 60,000 workers in a population of 1.3 million, can hardly be compared with that of Egypt, with at least five million industrial workers in a population of 50 million and among which are a far greater number in large workplaces operated by heavy industry and manufacturing.

There are other specific problems: Lebanese and Jordanian industries have been particularly affected by war, invasion and, in the Jordanian case—as the table above shows—by annexation, with the result that the working class has been fragmented. On the other hand in Saudi Arabia and some other Gulf countries the industrial workforce is now much larger than official figures suggest; in particular the statistics do not reflect the millions of emigrant workers travelling from Arab countries such as Egypt, and from Asia, to work in the oil economies.[17]

But such statistics do reflect the pace of change in the region and the growth of an industrial proletariat which in many countries numbers several million. The absolute number of workers in core industries is large: for example, by 1981 there were 1.5 million workers in manufacturing in Egypt, with more than another million in construction and transport; in Iraq there were 750,000 workers in manufacturing and construction; in Syria there were more than 500,000 workers in these sectors.[18] During the 1980s these figures have increased substantially.

The process of uneven development means that the industrial working class may merge with the urban poor and the agricultural proletariat—such is the case especially in North Africa and Egypt. This does not lessen the political potential of the proletariat as a class with the collective power to play the leading role in political life. Indeed, as events from the Russian revolution of 1917 to the Iranian revolution of 1979 have shown, at times of social crisis the working class in such countries plays the decisive role in the process of change.[19]

A history of struggle

One result of the bankruptcy of Stalinism has been that the written history of the workers' movement in the Middle East is particularly impoverished. Only in recent years have studies of parts of the workers' movement begun to appear; the record of Arab workers' struggles over some 60 years is largely hidden.[20]

This absence of an active proletariat is one of the most striking features of analysis of the Arab world from writers on the left. Thus one of the most influential studies of the Arab world written in the past 20 years—**The Arab Nation**, written by the Egyptian Samir Amin in the mid-1970s—finds space to refer to the proletariat only to dismiss it. Amin maintains:

In the Third World integration [into the imperialist system] has proletarianised and impoverished the broad masses, without managing to integrate them into the system of capitalist accumulation...[21]

As a result, Amin maintains, the proletariat has played a minor role in political change. Nationalism, under the leadership of 'proletarianised and popular masses, especially the rural ones' is the answer to the region's problems.[22]

Even in the late 1980s there is a deep scepticism about the potential of the Arab working class. Writing in 1989, Eric Davis argues against the analysis 'that tends to romanticise the historical role of the working class in the Arab world'.[23] He observes:

In what often seems a rush to locate revolutionary agency, such romanticisation only serves to reify and trivialise the political impact of workers and the conditions under which they must struggle.[24]

Such views assert and reassert a Stalinist tradition which has written the working class out of the political history of the region. It is contradicted by a long record of working-class struggle. Despite high levels of repression the working class has repeatedly shown its willingness to take on the forces of imperialism and the regimes.

As Israel was being established, Egyptian workers were resuming struggles they had first undertaken after the First World War.[25] A series of mass strikes forced the regime of King Faruk to the brink of defeat; significantly, this wave of activity was only ended by the king's declaration of war 'on behalf' of the Palestinians.[26] The struggles were renewed in the 1950s, when, in the absence of a socialist alternative, the beneficiary was the new petit bourgeoisie represented by the Free Officers around Nasser.

During the same period Iraq saw the rapid growth of a workers' movement centred on the oilfields, the port of Basra, the railways and the tobacco industry. There were repeated strikes during the 1950s until in 1959 the Communist Party finally aborted the movement. Nearby, in the Gulf states, the development of the oil industry produced major struggles. In 1953, 13,000 workers in the Saudi oilfields went on strike, largely under Palestinian leadership. Three years later there were further strikes leading to the expulsion of many activists.[27]

For much of the 1960s, which were the golden age of Arab nationalism, the movement was relatively subdued, anaesthetised by a combination of the nationalists' rhetoric and repression and the Communist parties' acquiesence.[28] However, towards the end of the decade the movement revived. Egypt was again the centre and by the early 1970s a series of struggles had affected almost every section of industry. These included waves of strikes in 1971, 1972 and 1976, culminating in the uprising of January 1977 that took the Sadat regime to the brink of defeat.

The 1977 events were a reminder of the power of workers in the region. Factories, mills, docks and offices emptied and millions poured onto the streets to oppose Sadat's policies. Despite his quick concession of the movement's demands, Sadat's government lost control in every major urban centre in the country. A complete lack of organisation on the left and Sadat's use of the army to put down the demonstrations just saved the regime.[29]

In succeeding years a string of revolts in North Africa showed that the regimes of the Maghreb were also vulnerable. General strikes in Tunisia in 1978 and 1981 and in Morocco in 1980 were followed by riots in both countries in 1984. In 1985 the focus moved to Sudan, where the role of workers in a rising mass movement against president Nimairi became so prominent that army officers seized power before the movement could widen and threaten their own interests. In 1988 it was the turn of Algerian workers, whose strikes precipitated the 'intifada' of October. In this first upsurge since the war of liberation against France, Algerian workers have shown that it is they who will set the pace in the struggle against the country's new ruling class—a warning to those who control the other Arab nationalist regimes in Syria, Iraq and Libya.

Such a record does not 'romanticise' the working class in the Arab world. It affirms the increasing weight of the working class during a period in which uneven development has created great instability. The pace of Arab workers' struggle is unlikely to slow. As the regimes' room for manoeuvre is narrowed by economic pressures, further upheavals can be expected. In particular, where the crisis of Arab nationalism is reflected by the break-up of state-owned industry and the advance of private and foreign capital—as in Egypt, Algeria, Iraq and even in Libya[30]—sudden explosions are likely. As the Iranian revolution of 1979 showed so dramatically, in a region where there is a tradition of political movements rapidly stimulating activity across national boundaries, such struggles are likely to have a highly destabilising effect.[31]

All the Arab regimes are vulnerable to movements from below which express the interests of millions who have not shared in the oil boom, in the privileges of the ruling families and bureaucracies, or in the wealth of those who profit from the 'opening' to Western capital. A continuing struggle against imperialism such as the Palestinian Uprising can act as a catalyst —as the Egyptian, Algerian and Jordanian rulers have found to their cost. But what will be the reaction of the Palestinian movement to such new waves of workers' struggle?

A new tradition

For the PLO leadership past struggles in the Arab countries have been a sideshow. They have sometimes felt that domestic unrest has been useful for bringing pressures on regimes with which Arafat has wanted to play what he has called 'tactical games'.[32] Under these circumstances the working class has been seen as a potential ally—but one that according to Fatah 'cannot be relied on'. On the other hand such struggles may be an embarrassment, even an obstacle, to Fatah's aim of raising support from the regimes. In most cases the PLO leadership has identified openly with the ruling class against the masses.[33]

For 30 years Fatah has trailed the regimes, despite the fact that such a strategy has never led to real pressure on the state of Israel. The greatest potential threat to Israel has come when the workers' movement has reached its highest point—when in 1977 the Egyptian workers threatened to remove Sadat. This raised the prospect that continuing political instability in Egypt might undermine the local ruling class and threaten to spread to other states, destabilising the whole structure of imperialism in the region. The absence of a revolutionary workers' leadership prevented the development of the 1977 movement; in future crises the existence of a Marxist current within the workers' movement could bring a different outcome.

For those Palestinians who have reached this conclusion the task becomes that facing all Arab socialists—how to establish a new socialist tradition in the region, one capable of building on the potential of the Arab working class. This means, first, re-asserting confidence in the revolutionary role of workers in the face of the Stalinist tradition with its substitutionist formulas. It means focusing on all the manifestations of workers' activity in the Arab countries—on strikes, occupations, demonstrations, bread riots, campaigns against repression and for union rights. Above all, it means setting out to build independent workers' parties whose ideas are rooted in the Marxist tradition.

Such a strategy has never been formally debated in the Palestinian movement. When radical nationalists have approached the question, they have raised two main points: the marginality of the Palestinians and the problem of the 'long view' canvassed by revolutionary Marxists.[34]

Palestinian workers have indeed been marginal within the Arab economies: the result of the regimes' anxiety to keep them outside areas of economic activity.[35] However this does not make the general involvement of Palestinians in Arab politics less relevant, rather it emphasises the need for it. Palestinian workers lack real political weight: in order to pursue their interest the Palestinian masses must engage with social forces which possess the power to confront Arab capitalism.

The first obstacle to overcome is that of ideas: the notion that Palestinian interests are strictly national interests—that events in the Arab capitals have no bearing on those in the West Bank or Gaza. For the Palestinians will continue to be a radicalising force throughout the region—there will be more *intifadas* which in part draw inspiration from Palestinian struggles. But there will also be Arab workers' movements with the power to bring change throughout the region and from which Palestinians cannot afford to stand aside.

The second obstacle to Palestinian integration in the Arab workers' movement has been Palestinians' scorn of the Marxists' long-term strategy. Armed struggle seemed to offer the prospect of an immediate engagement with the Zionist enemy, a chance to start the process of liberation after years of rhetoric from the Arab regimes. By comparision, the Marxist strategy of building up a revolutionary current in the working class by engaging in workers' struggles over many years seemed laborious. But within a few years the nationalist strategy had delivered up the Palestinian movement to the regimes.

The 'long view' does not offer the prospect of an immediate confrontation with Zionism, for its success can only be measured by the degree to which revolutionary ideas spread among workers—there are no short cuts to the construction of the party that can argue for such ideas. To succeed in this project means going back to basic principles of politics and organisation, but doing so among proletarian forces that have the potential for change—a sharp contrast to the effort to construct phoney alliances with the bourgeoisie, a class intrinsically alien to the interests of the mass of Palestinians.

Never has there been a better time for Palestinians to engage with the workers' movement. The crisis of nationalism has been evident for many years and the Stalinist tradition is at last being reassessed. In several Arab countries, notably Egypt, Marxists are looking afresh at the history of the Communist movement and beginning to build new forms of socialist organisation. These can establish a political current wholly independent of the old Communist parties, with their ties to Moscow and to the regimes. For the first time since the establishment of Israel, Palestinian socialists can work together with Arab revolutionaries opposed to the policies of imperialism East and West.

A new generation of Palestinian activists has emerged from the *intifada*. Its options are limited: to embrace the orthodox nationalism of Fatah or the 'radicalised' version of the Democratic and Popular Fronts and the Communist Party. Alternatively, it can look to the Islamic current—the Jihad or the Muslim Brotherhood's Hamas: organisations committed to the same petit-bourgeois nationalism which has failed the Palestinians. They are also more deeply compromised by the Islamic movement's relationship with the regimes—notably the Brotherhood's close link to the rulers of the Gulf states.

The aspirations of these organisations extend no further than the establishment of a ministate which cannot serve the interests of the majority of the Palestinian people. Israel's intransigence makes even the prospect of such a state unlikely. It also points up the inadequacy of an approach which does not challenge imperialism but constantly seeks accommodation with it—always to be bloodily rejected. The new generation of Palestinian activists which has made the *intifada* therefore faces the challenge of taking a new direction.

Workers' power

In May 1989 *al-Hadaf*, the newspaper of the Popular Front, discussed the dilemma facing the Palestinian movement. Writing only weeks after Jordan's 'intifada of the East Bank' it asked:

How are we Palestinians supposed to deal with our hinterland, with the backing which we receive from the Arab world? This ancient question keeps cropping up and remains unresolved. Arab backing consists of the support provided by the Arab masses for the Palestinian Revolution, and that given by the Arab regimes to the PLO. Which should have the priority, particularly when—as is so often the case—our relations with the Arab masses cost us the goodwill of the regimes, and vice versa?...

We exercise gladly our membership of all official Arab institutions. We are visibly pleased to attend anything from Arab summit conferences to meetings of Arab interior ministers, to meetings about the Arabsat [the Arab telecommunications satellite].

After these meetings we go and address public meetings and popular rallies at which we lament the failings of the current Arab situation, criticise the quiescence and silence of the Arab people and ask them—from sea to sea—to move and confront the imperialist-Zionist-reactionary plot.

And when the Arab masses do move, our hearts dance with joy. But no sooner does this happen than we find ourselves hurrying to voice our concern for the safety of the regime in question and the health of its leader, whom we shower with telephone calls and telegrams denouncing this latest plot against Arab security and order. Some of us even prove our good intentions by contributing some dollars to help rebuild that which the mass movement had damaged!

It is certainly a very difficult question. We try to be a well-behaved part of the Arab system and pay our dues for membership in the 'Club of Regimes' in order to avoid trouble with them. But when their unholy tactics and alliances end up squeezing us we look to the forgotten Arab masses for salvation. The masses in the meantime have been drowning in their own regional concerns and their struggle with everyday life.

Our incomplete faith in the capabilities and effectiveness of the Arab masses drives us nearer to the regimes. Our fear and distrust of the regimes, their intentions and promises, draw us closer to the masses for salvation. We end up in an unenviable position. The Arab masses may be understanding of our position and they excuse us up to a point. But the Arab regimes are prepared to be flexible about anything except this question.[35]

Al-Hadaf was unable to reach a conclusion:

So how can this be resolved? Perhaps in our end-of-Ramadan prayers we should beseech God to remove this 'misunderstanding' between the regimes and the people. It would certainly be the easiest and least costly solution.

Karl Marx argued that history never raises a problem unless there are the conditions present for its solution. Although the Palestinian problem has been most evident in the camps of Beirut or the villages of the West Bank, the solution lies elsewhere. The power to begin the process of change lies above all in the industrial cities of Egypt, the centre of Arab capitalism. A mass movement in Egypt can bring to power a class which has a real interest in confronting imperialism, not accommodating to it. When workers take the factories into their hands and peasants take the land, for the first time there can be an alternative to both Arab capitalism and the Zionist state.

The struggle with Israel and its backers will be long, bloody and tortuous, but it can take place on the basis of a strategy which both recognises that there can be no compromise with Israel —which is still the main guarantor of imperialist interests in the Middle East—and offers the prospect of a socialist, internationalist alternative for Arabs and Jews in Palestine. The question for Palestinian and Arab socialists is whether they will be prepared to adopt the only strategy which can offer a chance of removing both the regimes and imperialism's Zionist watchdog.

The potential of the Arab workers' movement is not in question; the problem confronting all Arab socialists is how to build a new revolutionary current which can offer real leadership in the political crises which are to come. For Palestinians this does not mean that resistance to the Israelis must be abandoned, but that the most urgent task becomes that of winning activists to revolutionary socialist ideas and to the practical task of building independent workers' parties. On one score Yasser Arafat has been right. He has admitted: 'Israel is the superpower of the region and we are resisting it with the equivalent of bows and arrows.'[36] It is time for the Palestinians to ask how they can participate in forging the weapon of workers' power.

Notes

INTRODUCTION

1. **The Independent** (London), 18 May 1989.
2. **The Independent**, 18 May 1989.

Chapter 1: INTIFADA

1. **Mideast Mirror** (London), 11 December 1987.
2. **Middle East Report** (Washington), number 152, May-June 1988 page 22.
3. **Mideast Mirror**, 11 December 1987.
4. **Mideast Mirror**, 22 December 1987.
5. **Middle East Report**, number 152, page 9.
6. **Middle East Report**, number 152, page 9.
7. **The Jerusalem Post**, 23 January 1988. (This and all references are to the international edition.)
8. **Mideast Mirror**, 14 January 1988.
9. Janet Abu-Lughod, 'The Demographic Consequences of the Occupation', in Naseer Aruri (editor), **Occupation: Israel Over Palestine** (London 1984), page 258.
10. **Middle East Report**, number 152, page 26.
11. **Merip Report** (Washington), number 74, January 1979, page 7.
12. **Middle East Report** number 152, page 36.
13. **Financial Times** (London), 13 January 1988.
14. **Middle East Report**, number 152, page 35.
15. **Middle East Report** number 152, page 37.
16. Report of the West Bank Data Base project, in **The Middle East** (London), August 1986.
17. **Middle East Report**, number 152, page 36.
18. **Middle East Report**, number 152, page 36.
19. **Middle East Report**, number 152, page 36.
20. **Middle East Report**, number 152, page 35.
21. **Middle East Report**, number 152, page 19.
22. **Middle East Report**, number 152, page 7.

23. **Middle East Report**, number 152, page 7.
24. **The Jerusalem Post**, 23 January 1988.
25. **The Jerusalem Post**, 23 January 1988.
26. **Middle East Report**, number 155, November-December 1988, page 39.
27. **Middle East Report**, number 155, page 39.
28. **Middle East Report**, number 154, September-October 1988, page 8.
29. *Ha'aretz*, (Tel-Aviv) 5 December 1988.
30. **Mideast Mirror**, 27 February 1989.
31. **New York Times**, 24 February 1988.
32. Quoted in **Middle East Report**, number 154, page 15.
33. **The Jerusalem Post**, 13 February 1988.
34. **The Jerusalem Post**, 13 February 1988.
35. **Middle East International** (London), 9 September 1988, page 19.
36. **Middle East International**, 9 September 1988, page 19.
37. **Middle East International**, 9 September 1988, page 19.
38. **The Jerusalem Post**, 5 March 1988.
39. Wolf Blitzer in **The Jerusalem Post**, 23 January 1988.
40. Kissinger's speech to a private gathering of American Jewish leaders, quoted in the **New York Times**, 6 March 1988, and reported in **Middle East Report**, number 152, page 11.
41. **Middle East Report**, number 154, page 14.
42. **Middle East Report**, number 154, page 14.
43. Text from **Middle East International**, 18 November 1988, page 23.
44. **Middle East International**, 16 December 1988, page 5.
45. **Middle East Report**, number 152, page 30.
46. **The Independent**, 18 May 1989.
47. **Mideast Mirror**, 17 July 1989.
48. **Mideast Mirror**, 5 July 1989.
49. **Mideast Mirror**, 5 July 1989.

Chapter 2: THE IMPERIALIST CONNECTION

1. Abram Leon writes: 'The highly tragic situation of Judaism in our epoch is explained by the extreme precariousness of its social and economic position. The first to be eliminated by decaying feudalism, the Jews were also the first to be rejected by the convulsions of dying capitalism. The Jewish masses find themselves between the anvil of decaying feudalism and the hammer of rotting capitalism.' (Abram Leon, **The Jewish Question** (New York 1970) page 226). Leon extends Marx's analysis of the Jewish predicament by examining the roots of anti-Semitism in the twentieth century—see especially chapter 6 of his book.
2. Some nationalist currents, such as the General Union of Jewish Workers of Lithuania, Poland and Russia—known as the Bund—at first rejected nationalism in favour of united working-class action against the Tsarist regime. But the Bund retreated to a position from which, like the Zionists, it called for separate Jewish organisation. The Marxists in Russia

contested the ideas of the Zionists and the Bund, arguing that anti-Semitism was not a condition of non-Jewish existence, as Jewish nationalism maintained, but a product of capitalism in crisis. The Marxists argued that a joint struggle of workers, including minorities such as the Jews, was necessary in order to change the society which produced such excrescences. See V I Lenin, **Critical Remarks on the National Question** (Moscow 1968), especially page 28. For a brief account of the emergence of the Jewish nationalist current, including the Bund, see Nathan Weinstock, **Zionism—False Messiah** (London 1979) chapter 2.

3. Herzl, in the **Complete Diaries of Theodore Herzl** (New York 1960) volume 4, page 1296.
4. Quoted in Weinstock, page 39.
5. Quoted in Weinstock, page 39.
6. Other areas canvassed for settlement by the Zionist movement and its sympathisers included Egypt (the Sinai Peninsula), Kenya and Cyprus—see Weinstock, page 41. According to Elmessiri, Madagascar, the 'Belgian' Congo, Mozambique, Iraq and Libya were also discussed by the Zionist leadership—see Abdelwahab M Elmessiri, **The Land of Promise** (New Brunswick 1977) page 95.
7. Weinstock, page 39.
8. Quoted in N Israeli, 'Israel and Imperialism', in Arie Bober (editor) **The Other Israel** (New York 1972) page 56.
9. See Weinstock, page 42.
10. Elmessiri, quoting Herzl's diaries, notes that the Zionist leader also tried to convince the Italian king, Victor Emmanual III, 'to channel the surplus Jewish immigration into Tripolitania, under the liberal laws and institutions of Italy'. (Elmessiri, page 97).
11. Quoted in Simha Flapan, **Zionism and the Palestinians** (London 1979) page 21.
12. Weinstock, page 96.
13. Flapan, page 22.
14. See Flapan, page 95, note 20.
15. The Anglo-Persian Oil Company, in which the British government held a 51 per cent stake, began exports from Iran in 1911. It supplied much of British military needs while making huge profits—no less than $200 million during its first 20 years of operation. See J Bhahrier, **Economic Development in Iran** (London 1971) chapter 8.
16. Britain, unable to contain a mass anti-colonial movement, was forced in 1924 to grant semi-independence to an Egyptian government under the bourgeois nationalist Wafd Party.
17. Flapan, page 22.
18. Flapan, page 22.
19. Flapan, page 22.
20. Barnet Litvinoff, **Weizmann** (London 1976) page 107.

21. The Zionist movement declared it sought 'A land without people for a people without land'—a phrase coined by Israel Zangwill, the British Zionist.

22. In 1914 population density in Palestine was 20.29 inhabitants per square mile; in Syria and Lebanon 8.53 per square mile; in Asiatic Turkey 10.67 per square mile (Weinstock, page 52). By 1922 there was a Jewish population of 83,790 in a total population of 752,048 (Doreen Warriner, **Land and Poverty in the Middle East** (London 1948) page 54).

23. Almost all the earliest settlers were dependent upon charitable support from Jewish organisations in Europe. There were no farmers and few workers (see Weinstock, page 53).

24. Weinstock, page 134.

25. Various ordinances eased Jewish immigration and the transfer of land from Arabs to Jews. They also limited traditional rights to enlarge Arab land holdings. See Weinstock, page 113.

26. Most land was bought from Palestinian absentee landlords. The main Jewish land agency, the Jewish National Fund (JNF), acquired 90 per cent of its land in this way. Much land remained unused, having been bought for the use of future migrants. By 1936, 20.3 per cent of JNF land was unused; meanwhile more than 30 per cent of rural Palestinians were landless (see Weinstock, page 127, and Flapan, page 68).

27. Flapan, page 68.

28. Weinstock, page 135.

29. Capitalist crisis, accompanied by the failure of mass workers' parties under Stalinist domination, allowed the fascist movement to surge forward. For a contemporary account of the process in Germany see Leon Trostsky, 'What Next?', in Trotsky, **Fascism, Stalinism and the United Front** (Bookmarks, London 1989) pages 73-204.

30. Zionist leaders entered agreements with Nazi Germany for the transfer of Jewish assets, and a limited number of German Jews, to Palestine (see Weinstock, pages 135-7).

31. British legislation such as the Aliens Act 1905 had long been an obstacle to the migration of Jews to Britain. In the US the racist Quota Act, passed in 1924, had the same effect.

32. Weinstock, page 138.

33. Weinstock, pages 135-6.

34. Weinstock, pages 137 and 144.

35. Even when construction could be organised far more cheaply using Arab labour the British administration used only Jewish workers (see Elia Zureik, 'Reflections on Twentieth-Century Palestinian Class Structure', in Khalil Nakhleh and Elia Zureik (editors) **The Sociology of the Palestinians** (London 1980) page 57).

36. Ronald Storrs, **Orientations** (London 1939) page 376.

37. From 1921 to 1937 a British diplomatic representative attended the inaugural session of every Zionist Congress (Weinstock, page 128).

38. The Mufti lost the election but with British help took office in the most powerful position in the Palestinian Arab political system (Weinstock, page 117.

39. Flapan, page 68.

40. Earlier proposals to limit immigration were set aside and increased numbers of Jews were admitted (Weinstock, page 120).

41. Most important was the success of a 50-day national strike in Syria, which compelled the French to promise independence.

42. Part of the city of Jaffa was blown up and houses were demolished in a number of villages. See Ghassan Kanafani, **Palestine: The 1936-39 Revolt** (London, undated) page 18.

43. Christopher Sykes, **Orde Wingate** (London 1959) page 107.

44. Kanafani, page 25.

45. According to Kanafani, 50 Zionist colonies were established between 1936 and 1939 (Kanafani, page 25).

46. Norman Bentwich, **Judea Lives Again** (London 1944) page 63.

47. The Jewish Defence Force, or *haganah*, was established in 1919 to defend Zionist settlements. The British administration supplied some arms and set up police posts to give settlements added protection (Weinstock, page 129).

48. The Jewish Settlement Police Force overlapped with the *haganah*. According to Moshe Dayan, who served with the force, both organisations liaised closely with the British. He recalled: 'The cooperation between the Mandatory government and the Jewish authorities opened up extensive possibilities to improve and broaden our own military training. Licensed weapons for supernumeraries [the Jewish Settlement Police Force] served as cover for the possession of illegal arms.' (Moshe Dayan, **Story of My Life** (London 1976) page 26).

49. Irgun Zvai Leumi was an offshoot of the Revisionist Movement, a right-wing, highly militaristic branch of the Zionist current established by Zev Jabotinsky. Between 1936 and 1939 Irgun launched a series of terrorist attacks on Arab communities (see Flapan, pages 96-120).

50. The 'Night Squads' became a training ground for Zionist military leaders. Wingate's deputy was Moshe Dayan, later Chief of Staff of Israel's armed forces.

51. Maurice Edelman, **Ben Gurion** (London 1964) page 107.

52. Wingate declared his interest in leading a Jewish army into battle (Edelman, page 106).

53. According to Edelman, 'Inside many an innocent-looking factory, like the leather factory of Yaakov and Lefkovits outside Tel-Aviv, arsenals began to grow, while the old Rehovoth wine presses became armouries concealing explosives' (Edelman, pages 107-8).

54. Weinstock, page 130.

55. Israel Zangwill, **The Voice of Jerusalem** (London 1921) page 291.

56. C Issawi and M Yeganeh, **The Economy of Middle Eastern Oil**

(London 1962) page 88.

57. See Bhahrier, chapter 8. By the late 1930s Anglo-Iranian was producing six million tons of oil from its Iranian oilfields. It also had smaller fields in Iraq (Bhahrier, page 158).

58. The first commercial fields in Saudi Arabia were discovered in 1938. Exports were soon under way, under the control of the US oil giants Texaco and Socal (**Merip Report** number 91, October 1980, page 24).

59. Most important, from the British viewpoint, was the pipeline which carried oil across Palestine from the Iraqi oilfields near Kirkuk to the port of Haifa.

60. Weinstock, page 205.

61. This produced a split which led to the establishment of a new group under Abraham Stern, which continued a policy of harassing British forces and attacking Arab communities.

62. Weinstock, pages 209-210.

63. Bentwich, page 137.

64. Bentwich, page 138.

65. Weinstock, page 207.

66. Michael J Cohen, **Palestine: Retreat From the Mandate** (London 1978) page 123.

67. According to Sayigh, the Zionist militia had 800 improvised armoured cars, two Sherman and two Cromwell tanks. It also had 21 second-hand light Auster aircraft, which were used to support isolated Jewish settlements and, during the war of 1948, to bomb Arab villages (R Sayigh, **Palestinians—From Peasants to Revolutionaries** (London 1979) page 73).

68. Weinstock, page 211.

Chapter 3: TOWARDS A STATE

1. Richard Crossman, **Palestine Mission—A Personal Record** (London 1946) page 141.

2. Crossman described the Egypt of 1946 as a society underneath which 'the volcano grumbled' (Crossman, page 114). For an account of the Egyptian movement during this period see Mahmoud Hussein, **Class Conflict in Egypt: 1945-1970** (New York 1973) part 1. In Iran a similar movement threatened the regime of Reza Shah. For a brief account of events in Iran see Phil Marshall, **Revolution and Counter-Revolution in Iran** (Bookmarks, London 1988) pages 18-22.

3. **Merip Report** number 91, page 24.

4. **Merip Report** number 91, page 24.

5. The oil company Socal pressed US President Roosevelt to back the Saudi monarch and in 1943 it was agreed that over four years he should receive $17.5 million (**Merip Report** number 91, page 24).

6. According to Crossman, a million Jews had entered the US in the ten years up to 1914 (Crossman, page 37).

7. Crossman, page 37.
8. By 1942 the Zionist movement in the US claimed to have attained its objective of representing 90 per cent of the American Jewish community. In 1942-43 the movement distributed over a million pamphlets and leaflets arguing the Zionist case for a state in Palestine (M Arakie, **The Broken Sword of Justice** (London 1973) pages 32-33).
9. According to Arakie: 'The campaign for a Jewish state in Palestine which the Zionist leadership in America now launched was one of the most brilliant and successful of such efforts ever to have taken place.' Much use was made of press and radio networks. He notes 'the entire absence of a comparable counter-campaign by the Arabs' (Arakie, page 33).
10. Delegates at the Biltmore Conference clearly understood the Balfour Declaration to have promised a Jewish state in Palestine. Their statement marked a conviction that the need for talk of compromise with the Arabs was over; henceforth the movement could press for 'maximalist' demands. According to Flapan, 'The Biltmore programme signified a basic change in relation to the Arab factor; it ignored it completely.' (Flapan, page 283).
11. Flapan, page 282.
12. Arakie, page 38.
13. The president of the Zionist Organisation of America, Rabbi Israel Goldstein, declared that the next step was to 'win the wholehearted approval of the American government and people with respect to Palestine, which has now become the program of the whole of American Jewry...' (quoted in Arakie, page 32).
14. 'Of all the Zionist formations, the Revisionists were least interested in the Arab question. The Arabs concerned them only as enemies, and as enemies they had to be treated without pity. In other words to be smashed, as there was no room for compromise.' (Flapan, page 114).
15. Figures such as Magnes argued for a bi-national state in Palestine. He saw the purpose of Jewish political activity as to establish 'a Jewish cultural centre' and argued against 'a home necessarily established on bayonets' (see Flapan, page 175).
16. Litvinoff, page 225.
17. Supporters of Jabotinsky were scathing about the 'gradualist' approach, ridiculing the '*dunam* to *dunam*, goat to goat' policy (Flapan, page 108)
18. Quoted in Bober, page 13.
19. Crossman recorded the calculating approach of the US government: 'In considering... whether to give overt support to Zionism, the American Administration has to consider the objections of powerful economic interests as well as of the Chiefs of Staff. Aviation and oil have in the past been able to exert considerable influence on American foreign policy, and I was not surprised to discover that, unspectacularly but systematically, they were pressing their... view in Washington.' (Crossman, page 51).
20. There is evidence that Nazi plans for the Holocaust—the extermination of Europe's Jews—were available to the US government by 1942 but were

suppressed for almost two years (see Arthur Morse, **While Six Million Died: A Chronicle of American Apathy** (New York 1965) chapter 1).

21. At this point Roosevelt was apparently still planning to secure a strong link to the Arab states, especially those of the oil-rich Gulf. In 1944 he told the Saudi monarch: 'I would take no action... which might prove hostile to the Arab people' (quoted in Arakie, page 42). For an account of Roosevelt's growing enthusiasm for the Zionist cause see Peter Grose, 'The President versus the Diplomats', in W Roger Lewis and Robert W Stookey (editors) **The End of the Palestine Mandate** (London 1986).

22. By 1946 the British administration in Palestine had mobilised a soldier or policeman for every 18 of the country's inhabitants (Weinstock, page 229).

23. Bernard Reich, **The United States and Israel: Influence in the Special Relationship** (New York 1984) page 3.

24. 'Some observers felt that the American delegation [to the UN], in their efforts to make clear to hesitant delegations the advantages of partition, lobbied with an energy more reminiscent of a national political campaign than of conventional diplomatic behaviour.' (Arakie, page 63).

25. The Zionist lobby campaigned frenetically, bringing great pressure on the US to use its leverage on other countries to secure their votes. According to David Horowitz of the Jewish Agency: 'The United States exerted the weight of its influence almost at the last hour [sic], and the way the final vote turned out must be ascribed to this fact.'(Arakie, page 64).

26. See Oles M Smolansky, 'The Soviet Role in the Emergence of Israel', in Lewis and Stookey, pages 61-78.

27. Weinstock, page 232.

28. In effect Palestine was at war from October 1947, when there was a general mobilisation of the *haganah*. Between 30 November 1947 and 1 February 1948, 864 people were killed, the majority being Arabs (Weinstock, page 234).

Chapter 4: THE PALESTINIAN RESISTANCE

1. Weinstock, page 58.

2. In the 1940s Warriner described 'that special phenomenon of the Middle East, the "city notable" '—'an absentee landlord whose main function is to provide credit and who does not interest himself at all in farming' (Doreen Warriner, page 15).

3. Weinstock, page 157.

4. The Christian population was concentrated in 23 main towns; most lived in Jerusalem, Haifa or Jaffa. In contrast only 25 per cent of Muslims were urbanised. Thus the Christians played an important role in commercial life and were well represented in the administrative layers (Ann Mosely Lesch, 'The Palestine Arab Nationalist Movement Under the Mandate', in Quandt, Jabber and Lesch, **The Politics of Palestinian Nationalism**

(Berkeley 1973) page 19).

5. Kanafani, page 9.

6. The great majority of Palestinian companies were 'ludicrously small. The Arab industrial sector amounted at most to 10 per cent of the global Palestinian industrial product.' (Nathan Weinstock in **Journal of Palestinian Studies**, volume 2, number 2, page 58).

7. There was a sharp contrast between the development of capital in Palestine and that in neighbouring Arab countries, which were also under European occupation. In Egypt the bourgeoisie was strong enough to challenge Britain by the early 1920s—a function of the pace at which indigenous capital had been concentrated. During this period, 'A domestic industrial and commercial bourgeoisie began to crystallise... Bank Misr [the first independent Egyptian Bank], founded in 1920, became the quintessential expression of Egyptian economic nationalism.' (Robert L Tignor, **State, Private Enterprise and Economic Change in Egypt, 1918-1952** (New York 1984) page 49). There was no Palestinian equivalent of the Egyptian Wafd Party, which demanded independence from Britain and pursued a programme of limited political reform.

8. Among the most notorious cases was that of the Sursuks, a family of absentee landowners and money-lenders who in 1872 had acquired 20 villages and 18,000 hectares of land in Galilee. In 1920 Sursuk sold this and other land to the Zionists' Palestine Land Development Company. Compensation to peasants made landless was ten shillings a head. There were 664 evictions (Weinstock, pages 127 and 163).

9. During the 1920s the Zionists made several attempts to deepen divisions in Arab society. They established Arab organisations which they hoped would exploit family feuds, competition between community leaders, and friction between nomads and farmers, Christians and Muslims and rural and urban settlements (Lesch, pages 18-19, and Flapan, pages 64-67).

10. According to Kanafani, al-Qassem had a well-developed strategy for Palestinian resistance. This was based on three stages: psychological preparation, the formation of clandestine groups and a network of committees, and armed revolt. Al-Qassem, who had been trained at the leading institution of the Muslim world, al-Azhar in Cairo, combined the idea of an Islamic response to imperialism with that of Arab nationalism. His slogan was 'Die as martyrs' (Kanafani, pages 15-17).

11. Al-Qassem's death had an impact out of all proportion to his military strength. His attempt to launch armed struggle was seen as a first effort to take the initiative against Britain and the Zionists. Huge numbers of people attended his funeral. A British report observed: 'Sheikh al-Qassem's funeral in Haifa was attended by very large crowds, and in spite of the efforts made to keep order, there were demonstrations and stones were thrown. The death of al-Qassem aroused a wave of powerful feelings in political and other circles in the country, and the Arabic newspapers agreed in calling him a martyr in the articles they wrote about

him.' (Quoted in Kanafani, page 16).

12. Thomas Hodgkin, **Letters from Palestine 1932-36** (London 1986) page 196.

13. Lesch, page 35.

14. Kanafani describes al-Quwukji as an 'adventurist nationalist'. Shortly after entering Palestine with his guerrillas he declared himself 'commander-in-chief' of the Revolt (Kanafani, page 18).

15. The majority of the guerrillas were dispossessed peasants who took to the hills armed with antique weapons. Their activity was usually initiated by the groups themselves; it varied from crop-burning and wire-cutting to armed engagements with units of British troops. According to Hodgkin (page 197): in Samaria, 'they carry on what almost amounts to guerrilla warfare against any detachment of British troops they come across.'

16. The Arab Higher Committee arranged for an 'intervention' by the Arab monarchs. It then distributed a statement: 'Inasmuch as submission to the will of their Majesties and Highnesses, the Arab kings, and to comply with their wishes, is one of our hereditary Arab traditions, and inasmuch as the Higher Arab Committee, in obedience to the wishes of their Majesties and Highnesses would only give orders that are in conformity with the interests of their sons and with the object of protecting their rights; the Arab Higher Committee, in obedience to the wishes of their Majesties and Highnesses, the Kings and Emirs, and from its belief in the great benefit that will result from their mediation and cooperation, calls on the noble Arab people to end the strike and the disturbances, in obedience to these orders, whose only object is the interests of the Arabs.' (Quoted in Kanafani, page 20).

17. George Antonius, **The Arab Awakening** (Beirut 1955) pages 406-7.

18. Hodgkin, pages 196-7. Hodgkin observed that the movement involved the whole of Arab society; even the clear-cut division between the sexes which made politics a male preserve began to break down: 'The present resistance to the Government is not confined to men: women and schoolboys and schoolgirls have initiated demonstrations and presented protests in many of the towns.' He added that British illusions about their Arab subjects were rudely shattered: 'British teachers have written shocked letters to the newspapers deploring the fact that the children they have trained to be nice little Anglophiles should now show a cloven hoof.' (Hodgkin, page 197).

19. Lesch, page 38.

20. Y Baer, 'The Arab Revolt of 1936', in **New Outlook** (Israeli bi-monthly) July-August 1966, page 56.

21. Large numbers of *haganah* officers were trained in 'counter-insurgency' operations by the British and ten special groups of 'Colony Police' were formed, composed of over 14,000 settlers. Each group was commanded by a British officer with a Jewish deputy appointed by the Jewish Agency (Kanafani, page 26).

22. Some small groups declared the newly formed party to be 'crypto-Zionist' and refused to join. They called for the abandonment of the Zionist project and full support for the Arab nationalist movement (Musa Budeiri, **The Palestine Communist Party 1919-1948** (London 1979) page 7).

23. 'Preliminary Draft Theses on the National and Colonial Questions', in **Theses, Resolutions and Manifestos of the First Four Congresses of the Third International** (London 1980) pages 76-81.

24. According to British police reports, by 1930 there were only 26 Arab members (see Budeiri, page 26). The Comintern formed the view that the party was not putting its best efforts into the attempt to break out of the Jewish milieu, the result of 'Jewish national chauvinism' within its ranks (Budeiri, pages 33-36 and 44).

25. Budeiri, page 28.

26. Budeiri, pages 33-36.

27. The PCP leadership accordingly convened a plenum under the slogan 'Arabisation plus Bolshevisation'. In line with the International's latest turn the party was to become a 'professional revolutionary organisation' oriented on the Arab masses (Budeiri, page 39).

28. Budeiri, page 70.

29. Budeiri, page 71.

30. Budeiri, page 69.

31. The new turn was imposed by the Stalinist bureaucracy as part of its effort to isolate Communist parties from criticism on the left which might have accompanied the disastrous consequences of the 'Third Period' and the purges which soon liquidated the survivors of the party which had led the revolution of 1917. Duncan Hallas comments: 'The Comintern was now to be swung, by Stalin's agents, to a position well to the *right* of the social democrat parties, to a position of class collaboration—precisely the position taken by the social democrats during and after the First World War and against which the founders of the Comintern had revolted. The "Peoples Front", systematic class collaboration with the "liberal" bourgeoisie, was now the order of the day—again, in the interests of Stalin's foreign policy.' (Duncan Hallas, **The Comintern** (Bookmarks, London 1985) page 141.

32. Budeiri, page 81.

33. Budeiri, page 82. When the PCP delegate to the Comintern Congress, Radwan al-Hilou, returned to Palestine, he argued that the party would never be able to lead the Arab masses unless it put itself at the head of the national struggle. The policy of leading the class struggle should be set aside (Budeiri, page 82).

34. Budeiri, page 90.

35. Budeiri, page 90.

36. Budeiri, page 96.

37. Those who split from the PCP set out to influence 'the progressive forces within Zionism' (Budeiri, page 113). However, all the left-Zionist

organisations were organically connected to the Zionist movement. There were a host of links to the mainstream, the most important of which was through the Histadrut. Following the PCP split in the late 1930s former Jewish members who remained active found themselves in a milieu in which internationalism had long before been rejected.

38. In 1939 a small number of former PCP members formed a group based on the principles of the Fourth International, which Leon Trotsky and his supporters had established to maintain Marxist principles in the face of the Stalinist degeneration. The Trotskyists argued for solidarity with the Arab nationalist movement, an end to Jewish immigration and to Jewish land purchases, and for an Arab national government in Palestine (Weinstock, page 199).

39. Budeiri, page 131.

40. In 1943 there was a further split in the PCP. In a development which foreshadowed the events of 1948 the party collapsed along national lines. A new Jewish party declared itself in favour of a 'democratic' state, which was not described as Arab or Jewish but carefully left ambiguous. Arab members of the PCP formed the National Liberation League, later to be the nucleus of the Jordanian Communist Party (Budeiri, pages 153-171).

41. Walid Khalidi, 'Plan Dalet, the Zionist Masterplan for the Conquest of Palestine, 1948', in **Middle East Forum**, November 1961.

42. Twenty years later the Zionist historian Arie Yitzakie wrote: 'In the first months of the "War of Independence", *Haganah* and Palmach troops carried out dozens of operations of this kind, the method being to raid an enemy village and blow up as many houses as possible in it. In the course of these operations many old people, women and children, were killed whenever there was resistance.' (Quoted in David Hirst, **The Gun and the Olive Branch** (London 1978) page 140). Sayigh lists some of the lesser-known incidents. She comments: 'Deir Yassin was not an isolated, inexplicable atrocity in a war of defence against Arab invasion, as Zionist propaganda alleged, but part of a systematic campaign to terrorise the Palestinian peasants and force them to give up resistance.' (Sayigh, page 75).

43. The Zionist movement habitually spoke of 'cleansing' Palestine of the Arab inhabitants. For example, Yigal Allon, later a member of successive Labour Party governments, wrote that in 1948, 'We saw a need to clean the inner Galilee and to create a Jewish territorial succession in the entire area of the Upper Galilee...' (Yigal Allon, **The Book of the Palmach**, quoted in Sayigh, page 77).

44. There was no legal source of weaponry; the main source was the *bedouin*. As in 1936 the Palestinian resistance fought mainly with antique hunting weapons (Sayigh, page 78)

45. Palestinians named the force *al-jaysh al-rikad*—'the run-away army' (Sayigh, page 79).

46. The Arab 'army' was a token force. It had only 22 light tanks and a handful

of aircraft—no match for the Zionist militias. Its main function was to provide evidence that Arab rulers anxious to come to a negotiated settlement with the Zionists were backing the Palestinian cause. In fact, the rhetoric which surrounded the Arab troops' entry into Palestine concealed their inadequacy and helped to disorient Palestinians who were expecting a massive Arab response to the Zionist offensive (Sayigh, page 81).

47. Of 1.3 million Arab inhabitants, the Zionist militias had displaced 900,000. The settlers now came into possession of scores of Arab towns, hundreds of villages and an estimated 10,000 Arab-owned stores, workshops and other businesses. In addition they seized more than half the country's valuable citrus orchards (Hirst, pages 142-3).

Chapter 5: ISRAEL AND THE UNITED STATES AFTER 1948

1. M Machover and A Orr, 'The Class Character of Israeli Society', in Bober, page 94.
2. Machover and Orr, in Bober, page 94.
3. Machover and Orr, in Bober, page 94.
4. Machover and Orr, in Bober, page 95.
5. During the first five years after the establishment of the state almost 700,000 immigrants arrived in Israel. They included almost the entire Jewish populations of Iraq and Yemen and large numbers from North Africa, Romania and Poland. In 1949, 266 immigrants arrived for every 1,000 inhabitants. Elisha Efrat comments: 'These figures are phenomenal due not only to the high level of immigration but also to the ability of the small existing population to absorb and integrate so many newcomers...' (E Efrat, **Urbanisation in Israel** (London 1984) page 22).
6. Machover and Orr, in Bober, page 96.
7. Thomas A Bryson, **Seeds of Mideast Crisis: The United States' Diplomatic Role in the Middle East During World War II** (Jefferson 1981) page 43.
8. Bryson, page 179.
9. Bryson, page 179.
10. George E Kirk, **A Short History of the Middle East** (New York 1960) page 231.
11. The US was particularly anxious about the situation in Iran, which threatened its newly established oilfields in the Arabian peninsula. In Iran a mass movement based in the oilfields of Khuzistan had grown with astonishing speed. The Tudeh was in a position of enormous influence: in June 1946 the British ambassador to Iran reported that, 'at the present time the security of the [Abadan] refinery and fields and the safety of the British personnel, depends on the good will and pleasure of the Tudeh Party.' (Quoted in Ervand Abrahamian, **Iran Between Two Revolutions** (Princeton 1982) page 362).

12. Bryson, page 177.
13. Bryson, pages 176-180.
14. Reich, page 148.
15. Efrat, page 32.
16. Czechoslovak arms sales to Israel reflected Russia's continued willingness to back Israel, despite Moscow's 'anti-imperialist' rhetoric (see Roger F Pajak, 'West European and Soviet Arms Transfer Policies in the Middle East', in Milton Leitenberg and Gabriel Sheffer (editors) **Great Power Intervention in the Middle East** (New York 1979) page 160).
17. Kirk, page 274.
18. Henry Longhurst, official historian of the Anglo-Iranian Oil Company, quoted in Kermit Roosevelt, **Countercoup: The Struggle for Control of Iran** (New York 1970) page 102
19. *Ha'aretz*, 30 September 1951, quoted in Bober, pages 16-17.
20. For several years after 1952 Nasser and the ruling group were undecided as to their orientation towards the West. As late as 1955 Nasser seemed content to pursue a policy of military cooperation with the West while he carried out domestic reforms. However, 'At that time Britain and the United States were... obsessed with the formation of military pacts against possible Soviet invasion or Communist subversion'. They regarded Cairo with great suspicion and refused Egypt economic aid, setting the scene for confrontation over the Suez Canal. (Robert Stephens, **Nasser** (London 1973), page 143).
21. Reich, page 148.
22. The Pact was built around what remained of direct British influence among the Arab states and in South Asia. All the Arab League states were invited to join; none did.
23. Quoted in Elizabeth Monroe, **Britain's Moment in the Middle East 1914-71** (London 1981) page 113.
24. Moshe Dayan, **Diary of the Sinai Campaign** (London 1965) page 207.
25. Nasser wished for the unification of Egypt and Syria as the nucleus of a 'pan-Arab union'. The two countries joined in a United Arab Republic (UAR)—but its failure was evident long before the two countries' separation in 1961. Nasser had sought to dictate the terms of unification —in effect, the bureaucracy which had ruled Egypt since 1952 sought to extend its control to Syria, a prospect the Syrians rejected. Nonetheless, the formation of the UAR raised expectations throughout the Arab world, where it was seen as an assertion of Arab identity against imperialism. It played a part in precipitating the Lebanon events of 1958 and encouraged the nationalist movement in Iraq. It also caused alarm in the West, where for a time it seemed that Nasser had become the leader of a growing anti-imperialist bloc.
26. The conflict was an expression of the contradictions built into the Lebanese political system by French imperialism. In the 1940s, France formalised a system in which the wealthy Maronite Christian minority

controlled a mostly poor Muslim majority. When, in 1958, Nasser declared that the UAR would be a centre of support for Arab nationalism, many Lebanese Muslims raised the call for union with Syria (and therefore with Egypt). The Chamoun government turned to the US for support, while the nationalist movement took up an increasingly determined anti-imperialist position. There was a general strike and fighting with the Lebanese army.

27. Joseph Churba, **The Politics of Defeat: America's Decline in the Middle East** (New York 1977) page 77.
28. Churba, page 78.
29. Churba, page 78.
30. Reich, page 180.
31. Arnold Rivkin, **Africa and the West** (New York 1961) page 63.
32. Between 1958 and 1970 Israel sent almost 4,000 development workers to Africa, Latin America and Asia, and trained almost 14,000 specialists from these countries in Israel (Samuel Decalo, 'Afro-Israeli Technical Cooperation', in Michael Curtis and Susan Aurelia Gitelson, **Israel in the Third World** (New Jersey 1976) page 93).
33. The relationship went back to 1948 when Weizmann sought the support of South African leader General Jan Christian Smuts. Two years later Israeli prime minister Moshe Sharrett visited South Africa. Despite strains over Israeli links with Black African countries the two states again grew close and by 1967 a South African military mission was in Israel 'to study tactics and use of weapons' during the June war (Richard Stevens and Abdelwahab M Elmessiri, **Israel and South Africa** (New York 1976) pages 62-70).
34. Reich, page 148.
35. Reich, page 148.
36. Reich, page 148.
37. Reich, page 156.
38. For example, Abba Eban's speech to the UN immediately after the June 1967 war. He declared: 'All the conditions of tension, all the impulses of aggression in the Middle East have been aggravated by the policy of one of the Great Powers.' (quoted in Walter Laquer (editor) **The Israel-Arab Reader** (New York 1976) page 208).
39. **The Times** (London) 5 February 1971.
40. **The Times**, 5 February 1971.
41. **The Economist** (London) 10 June 1967.
42. Robert J Donovan and the staff of the Los Angeles Times, **Six Days in June** (New York 1967) page 155.
43. Donovan, page 155.
44. Reich, page 179.
45. According to Reich: 'Israel provided the United States with valuable military information and intelligence as captured Soviet equipment facilitated US countermeasures against similar weaponry in Vietnam...'

(Reich, page 180). A relationship soon developed— by the 1973 war the Middle East was regarded as a regular testing ground for superpower weaponry. Churba records: 'American defense manufacturers and security analysts received a steady flow of information from Israel on the performance and effectiveness of both American and Soviet equipment and parts used in the Yom Kippur war.' (Churba, page 116).

46. Yair Evron, 'Great Powers' Military Intervention in the Middle East', in Leitenberg and Sheffer, page 31.
47. Dayan, **The Story of My Life**, page 350.
48. Reich, page 180.
49. Churba, page 33.
50. Reich, page 148.
51. Speaker of the US House of Representatives McCormack, quoted in **The Times**, 5 February 1971.
52. According to US diplomat David Nes: 'qualitatively, America has provided aircraft, missiles, and electronic systems of greater sophistication and greater strike capability than those furnished [to] our Nato and Seato allies.' (Quoted in **The Times**, 5 February 1971).
53. Quoted in **The Times**, 5 February 1971.
54. Reich, page 163.
55. **Business Week** (New York) 26 September 1970.
56. John M Lee, in the **New York Times**, 2 January 1971, quoted in Dick Roberts, **US Oil and Mideast Imperialism** (New York 1971) page 4.
57. Roberts, page 6.
58. In 1970 Libya compelled US oil companies operating in the country to cut production; meanwhile Algeria nationalised the major foreign operators. This was the signal for concerted action to raise oil prices throughout OPEC.
59. Churba, representing the most hawkish of US foreign policy analysts, argued that this 'was in direct opposition to American national security interests' (Churba, page 159).
60. Reich, page 165
61. Reich, page 148.
62. Reich, page 169.
63. These advances did not not, however, allow Israel to become independent of the US for its arms supplies. Even ten years later, Israel was 'dependent on the United States for its most sophisticated weapons systems and for some of the advanced components of its indigenous products, a condition that is not likely to be be altered in the near future' (Reich, page 172).
64. *Davar* (Israeli newspaper), 17 December 1982, quoted in Noam Chomsky, **The Fateful Triangle: The United States, Israel and the Palestinians** (London 1983) page 17.
65. **Los Angeles Times**, 18 August 1981, quoted in Chomsky, page 83.
66. The policy of *infitah*—the 'opening' or 'open door'—aimed at the reintegration of the country into Western capitalism. It was based on the

break-up of Nasser's industrial and commercial monopolies and the encouragement of Egyptian and foreign private capital. Sadat also broke Egypt's relationship with the Eastern bloc—which had been the country's main source of arms and heavy industrial investment since the mid-1950s—and entered the pro-Western bloc of Arab states centred on the Gulf regimes.

67. **Merip Report**, number 71, October 1978, page 23. Iran was not capable of absorbing the vast quantity of weapons ordered; the value of those delivered may not therefore have reached the levels agreed.

68. Reich, page 181.

69. **Defence and Foreign Affairs** (Washington) August 1983, page 40.

70. Reich, page 148.

71. Reich, page 148.

72. Between 1949 and 1959 world Jewry, mostly American Jews, provided more than 47 per cent of Israel's capital imports. Between 1970 and 1979 US government assistance—at $13.1 billion—dwarfed private Jewish assistance, which was some $5 billion. (**The Jerusalem Post** (International Edition) 17-23 August 1980, quoted in R D McLaurin, Don Peretz and Lewis W Snider, **Middle East Foreign Policy** (New York 1982) page 184).

73. **Defence and Foreign Affairs**, August 1983, page 40.

74. US Arms Control and Disarmament Agency (USACDA), **World Military Expenditures and Arms Transfers 1971-1980** (Washington 1983) Part B.

75. USACDA, Part B.

76. Their examination of messages exchanged between Israel and the US in the days before the invasion led them to conclude of the final, key letter from US secretary of state Alexander Haig to Israeli prime minister Menachem Begin that it was 'a highly significant document because it reveals the mild tone of the official American admonitions and the indulgent language employed in conveying them even at this late stage in the progress toward war'. Haig assured Begin that 'no one has the right to tell Israel what decision she must make in order to defend her people' (Ze'ev Schiff and Ehud Ya'ari, **Israel's Lebanon War** (London 1985) page 75).

77. The US regarded Syria as Moscow's proxy in the Middle East and the main obstacle to the reintegration of its most important Arab ally, Egypt, into the mainstream of Arab diplomacy—Egypt had been expelled from the Arab League for concluding a peace agreement with Israel in 1979. Washington was also prepared to back almost any initiative which reduced Palestinian influence, which it regarded as a destabilising factor in the region (see Schiff and Ya'ari, chapter 4).

78. **Middle East Reporter** (Beirut) 23 August 1985, quoted in Tabitha Petran, **The Struggle Over Lebanon** (New York 1987) page 347.

79. The 'Arabists' had had a presence in Washington since the 1940s, when

they had cautioned against American backing for the establishment of Israel. Over the succeeding 30 years their voice had hardly been heard amid the din of support for Israel. However, by the early 1980s, following the fall of the Shah in Iran and with the Gulf oil boom at its height, those who argued the case of the Arab Gulf states as the real focus for the US in the Middle East began to gain some ground. During the closing stages of the Gulf war they gained greater influence. For an account of the 'Israel-centric' and 'Arab-centric' lobbies at work during the late 1980s, see Eric Hoogland, 'Factions behind US Policy in the Gulf', in **Middle East Report**, number 151 (March-April 1988) pages 29-31.

80. **Merip Report** number 116 (September 1983), page 29.
81. **Defence and Foreign Affairs**, August 1983, page 40.
82. **Christian Science Monitor**, 3 February 1984.
83. **The Jerusalem Post**, 23 January 1988.
84. The US has turned aid on and off in line with the political demands it has made on potential recipients. In March 1989, for example, it withheld a vital $230 million loan to Egypt in order to compel the Egyptian government to implement economic policies advocated by the International Monetary Fund (see **Mideast Mirror**, 29 March 1989).
85. Reich, page 178.
86. Churba, page 29.

Chapter 6: THE PALESTINIAN DIASPORA

1. J Abu-Lughod, 'The Demographic Transformation of Palestine', in I Lughod, **The Transformation of Palestine** (Evanston 1971) page 155.
2. Figures collected by the United Nations Relief and Works Agency (UNRWA) (from E Hagopian and A B Zahlan, 'Palestine's Arab Population: The Demography of the Palestinians', in **Journal of Palestine Studies** (Beirut) number 12, pages 51-54).
3. Hagopian and Zahlan, page 54.
4. At the formal, diplomatic level, the Palestine 'problem' was seen as one of rehabilitation of the victims of war. UNRWA's mandate charged the organisation with care of the 'refugees'—the hundreds of thousands of dispossessed.
5. Pamela Ann Smith, **Palestine and the Palestinians** (London 1984) pages 87-100.
6. Smith, page 223.
7. Smith, page 120.
8. Smith, pages 172-3.
9. Hagopian and Zahlan, page 54.
10. Avi Plascov, **The Palestinian Refugees in Jordan 1948-1957** (London 1981) page 2.
11. In Lebanon ' Palestinians were placed in an indeterminate category, neither "foreigners" nor "nationals", and were excluded from joining the

army or entering public service' (Sayigh, pages 111-112).

12. Sayigh, pages 131-3, and Plascov, pages 50-59.
13. Smith, pages 115-116.
14. Smith, pages 172-3. For an evocative account of the problems faced by Palestinian workers in the Saudi oilfields see Fawaz Turki, **The Disinherited** (New York 1971) pages 85-92.
15. Fred Halliday, **Arabia Without Sultans** (London 1974) pages 66-7.
16. Smith, page 173-4.
17. Eric Rouleau, ' The Palestinian Diaspora in the Gulf ', in **Merip Report**, number 132 (May 1985), page 14.
18. Rouleau, page 14.
19. As late as 1985 a majority of judges in the UAE were Palestinians. 'They are also numerous among journalists (both print and electronic media), doctors, engineers, architects, and top management of oil companies and private business.' (Rouleau, page 14).
20. David Lynn Price, **Oil and Middle East Security** (Beverly Hills 1976) page 35.
21. Pamela Ann Smith, 'The Palestinian Diaspora 1948-1985', in **Journal of Palestine Studies** (Washington) number 57, page 95.
22. Smith, **Palestine and the Palestinians**, pages 129-137.
23. According to Khalid al-Hassan, also a founder of Fatah, Arafat's father came from the 'poor side' of the Husseini clan. Arafat's mother came from the Abu Saud family, one of the wealthiest families in Jerusalem (Alan Hart, **Arafat: Terrorist or Peacemaker?** (London 1984) page 68).
24. Alain Gresh, **The PLO: The Struggle Within** (London 1988), page 25.
25. According to Hart, Salah Khalaf was 'an enthusiastic member' of the Muslim Brotherhood (see Hart, page 86). Khalaf himself related that he had 'a certain sympathy' for the Muslim Brotherhood, although, he maintained, he was never a member (see Abu Iyad, **My Home, My Land** (New York 1981) page 20). Khalil al-Wazir also had connections with the Brotherhood (see Hart, page 101).
26. Arafat is said to have come to the conclusion that 'the Palestinians had been betrayed by the weakness and corruption of the Arab regimes' (Hart, page 87).
27. Iyad, page 38.
28. Hart, page 127.
29. Iyad, page 38.
30. Iyad, page 39.
31. Hart, page 127.
32. Price, page 71.
33. Hallas, page 125.
34. The Stalinist theory was not new. At the turn of the century it had been the approach of whole European Marxist current. Leon Trotsky's theory of permanent revolution, which rejected the notion of the necessity of 'stages' in revolutionary change, was then confirmed by events in Russia

in 1905 and again by the upheaval of 1917. The Communist International subsequently based its approach to change in the 'colonial' world on Trotsky's approach. For an account of the debate on 'stages' and the permanent revolution, see Hallas, pages 7-28.

35. Quoted in G G Kosach, 'Formation of Communist Movements in Egypt, Syria and Lebanon in the 1920s and 1930s', in R Ulyanovsky (editor) **The Revolutionary Process in the East** (Moscow 1985) page 222.

36. **Theses, Resolutions and Manifestos**, page 80.

37. Despite the leading position of the Chinese Communist Party (CCC) in a mass strike movement, the Comintern instructed it to confine itself to 'democratic demands' and to enter a 'bloc of classes' with the bourgeois nationalists of the Kuomintang (KMT). At the first opportunity the KMT slaughtered CCC activists and thousands of worker militants in the strike centre, Shanghai (see Hallas, pages 20-26, and Nigel Harris, **The Mandate of Heaven: Marx and Mao in Modern China** (London 1978) pages 3-15).

38. Bagdash, **The Communist Party in the Struggle for Independence and National Sovereignty** (Beirut 1944), quoted in Tony Cliff, **The Struggle in the Middle East** (London 1967).

39. By 1947 there were more than 350,000 industrial workers in Egypt, the majority employed in 583 large factories (see Joel Beinin and Lachary Lockman, **Workers on the Nile** (New Jersey 1987) page 265). The record of working-class struggle went back to the period before the First World War. Workers had also been a key element in the mass anti-colonial movement which had forced British concessions in 1924 (see Beinin and Lockman, pages 48-121).

40. Henri Curiel, one of the founders of the Communist current which re-emerged in the 1930s (see Giles Perrault, **A Man Apart: The Life of Henri Curiel** (London 1987) page 110).

41. By the early 1950s the Communists had split into three groups. When the Free Officers' coup took place, two of these—Workers' Vanguard and al-Raya (The Flag) backed Moscow's line that the officers had imposed a 'fascist military dictatorship'. The third group, the Democratic Movement for National Liberation (DMNL), supported the nationalists as part of the expected 'national democratic revolution'. Debate over the character of the regime continued among the groups, and the splits and fusions which developed from them, throughout the 1950s (see Joel Beinin, 'The Communist Movement and National Political Discourse in Nasirist Egypt', in **Middle East Journal** (Washington) volume 41, number 4, page 574).

42. Beinin, page 577.

43. In effect the party ceased to operate in 1959. In 1964 the regime offered a deal—Communists would be released from prison if the party (a unified organisation had been created in 1955) would dissolve and its members would enter the sole legal political party, Nasser's Arab Socialist Union.

The deal was agreed and the party liquidated. For the next decade informal, clandestine networks of militants continued hesitant activity; 'the Left' had all but disappeared.

44. The call never came—instead the party backed off and allowed 'progressive' elements among the nationalists in the army to carry out a coup—an initiative widely believed by party members to have stemmed from intervention by Moscow. In 1967 the party issued a fierce self-criticism: 'We let slip through our fingers [in 1959] a historic opportunity and allowed a squandering of a unique revolutionary situation to the detriment of the people... Our party [had become] the master of the situation... and should have gone on to conquer power... even though civil war and foreign intervention appeared possible, if not unavoidable... Had we seized the helm and without delay armed the people, carried out a radical agrarian reform, secured the masses in their interests, granted to the Kurds their autonomy and, by revolutionary measures, transformed the army into a democratic force, our regime would have with extraordinary speed attained to the widest popularity and would have released great mass initiatives, enabling millions to make their own history.' (From an internal party circular entitled 'An Attempt to Appraise the Policy of the Communist Party of Iraq in the Period July 1958-April 1965', quoted in Hana Batatu, **The Old Social Classes and the Revolutionary Movements of Iraq** (Princeton 1978) page 904).

45. On 8 February 1963 Baghdad radio broadcast Order Number 13 which called for a massacre of Communists. It concluded: 'Faithful sons of the people are called upon to cooperate with the authorities by informing on these criminals and annihilate them.' Despite resistance from the Communist Party and workers' organisations, between 3,000 and 5,000 party members were massacred (U Zaher, 'Political developments in Iraq', in **Saddam's Iraq** (London 1986) page 32).

46. In accordance with Moscow's 'peace strategy' of the late 1940s, the Lebanese Communist Party undertook to win signatories to a 'peace platform'. This took in leftist, liberal and right-wing politicians including Pierre Gemayal, founder of the *Phalange Libanaises*, a paramilitary organisation which mimicked the European fascist organisations, coming complete with a racist theory of Maronite superiority (see Walter Laquer, **Communism and Nationalism in the Middle East** (London 1956) page 164).

47. See Marshall, pages 24-6.

48. Palestine had been the touchstone for anti-imperialists throughout the region. When Moscow recognised the state of Israel in 1948 there was therefore consternation among the majority of Communists. However, in Iraq the party slavishly followed Moscow's line. In Egypt the Democratic Movement for National Liberation (DMNL)—one of the largest components of the Communist current—also backed the Zionist state. The DMNL had never rejected the Zionist presence in Palestine and

argued for a bi-national state (see Beinin and Lockman, page 352, and Perrault, pages 147-9).

49. J F Devlin, **The Baath Party: A History from its Origins to 1966** (Stanford 1976) page 28.

50. Devlin, page 33.

51. J Nottingham, 'A Study of the Ideology of Palestinian Nationalism' (unpublished thesis, University of Durham 1969) page 30.

52. **PFLP Bulletin**, number 33 (Beirut 1979), page 5.

53. Hart, page 152.

Chapter 7: FATAH AND THE LEFT

1. UNRWA report, quoted in **What Is the PLO?** (Beirut 1972) page 91.

2. Fatah believed that it might lose members to the PLO and for a while sought to come to an accommodation with the leadership (see Hart, page 167).

3. The raid marked the first act of *al-thawra*—the 'revolution'. Since 1965 the term has been used by Palestinians to describe the armed struggle, the mobilisation or 'awakening' of the Palestinian people, and most commonly, the resistance movement itself.

4. Iyad, page 20.

5. Hart, page 153.

6. Hart, page 153.

7. Nottingham, page 50.

8. Gresh, page 15.

9. Hart, page 123.

10. Salah Khalaf later maintained that Fatah 'harboured no illusions' that it could overcome Israel. 'But we believed that it was the only way to impose the Palestine cause on world opinion, and especially the only way to rally our masses to the people's movement we were trying to create' (Iyad, page 35).

11. Hart, page 157.

12. Iyad, pages 68-69.

13. Iyad, page 55.

14. Hart's assessment of the views of those who attended Fatah's first congress in 1967 (see Hart, page 236).

15. See Walid Kazziha, **Revolutionary Transformation in the Arab World: Habash and His Comrades From Nationalism to Marxism** (London 1975) pages 65-86.

16. Changes had been taking place in the Arab National Movement (ANM) since the early 1960s, when, in an attempt to analyse the failure of the union of Egypt and Syria, some members began to criticise Nasser from the left. Habash at first opposed this group for what he called 'infantile leftism' (see John K Cooley, **Green March, Black September** (London 1973) page 143). In 1967 the PFLP was formed, partly on the basis that the Habash group had been won to Marxism. In fact it had made a

rhetorical move to the left to keep pace with the more radical tone of those members led by Naif Hawatmeh (see Kazziha, page 87).

17. These perspectives are laid out in an interview with Habash, 'Why the PFLP?' in **PFLP Bulletin** (Beirut) number 33, pages 3-6.

18. The DFLP split from the PFLP in 1969 after an intense conflict between the Habash and Hawatmeh groups. The latter argued for the adoption of 'the ideology of the proletariat'; in fact, the two groups shared much the same radical nationalism (see Kazziha, pages 87-91).

19. Nottingham, page 151.

20. Fatah declared that it was determined to 'convince the Arab nation that there are among them people who do not retreat and run away. Let us die under the tank tracks. We shall change the course of history in the area and no one will blame us for that' (Fatah leader Hani al-Hassan, quoted in Hirst, page 284). The clash resulted in heavy Palestinian casualties but the fact that the guerrillas had put up vigorous resistance to the Israeli army in hand-to-hand battles was of enormous symbolic significance, especially as King Hussein refused to oppose the Israelis other than by giving the Palestinians some covering artillery fire (see Cooley, pages 100-102).

21. Cooley, page 101.

22. Over the next few weeks 20,000 Egyptians offered their services as *fedayeen*; 1,500 Iraqis volunteered within a week (Hirst, page 285).

23. The PLA had been established by Shuqeiry's PLO. It was to raise 'Palestinian' regiments in each Arab country, which were to be under the control of the regimes. Few units were formed but some were of use to Fatah when it took over the PLO. Other units of the PLA continued to be used *against* the PLO well into the 1970s.

24. Cooley, page 112.

25. Hart, page 304.

26. Iyad, page 74.

27. Iyad, page 81.

28. El-Rayyes and Nahas, **Guerrillas for Palestine** (Beirut 1974) page 39.

29. The majority of the population of the Jordanian capital, Amman, and of the north of the country was of Palestinian origin and in these areas the PLO had its bases. However, the political generalisation stimulated by the rising confidence of the Palestinian movement seems to have drawn in some Jordanians 'proper'—indigenous East Bankers. This may have been a factor in Hussein's final decision to attack the PLO.

30. On 12 September the PFLP exploded Swissair, TWA and BOAC jets at Dawson's Field airstrip, creating an international storm over Palestinian tactics (see Cooley, page 113, and Willam B Quandt, 'Political and Military Dimensions of Contemporary Palestinian Nationalism', in Quandt, Jabber and Lesch, pages 125-6).

31. Cooley, page 114.

32. Israel and the US had made clear they would back Hussein against the

PLO and would engage Syria if it moved in support of the Palestinians. Syria pulled back, leaving the Palestinians alone to fight off the Jordanian attack.

33. Cooley, page 117.
34. Iyad, page 76.
35. Iyad, page 76.
36. Iyad, page 76.
37. Salah Khalaf concluded that the Palestinian movement had departed from the Fatah strategy: it had been guilty of 'repeated errors of judgment... blunders and excesses and... provocations. By the very nature of things confrontation was inevitable' (see Iyad, page 74).

Chapter 8: A STATE WITHOUT A TERRITORY

1. Smith, **Palestine and the Palestinians**, page 141-2.
2. Much of Intra Bank's holdings were sold off to the governments of Kuwait, Bahrain and Lebanon, creating further bitterness among former employees and Palestinian clients. Many of them concluded that an investment in the PLO was their best hope of safeguarding their capital.
3. Hart, pages 288-296.
4. Hart, page 288.
5. Petran, page 92. Malcolm Kerr concurred; he observed that most Gulf states found little difficulty providing finance for the PLO: 'There was no harm in raising money in their kingdoms for the Fidayin—that is to say, the god-fearing Fidayin of Fat'h, not the aetheists of al-Sa'iqa and the PFLP—providing the Fidayin really directed their fire against Israel rather than the Jordanian monarchy, and providing the protraction of the struggle did not eventually unsettle Arab society closer to home.' (Malcolm H Kerr, **The Arab Cold War: Gamal 'Abd al-Nasir and His Rivals 1958-1970** (New York 1971) page 139).
6. Al-Saiqa was the military wing of Vanguards of the Popular War of Liberation, which had been established in 1967 among Palestinian members of the Baath Party in Syria.
7. The Arab Liberation Front (ALF) was established in 1969, largely in response to the formation of al-Saiqa by Iraq's Baathist rivals in Syria. Unlike the latter, which had a number of Palestinian activists, the ALF was composed mainly of mercenaries from Iraq, Lebanon and Jordan. It had no base in the Palestinian camps (see El-Rayyes and Nahas, pages 55-8).
8. Petran comments: 'The growing popular appeal of the resistance movement after the 1967 war prompted each Arab regime to create its own "Palestine resistance" organisation. Such organisations had little, if anything, to do with the Palestinian cause. They were intended to advance the aims of their patrons in inter-Arab conflicts and to contain and limit the local influence of the authentic resistance.' (Petran, pages 92-93).
9. During the October 1973 war OPEC had forced up oil prices by 70 per

cent, from $3.01 a barrel to $5.12 a barrel. In December 1973 the organisation forced a further rise of 128 per cent, taking the price to $11.65 a barrel. In addition, during the war the Arab states had imposed an oil boycott on the US and the Netherlands.

10. In 1967 Fatah had rejected the idea of 'liberating' a portion of Palestine. Even in November 1973 it issued a statement insisting that its strategic objective was 'liberation and the building of a democratic state in the whole of Palestine' (see Gresh, pages 141-2).

11. In January 1974 Fatah publicly called for a 'national authority' in occupied Palestine (see Gresh, page 143).

12. In fact Naif Hawatmeh of the Democratic Front had been the first to argue openly for a 'national authority'. In December 1973 he called for 'a struggle... to assert the independent presence of our people in every part of its land from which Israeli forces withdraw, whether as a result of force, the threat of force or a settlement imposed by the forces active in the area' (Gresh, page 139). In plain language this meant the PLO should accept a ministate in the West Bank and Gaza. But the Democratic Front could not bring the issue before the whole movement; for this Fatah's agreement was essential. A few weeks after Hawatmeh's speech Fatah raised the issue, giving it 'legal' status in the PLO.

13. Hart, page 379.

14. Hart, page 379.

15. Iyad, page 142.

16. In February 1974 the PLO Central Council introduced a 'working paper' which called for Arab and international recognition of the right of Palestinians to 'establish a national authority on any lands that can be wrested from Zionist occupation (see Hart, page 378). Only in 1977 was Arafat given an official PNC mandate to negotiate for a ministate.

17. Resolution of the Arab summit held in Rabat, Morocco, on 28 October 1974. The resolution added: 'The Arab states are pledged to uphold this authority, when it is established, in all spheres and at all levels.' (see T G Fraser, **The Middle East 1914-1979** (London 1980) page 136).

18. Hirst, page 333.

19. Arafat closed his speech by declaring: 'Today I have come bearing an olive branch and a freedom fighter's gun. Do not let the olive branch slip from my hand. I repeat: do not let the olive branch slip from my hand.' (Fraser, page 139).

20. Iyad, page 147.

21. Sameer Y Ibrahim, 'The Development and Transformation of the Palestine National Movement', in Aruri, page 409.

22. The oil embargo imposed on the US and the Netherlands during the October war proved that the Arab states had the potential to act together and to exert enormous influence over the Western economies. However, their action was short-lived and was not repeated.

23. See Petran, pages 126-133. One member of the Lebanese Communist

Party (LCP) later recalled: 'The government and the employers were on the run. We on the left were the only force organised enough to take decisive action. But the party wouldn't do it—it was afraid that non-parliamentary action would be seen as "illegitimate". So we did nothing and the chance passed. But those were "our days".' (Conversation with LCP members in Cairo, April 1986).

24. Cooley estimates, conservatively, that there were about 200,000 Palestinians in Lebanon before the civil war—7 to 8 per cent of the country's population. All population figures for Lebanon are highly unreliable; the real figure for Palestinians in the country may have been closer to 350,000 (see John K Cooley, 'The Palestinians', in P Edward Haley and Lewis W Snider, **Lebanon in Crisis** (Syracuse 1979) pages 21-54).

25. According to Cooley: 'During this period Arafat and the PLO leadership repeatedly pledged they would respect Lebanese sovereignty under the Cairo Agreement (of 1969, which gave the PLO the right to run affairs in Palestinian camps in Lebanon) and that they would not get involved in Lebanese affairs or support one faction against another.' (Cooley; in Haley and Snider, page 35).

26. By May 1976 the Syrians had launched a full-scale onslaught on the PLO more savage than anything since King Hussein's Black September attack and far more damaging to the Palestinians than any Israeli offensive. Israeli prime minister Yitzak Rabin commented: 'Syria is currently in a state of war with al-Fatah. Its forces killed last week in Lebanon more al-Fatah elements than the Israeli army has killed in two years' (quoted in Cooley, in Haley and Snider, page 41).

27. The weaker the state of Palestinian guerrilla forces, the stronger became the influence of Arab regimes within the smaller groups and the larger became the number of 'mercenaries'.

28. Palestinian activists perceived the PLO as having become infected by 'the Lebanese disease', especially by the syndrome of loyalty to the *zaims*—hereditary clan leaders who dominated Lebanese politics. Activists drew parallels between the status of leading members of the PLO and Lebanese figures such as Phalange chief Pierre Gemayal and Druze leader Kamal Jumblatt (conversations with guerrilla activists in Beirut, 1981).

29. PLO headquarters was increasingly seen as overloaded with comfortable bureaucrats who were becoming corrupted by the comforts of life in Beirut (conversations with members of the Popular Front and Democratic Front, Sidon and Tyre, Lebanon, 1981).

30. According to American government figures, no less than 8,300 PLO fighters and 3,600 PLA and Syrian troops left Lebanon (see Petran, page 282).

31. Both Lebanese and Palestinians were victims of the slaughter which the occupying Israeli forces had tacitly encouraged (see Petran, page 288, and Schiff and Ya'ari, pages 250-285).

32. Guerrillas were sent mainly to Algeria, Tunisia, South Yemen and Sudan. All were isolated from the local population, sometimes under armed guard. In Tunisia, for example, the PLO was permitted to establish a new headquarters; ostensibly this was in the capital city, Tunis—in fact PLO offices were 35 kilometres from the capital on an isolated beach.

33. Amal emerged from the Movement of the Disinherited, the first organisation in Lebanon to represent the interests of the mass of the Shia population. By the late 1970s, Amal was under Fatah influence but, according to Lebanese sources, by the early 1980s it was said to have factions loyal to Syria, the Lebanese *Deuxième Bureau*, Iran and Israel, as well as to Fatah—an index of the speed with which competing powers sought to penetrate new Lebanese organisations they hoped to manipulate. My information came from discussions with Lebanese activists, including Shiites, in southern Lebanon in 1982. For an account of the development of Amal see Petran, pages 263-7.

34. Petran, page 362.

35. In Shatilla camp 200 Palestinian youths fought off thousands of militiamen (see Petran page 363).

36. By 1986 only the Palestinian camp at Ain al-Hilweh, near Sidon, with a population of about 50,000, remained as a mass base for the mainstream PLO, and this was under pressure from Israeli forces in the south and Syrians to the north and east.

Chapter 9: THE OCCUPIED TERRITORIES

1. From its earliest years the Zionist movement has referred to Palestine as *Eretz Israel*—the land of Israel. This Hebrew term has designated an imagined ancient Jewish kingdom covering large areas of the Levant—an area which, the Zionists argued, they were entitled to 'reclaim' for world Jewry. The area has varied in extent according to the aspirations of the Zionist current concerned. Carta's **Historical Atlas of Israel**, published in Jerusalem in 1977, provides a semi-official modern view of *Eretz Israel* through a series of of maps which cover areas under Jewish kingdoms of the 14th to 13th centuries BC. These include Lebanon, most of Syria and modern Jordan, and all of Palestine (see pages 8-10).

2. The two groups of settlements served the purpose of securing a strategic base in the best cultivable land of the Jordan valley, opened access to water resources and created a barrier between the two main populated areas of the East and West banks of the River Jordan. The two areas were connected by a 'security corridor', the Allon Road.

3. Ibrahim Matar, 'Israeli Settlements and Palestinian Rights', in Aruri, page 121. Most of the land was seized from its Palestinian owners. In 1982 Israel's deputy minister of agriculture was asked by the newspaper *Ha'arets* how land was acquired in the West Bank. ' "There are various methods," he replied with a smile. "More than this I can't say".' (Quoted in **Merip Report** number 116, page 8).

4. Matar, in Aruri, page 120.
5. Peter Demant, 'Israeli Settlement Policy Today', in **Merip Report**, number 116, page 9.
6. Sarah Graham-Brown, 'The Economic Consequences of the Occupation', in Aruri, page 172.
7. **Middle East Report** number 152, page 26.
8. Quoted in Matar, in Aruri, page 120.
9. Quoted in Matar, in Aruri, page 124.
10. Joe Stork, 'Water and Israel's Occupation Strategy', in **Merip Report** number 116, page 19.
11. Stork, page 21.
12. Stork, page 22.
13. The impact in Gaza, where 45 per cent of agriculture relies on irrigation, has been extremely serious. Unless water consumption is reduced the aquifer could become saline (Graham-Brown, in Aruri, page 178).
14. Improved irrigation methods increased agricultural productivity in some areas, though Israeli water policy has generally blocked such developments (Graham-Brown, in Aruri, page 177).
15. Sarah Graham-Brown, 'Report from the Occupied Territories', in **Merip Report**, number 115, page 6.
16. Sara Roy, 'The Gaza Strip: A Case of Economic De-Development', in **Journal of Palestine Studies**, number 54, pages 60-61.
17. Richard Locke and Anthony Stewart, **Bantustan Gaza** (London 1985) page 21.
18. In the pre-1948 period the Zionists' 'parallel economy' had prevented the development of industry; even by the 1960s this was still based on small-scale production in wood, glass, pottery, food-processing, cigarettes and matches (see Graham-Brown, in Aruri, page 193).
19. Quoted in Sheila Ryan, 'Political Consequences of Occupation', in **Merip Report** number 74 (January 1979), page 3.
20. Graham-Brown, in Aruri, page 207.
21. Graham-Brown, in Aruri, page 206.
22. Ryan, page 6.
23. By 1977 Israel had benefited to the extent of between 2.5 billion and 3 billion Israeli pounds (report in the Israeli newspaper *Al Hamishmar*, quoted in **Merip Report** number 74, page 17).
24. Graham-Brown, in Aruri, page 206.
25. Israeli Central Bureau of Statistics figure, quoted in Ryan, page 7.
26. In Gaza one Arab bank was allowed to reopen, but was permitted only to do business in Israeli shekels (Graham-Brown, in Aruri, page 198).
27. Graham-Brown, in Aruri, page 194.
28. Graham-Brown, in Aruri, page 195.
29. **Financial Times**, 13 January 1988.
30. In the 1960s the West Bank had traded with Israel but the bulk of imports and exports were exchanged with Jordan. By 1980, 88 per cent of imports

came from Israel and 59 per cent of exports went to Israel. For Gaza the figures were 91 per cent and 76 per cent (Graham-Brown, in Aruri, page 204).

31. Israel's 'iron fist' policy was first practised in Gaza in 1971 under then Chief of Staff Ariel Sharon (for details see Locke and Stewart, pages 11-12).

32. Ann Lesch, 'Israeli Deportation of Palestinians From the West Bank and Gaza 1967-1970', in **Journal of Palestine Studies** number 30.

33. Salim Tamari, 'Israel's Search for a Native Pillar: The Village Leagues', in Aruri, page 378. See also Moshe Ma'oz, **Palestinian Leadership on the West Bank** (London 1984) chapter 8.

34. Tamari, page 379.

35. Joost Hilterman, 'Workers Under the Iron Fist', in **The Middle East** (London) May 1986, page 13.

36. Meron Benvenisti, reported in Hugh Scofield, 'A Study in Neglect', in **The Middle East**, August 1986, page 10.

37. **The Middle East**, August 1986.

38. **The Middle East**, August 1986.

Chapter 10: THE UPRISING

1. **Middle East Report** number 152, page 8.

2. Eban in the **New York Times**, quoted in **Middle East International**, 20 January 1989, page 16.

3. Sayigh, pages 164-167.

4. **Middle East Report** number 152, page 13.

5. Major General Amram Mitzna, quoted in **Middle East Report** number 154, page 11.

6. Palestine Human Rights Information Centre, quoted in **Palestine Solidarity** (London) number 36-37, page 6.

7. Amnesty International, **Israel and the Occupied Territories: Administrative Detention During the Palestinian Intifada** (London, June 1989).

8. **The Guardian** (London) 9 December 1988.

9. In late January 1988 the Peace Now movement called a rally in Tel-Aviv against policy in the Occupied Territories. Some 30,000 attended—a substantial number for Israel but a fraction of the massive crowds that had gathered for Peace Now rallies against the 1982 invasion of Lebanon. More serious for the Israeli government was the tide of criticism from Zionist leaders abroad; so sustained was criticism from the leaders of Jewish organisations in the US that Israel's consul-general in New York attacked them for 'comforting Israel's enemies' (**The Jerusalem Post**, 13 February 1988).

10. **Middle East International**, 2 December 1988, page 23.

11. **Middle East International**, 18 November 1988, page 23.

12. **Middle East Report**, number 154, page 8.

13. In the Marxist tradition the term 'dual power' has a specific meaning. Leon Trotsky wrote: 'The historic preparation of a revolution brings about, in the pre-revolutionary period, a situation in which the class which is called on to realise the new social system, although not yet master of the country, has actually concentrated in its hands a significant share of the state power, while the official apparatus of the government is still in the hands of the old lords. That is the initial dual power in every revolution.' (Leon Trotsky, **History of the Russian Revolution**, volume 1 (London 1967) page 203). No such situation had come about during the *intifada*; while there was a high level of Palestinian organisation, the Uprising had not 'concentrated in its hands a significant share of the state power'.

14. **Democratic Palestine** (Damascus) number 29, page 7.

15. **Democratic Palestine**, number 29, page 7.

16. Figure from the Bank of Israel, reported in **Mideast Mirror**, 1 June 1989, page 2.

17. **Jerusalem Post**, 23 January 1989.

18. **Middle East Report** number 154, page 15.

19. **Jerusalem Post**, 23 January 1989.

20. The **Jerusalem Post** greeted the mobilisation of students to pick the citrus crop as the return of *avodah ivrit*—Jewish labour (**Jerusalem Post**, 30 January 1988). Israeli labour contractors brought forward plans to import 10,000 foreign workers, arguing that rising unemployment meant Israel would need fewer workers and that such numbers would be adequate to deal with further strikes by Palestinian workers (see **The Jerusalem Post**, 6 February 1988).

21. **Mideast Mirror**, 1 June 1989.

22. **Mideast Mirror**, 1 June 1989.

23. Figures given by Brigadier General Michael Navon, economic adviser to the chief of the Israeli general staff (**Mideast Mirror**, 12 July 1989).

24. **Jerusalem Post**, 30 January 1988.

25. The level of strike action among Jewish workers in Israel has been remarkably high, especially among dockers, transport workers and in state sectors including health and education. In those areas of the Israeli economy from which Palestinian labour has been excluded strikes continued during the Uprising. In February 1988, for example, a stoppage involving 10,000 health workers paralysed the country's 32 state hospitals (**The Jerusalem Post**, 20 February 1988).

26. Machover and Orr, page 91.

27. **The Guardian**, 9 December, 1988.

28. The Palestinian Communist Party was established in 1982. It emerged from the Jordanian Communist Party (JCP), which had long maintained a small cadre of members in the West Bank. The JCP had been formed in 1951 from the National Liberation League, the rump of the original Palestine Communist Party which had finally split into Arab and Jewish sections in 1943. From the late 1960s the JCP argued that in the West

Bank guerrilla struggle was not the main issue and concentrated on economic and social issues. Against bitter opposition from PLO activists it argued strongly for the establishment of a ministate in the Occupied Territories. During the 1970s and early 1980s it was able to build a small but influential base in the West Bank and when the *intifada* began the new PCP was able to play an important mobilising role and became a member of the Unified Command of the Uprising. However, it has accepted that the PLO plays the leading role in directing the movement. See Alain Gresh, 'Palestinian Communists and the *Intifada*' (review article), in **Middle East Report** number 157 (March- April 1989) pages 34-6.

29. **Middle East Report** number 154, page 21.
30. See Phil Marshall, 'Islam: Oppression and Revolution', in **International Socialism** number 2:40 (London 1988) pages 38-44.
31. **Jerusalem Post**, 6 February 1988.
32. For an account of the Brotherhood's early activities see Richard P Mitchell, **The Society of the Muslim Brothers** (London 1969). On recent developments see **Middle East International**, 9 September 1988.
33. **Middle East International**, 9 September 1988.

Chapter 11: IMPACT OF THE *INTIFADA*

1. The Palestinian Declaration of Independence, issued on 15 November 1988, asserted: 'The massive national uprising, the *intifada*, now intensifying in cumulative scope and power on occupied Palestinian territories [has] elevated consciousness of the Palestinian truth and right into still higher realms of comprehension and actuality... Because of the *intifada* and its revolutionary irreversible impulse, the history of Palestine has therefore arrived at a decisive juncture.' (**Middle East International**, 18 November 1988).
2. Account of eyewitnesses recounted in Cairo, April 1986.
3. **Middle East Report** number 152, page 51.
4. **Middle East Report** number 152, page 51.
5. **Middle East Report** number 152, page 51.
6. **Middle East Report** number 152, page 47.
7. **Middle East Report** number 152, page 47.
8. **Middle East Report** number 152, page 51.
9. **Middle East Report** number 152, page 52.
10. **Middle East Report** number 152, page 51.
11. **Mideast Mirror**, 7 January 1988, and **Middle East Report** number 152, page 51.
12. **Middle East Report** number 152, page 51.
13. **Mideast Mirror**, 10 February 1988.
14. **Mideast Mirror**, 10 February 1988.
15. **Middle East Report** number 152, page 52.
16. **Middle East Report** number 152, page 52.

17. Even the most polite bourgeois analysts have been compelled to record the impact of the economic policy adopted by President Sadat—*infitah* or the 'open door'—which from 1974 exaggerated the already deep inequalities in Egyptian society. For example, according to Raymond Hinnebusch, in the mid-1970s a new 'parasitic bourgeoisie' emerged, and 'The explosion of conspicuous consumption at the top fed a growing perception that class gaps were widening, the rich getting richer and the poor poorer.' (Raymond A Hinnebusch Jnr, **Egyptian Politics Under Sadat** (Cambridge 1985) page 70).

18. **Middle East Report** number 152, page 45.

19. **Middle East Report** number 152, page 45.

20. In Egypt, as in many Arab countries, lawyers', doctors' and engineers' associations have been important areas of political activity for the radicalised petit bourgeoisie and an area of conflict between the left, nationalists and the Islamic current. The lawyers' strike, which also involved judges, paralysed the legal system for a day. Two days later the doctors' association organised a solidarity rally in Cairo attended by 3,000 people (**Middle East Report** number 152, page 45, and **Mideast Mirror**, 4 January 1988).

21. See Marshall, in **International Socialism** 2:40, pages 28-31.

22. On 1 January hundreds of people in Mehalla al-Kubra assembled after Friday prayers and demonstrated in solidarity with the Palestinians. After a march to the local headquarters of the ruling National Democratic Party, they burned an Israeli flag. Five demonstrators were arrested (report of an Egyptian journalist, given in London, September 1988, and **Middle East Report** number 152, page 45).

23. **Mideast Mirror**, 4 January 1988. The government's furious response indicated its anxiety over the spread of demonstrations to major industrial centres and, in particular, to Mehalla al-Kubra, which since the 1930s had a record of militancy and a reputation for being a stronghold of the left.

24. **Mideast Mirror**, 4 January 1988.

25. **Mideast Mirror**, 5 January 1988.

26. **Mideast Mirror**, 6 January 1988.

27. **Mideast Mirror**, 11 January 1988.

28. **Mideast Mirror**, 12 January 1988.

29. **Mideast Mirror**, 12 January 1988.

30. **Mideast Mirror**, 12 January 1988.

31. **Middle East Report** number 152, page 51.

32. **Mideast Mirror**, 1 February 1988.

33. The summit reflected the turnround in the PLO's position since the start of the Uprising. At the November 1987 summit the Palestinian issue had been marginalised; now Palestine was again at the centre of events with the 21 Arab states pledging over $350 million in support for the year, in addition to individual state donations (see **The Independent** (London)

10 June 1988).

34. For an analysis of the US strategy in the Gulf see Phil Marshall, 'A Test of Strength', in **Socialist Worker Review**, number 104 (London December 1987), and Alex Callinicos, 'Socialists and the Gulf War', in **Socialist Worker Review**, number 113 (September 1988). The PLO had supported the Khomeini government after the fall of the Shah in 1979; indeed Yasser Arafat was the first foreign leader to fly to Tehran to greet Khomeini. However, within a few years the PLO was firmly aligned with Iraq against Iran in the Gulf war.

35. In 1977 the US had imported 8.6 million barrels per day (b/d); by 1985 this figure had fallen to 4.3 million (**Time** (New York) 14 April 1986).

36. There was general satisfaction in the US at the move away from Middle East suppliers. **Time** magazine noted the fall in imports and added: 'Even better, much of that [reduced] supply came from such newly expanded sources as Mexico and Britain rather than from the volatile Persian Gulf countries.' (**Time**, 14 April 1986).

37. US Department of Energy and Department of Commerce statistics, quoted in **Middle East Report** number 155, pages 27-9.

38. In 1985 the US required 15.7 million barrels per day (b/d); by 1988 the figure had risen to 17.7 million b/d (US Department of Energy statistics, in **Middle East Economic Digest** (London) 7 April 1989).

39. **Middle East Economic Digest**, 7 April 1989.

40. **Time**, 14 April 1986.

41. **Middle East Report** number 155, page 28.

42. Consumption would remain between 17.2 and 17.7 million barrels per day (b/d). Domestic production would fall to 8.5 million b/d by 1992 (**Middle East Economic Digest**, 7 April 1989).

43. **Middle East Economic Digest**, 7 April 1989.

44. Oil exploration had slowed during the recession and when in the mid-1980s the price had fallen below $10 a barrel, exploration was abandoned in some areas. In established oilfields such as the North Sea and Central America there were few new finds; in the Far East expectations that fields off the Chinese coast might supply Japan and the South East Asian economies had collapsed. Cheap, accessible Gulf oil again seemed the obvious source of supply.

45. **The Independent**, 8 October 1988.

46. For an account of the development of Algerian state capitalism, see Rachid Tlemcani, **State and Revolution in Algeria** (London 1986) parts 3 and 4.

47. See Jon Marks, 'Opening up Algeria', in **The Middle East**, June 1985, pages 48-49.

48. **The Independent**, 7 and 8 October 1988.

49. **Mideast Mirror**, 7 October 1988.

50. **Mideast Mirror**, 7 October 1988.

51. **Mideast Mirror**, 7 October 1988.

52. In January 1986 the cities of Tunisia erupted in protest over price rises imposed on basic commodities. Within hours there were similar demonstrations in Morocco. In both countries the army was called in to crush the protests (see **The Middle East**, March 1986).
53. Reported in the Saudi newspaper *Al-Sharq al-Awsat* and recorded in **Mideast Mirror**, 10 October 1988.
54. **Mideast Mirror**, 10 October 1988.
55. **Mideast Mirror**, 10 October 1988.
56. **Mideast Mirror**, 11 October 1988.
57. **Mideast Mirror**, 12 October 1988.
58. **Mideast Mirror**, 10 October 1988.

Chapter 12: THE 'PSEUDO-ENTITY'

1. **A Handbook to the Palestine Question** (Beirut 1969) page 184.
2. **A Handbook to the Palestine Question**, page 188.
3. Gresh, page 66.
4. Gresh, page 108.
5. Gresh, page 108.
6. Gresh page 108.
7. Gresh quotes a member of the Front's politburo to the effect that, despite the organisation's sharp move to the left in 1969 and its call for the Palestinian movement to take power in Jordan in 1970, 'leftist' elements were removed in 1971. (Gresh, page 138).
8. The Front often spoke of 'intermediate' or 'transitional' slogans (see Gresh, page 140, and Fuad Faris, 'A Palestinian State?', in **Merip Report** number 33, pages 3-27). Use of such terms was sometimes seen by the left in the West as evidence of the Front's move towards a 'Trotskyist' approach. Nothing could have been further from the truth, though the use of the terms may reflect the fact that from the late 1960s the Front had regular contact with European organisations which saw themselves as standing in the Trotskyist tradition and that it seemed prepared to use 'Trotskyist' terminology without reference to its original context and meaning.
9. Gresh, page 147.
10. Gresh, page 147.
11. Gresh, page 148.
12. Gresh, page 148.
13. Iyad, page 142.
14. Yasser Arafat used middle-ranking members of the organisation such as Said Hammami and Issam Sartawi to float the idea of a ministate solution with Israelis, including then leading 'dove' Uri Avnery. Hammami was assassinated in 1978, Sartawi in 1983 (see Gresh, pages 144-5, and Hart, pages 392-4).
15. Faiz Abu Rahma, former head of the Gaza Bar Association, quoted in **Middle East International**, 18 November 1988.

16. **Mideast Mirror**, 3 March 1988.
17. **Mideast Mirror**, 22 March 1988.
18. George Habash, leader of the Popular Front, expressed reservations about the declaration but did not oppose it.
19. Bassam Abu-Sharif interviewed for the Popular Front in Beirut in August 1977 (**International Discussion Bulletin** number 5 (London 1977) page 5).
20. **The Independent**, 18 May 1989.
21. **Mideast Mirror**, 1 February 1989.
22. Gush Emunim, 'The Bloc of the Faithful', emerged in 1974 from the ultra-nationalist National Religious Party. The organisation was committed to unlimited settlement of all areas of *Eretz Israel* on the basis of a divine right to the land. Its method of settlement—described in Hebrew as *hichnachalut*, literally 'colonisation'—has involved squatting and, if necessary, violent opposition to all those who oppose them. Members of Gush Emunim have been among those most insistent that the population of the Occupied Territories be 'transferred' in order to allow unhindered Jewish settlement (see David Newman, **Jewish Settlement in the West Bank: The Role of Gush Emunim** (Durham 1982).)
23. In an interview with **Time** magazine, quoted in **Mideast Mirror**, 10 April 1989.
24. Sharon has been the most insistent proponent of the 'Jordanian option'—the idea that a Palestinian state already exists in Jordan and that Israel should 'encourage' the Arab population of Palestine to move there. In May 1989 he commented that if Arabs wanted Palestine 'they would find it in Jordan', where the population was Palestinian, 'but all rights to this country, to the land of Israel and especially Judea and Samaria [the West Bank], are Jewish' (**The Times**, 19 May 1989).
25. **Mideast Mirror**, 4 January 1988.
26. Nadav Safran, 'The Jordanian Option', in **Movement** (Boston) November 1984, quoted in Naseer Aruri, 'The PLO and the Jordanian Option', in **Third World Quarterly** (London, October 1985) page 903.
27. Mark A Heller, **A Palestinian State: The Implications for Israel** (London 1983), page 138.
28. **Mideast Mirror**, 20 February 1989.
29. **Middle East International**, 6 June 1989.
30. **A Handbook to the Palestine Question**, page 188.
31. Gresh, page 66.
32. According to PLO Executive Committee member Mahmoud Abbas (Abu Mazen) by January 1989 the PLO and US representatives had discussed only one issue—'terrorism' (**Mideast Mirror**, 25 January 1989).
33. **Mideast Mirror**, 25 January 1989.
34. **Mideast Mirror**, 25 January 1989.
35. **Mideast Mirror**, 19 April 1989.

36. **Middle East International**, 28 April 1989.
37. **Middle East International**, 28 April 1989.
38. King Hussein, who was visiting Washington at the time of the demonstrations, was immediately offered an increase in economic aid from $15 million to $35 million. US president Bush also raised the prospect of increasing military aid from $10 million in 1988 to $48 million in 1989 (**The Guardian**, 21 April 1989).
39. Report in the Israeli newspaper *Ha'arets* (quoted in **Mideast Mirror**, 24 April 1989).
40. Quoted in **Middle East International**, 26 May 1989.
41. **The Times**, 25 April 1989.
42. Hundreds were arrested but there was not even token protest from the PLO (**Middle East International**, 28 April 1989). Indeed, the Palestinian leadership aligned itself with the Jordanian monarch: according to **The Guardian**, 'King Hussein saw fit to pay unprecedented tribute to the PLO for the "vital role" it played in "calming the riots".' (**The Guardian**, 8 May 1989).
43. **Middle East International**, 4 November 1988.

Chapter 13: PALESTINE AND THE ARAB REVOLUTION

1. The Fronts were certainly Stalinist in orientation, though they were not tied to the Soviet Union in the manner of most Communist parties. In the 1960s and early 1970s the sole 'Palestinian' Communist party, the Jordanian Communist Party (JCP), which operated in the West Bank, had little impact on the burgeoning nationalist movement. One reason may have been its subservience to Moscow. At this stage Russia was troubled by the 'terrorist' character of the armed Palestinian resistance and in 1974 a leading member of the JCP, writing in Moscow's **World Marxist Review**, criticised the influence of 'Maoist and Trotskyist ideas and slogans' such as 'everything comes from the barrel of a gun'. The PLO was attacked for 'adventurist actions' (see Galia Golan, **Yom Kippur and After: The Soviet Union and the Middle East Crisis** (Cambridge 1977), page 235). The Popular and Democratic Fronts, even though they had absorbed much of the Stalinist tradition, were at least not brought under such direct pressures.

2. References to the 'sacred cause' of Palestine became a routine device for directing attention away from domestic issues. In Egypt, for example, following the failure of union with Syria in the early 1960s and with economic problems deepening, the media took to increasingly assertive declarations that war with Israel was on its way; meanwhile President Nasser used the newly created PLO to try to control the growing Palestinian nationalist movement (Raymond William Baker, **Egypt's Uncertain Revolution Under Nasser and Sadat** (Cambridge, Massachusetts 1978) pages 118-119).

3. Some sections of the movement of course were creations of the regimes

established specifically to deepen Palestinian dependence, and even in 'independent' Fatah there were factions tied to various Arab capitals. Khalil al-Wazir, for example, who was responsible for securing the first arms and finance from Saudi Arabia, was subsequently viewed by most Palestinian activists as the man who kept open the channels to Riyadh. Between 1979 and 1989 alone the PLO received $850 million from the Saudis and in 1988 Saudi King Fahd promised the organisation $6.02 million a month to finance its work in the Occupied Territories, in addition to the Saudi contribution paid through the Arab League **(Mideast Mirror,** 16 February 1989).

4. Hart, page 267.
5. Hart, page 342.
6. Hart, page 342.
7. Trotsky's approach was first spelt out in **Results and Prospects,** published in 1906; it was developed 23 years later in **The Permanent Revolution** (see Leon Trotsky, **The Permanent Revolution and Results and Prospects** (New York 1969)).
8. For a brief account of the process by which Stalinism re-established the 'stages' theory see Duncan Hallas, **Trotsky's Marxism** (London 1979) chapter 1.
9. See Hallas, **The Comintern,** especially chapter 5.
10. The Egyptian party was formed during the wave of workers' struggles which followed the First World War and was soon crushed by the nationalists of the first Wafd government. See Beinin and Lockman, pages 137-154.
11. See **Theses, Resolutions and Manifestos,** pages 76-81.
12. 'Abu Lutf Answers Questions', in L Kadi (editor) **Basic Political Documents of the Armed Palestinian Resistance Movement** (Beirut 1969) page 102.
13. Roger Owen, 'The Arab Economies in the 1970s', in **Merip Report** number 100-101 (October-December 1981), page 4.
14. Joe Stork, 'Ten Years After', in **Merip Report** January 1984, page 5.
15. E Longuenesse, *'Structures Sociales et Rapports de Classe dans les Sociétés du Proche-Orient Arabe',* in *Peuples Mediterranéens,* number 20 (Paris 1982), page 167.
16. **World Bank Development Report** (Washington 1983).
17. By the mid-1980s there were estimated to be 3.5 million migrant workers in the main Arab labour-importing countries— Bahrain, Kuwait, Libya, Oman, Qatar, Saudi Arabia and the UAE. Of these 1.8 million were Arabs, the majority from Egypt (Susannah Tarbush, 'The New Nomads: Manpower in the Gulf', in **The Middle East,** February 1983, pages 29-34).
18. International Labour Organisation, **Yearbook of Labour Statistics** (Geneva 1981).
19. For an account of the role of workers in the Iranian revolution see Assef

Bayat, **Workers and Revolution in Iran** (London 1987); Phil Marshall, **Revolution and Counter-Revolution in Iran**, pages 38-52.

20. Two studies which break new ground cover the history of the Egyptian working class: Beinin and Lockman's **Workers on the Nile** and Ellis Goldberg's **Tinker, Tailor and Textile Worker: Class and Politics in Egypt, 1930-1952** (Berkeley 1986). There is little or no literature in Arabic or other languages on other Arab countries.

21. Samir Amin, **The Arab Nation** (London 1978) page 84.

22. Amin, page 86.

23. Eric Davis in a review of Goldberg's **Tinker, Tailor**, in **Middle East Report** number 156, pages 40-41.

24. Davis, page 41.

25. During the colonial period Arab workers played a leading role in the anti-imperialist movement, notably in Egypt. See Beinin and Lockman, especially chapters 3, 4, 5, 9, 10 and 11.

26. See Mahmud Hussein, **Class Conflict in Egypt: 1945-1970** (New York 1973) page 74.

27. On Iraq, see Batatu, page 904; on Saudi Arabia see Halliday, pages 66-7.

28. Despite the apparant quiescence of the Egyptian movement in the 1950s Beinin shows that the level of industrial disputes remained extremely high. Between 1952 and 1958 the annual average of disputes (including all types of grievances) was 45,635—a level three times that of the period 1945-51, when industrial struggle was at a mass level. However, these largely localised disputes did not produce a movement of generalised opposition to the Nasser regime (see Joel Beinin, 'Labour, Capital and the State in Nasserist Egypt', in **International Journal of Middle East Studies** (Utah, February 1989) volume 21, number 1, page 77).

29. For accounts of the Egyptian events see N Lachine, 'Class Roots of the Sadat Regime', in **Merip Report** number 56 (April 1977) pages 3-7, and **International Socialism**, number 1:76 (March 1977).

30. All these countries have introduced 'liberalisation' policies; in Egypt and Algeria this has been followed by the emergence of import and commission agents, the rapid advance of the domestic bourgeoisie and increasing impoverishment of the mass of the population. One result has been the eruption of massive anti-regime demonstrations.

31. The Iranian events were followed by a resurgence of the Kurdish movement in Iran and Iraq, a renewal of the Iraqi opposition, and the emergence of (mainly Shiite) opposition groups in Saudi Arabia, Bahrain and Kuwait. The whole Gulf area went into a period of instability which only ended with the defeat of Iran in the Gulf war in 1988.

32. Hart, page 354.

33. Salah Khalaf admits: 'Faced with a situation of conflict within a given country, more often than not we opted to safeguard our relations with the regime in power at the expense of our relations with the masses who

contested it.' (Iyad, page 221).

34. Fatah has long used the fact of Palestinian 'marginality' to question the applicability of the Marxist approach to the Palestine question. In 1969 Salah Khalaf attacked the 'Marxist' analyses of the Palestinian movement offered by the Popular and Democratic Fronts. He commented: 'Did Karl Marx discuss the question of the class of refugees that has emerged among the Palestinian people? The refugee was a labourer working in his own country but is now unemployed... there is a class of refugees... that cannot be defined according to classical lines.' (See Kadi, page 68). The Fronts too were conscious of the problem. In its August Programme of 1968 the opposition faction of the Popular Front—soon to become the Democratic Front—argued that the weakness of the Palestinian movement was partly a result of 'the contradictions of the Palestinian problem and the large number of nonproductive human beings among the dispersed Palestinian population' ('The August Programme', in R Stetler (editor) **Palestine: The Arab-Israeli Conflict** (San Francisco 1972) page 198).

35. **Middle East International**, 26 May 1989.

36. Hart, page 335.

Index

Camp David: 180
Canada: 81
Cecil, Sir Robert: 33
Chadli, Benjedid: 173-5, 193-5
Chamoun, Camille: 79
China: 119-20
Churchill, Winston: 38
Churba, Joseph: 79-80, 84, 93
CIA: 82
Communist International: 66-7, 107-9, 196
Communist Party
—of Egypt: 110
—see also Egyptian Communist Party
—of Iraq: 110, 201
—see Jordanian Communist Party
—see Palestine Communist Party
—see Palestinian Communist Party
Composite Air Strike Force (American): 79
Consolidated Contractors Company: 102
Contracting and Trading Company: 102
Cooley, John: 123
Crossman, Richard: 49
Cuba: 119
Czechoslovakia: 76, 79

Daoud, Abu: 214
Daoud, General Muhammad: 126
Davis, Eris: 201
Dayan, Moshe: 78, 84
Deir Yassin: 71
Defence Procurement Act: 85
Democratic Front for the Liberation of Palestine (DFLP): 121-2, 124, 126, 131-2, 135-6, 159-60, 179, 181, 189, 193-4, 205
Democratic Movement for Peace: 147
Deuxieme Bureau: 98

East Bank: 95, 123, 188-9
Eastern Europe: 30, 33, 50-1
East India Company: 31
Eban, Abba: 150
Edelman, Maurice: 42
Eden, Anthony: 78
Egypt: 15, 19, 38, 40, 45-6, 50, 54-5, 61, 76-80, 82, 87-8, 95, 104, 110, 112, 116, 122, 125, 164, 166-8, 170, 172-5, 192, 194, 196-203, 205, 207
Egyptian Bar Association: 167

Egyptian Communist Party: 196
—see also Communist Party of Egypt
Eisenhower Doctrine: 79
Eretz Israel: 23

Faisal, King: 34, 130, 194
Fahd, King: 174
Faruq, King: 116, 201
Fatah, al-: 103-6, 113, 115-37, 151, 153, 158-61, 163, 169, 176- 83, 189-96, 203, 205
Fez University: 165
FLN (Algeria): 173-4
French imperialism: 30, 32-3, 40, 46, 50, 61, 78-9, 81, 115, 119
Ford, Gerald: 83

Galilee: 72
Gass, Oscar: 73
Gaza: 9-10, 13-27, 72, 78, 83, 91, 95, 120-1, 132-3, 139, 141-59, 163, 172, 178-9, 182, 185-7, 194, 204
Gemayal, Pierre: 111
General Accountin Office: 90
German imperialism: 32-3, 37, 45, 73-4, 79
Giap, General: 120
Golan Heights: 83, 139
Graham-Brown, Sarah: 143, 145
Green Hand: 60
Gresh, Alain: 118
Gush Emunim: 184

Habash, George: 112, 165, 181, 193-4
Haganah: 42, 46, 55, 72
Haifa: 46, 58
Haifa Muslim Society: 61
Hallaj, Muhammad: 190
Hallas, Duncan: 107
Hamas (Islamic Resistance Movement): 160, 205
Hammuda, Yahya: 122
Harkabi, Yehoshafat: 22
Hart, Alan: 133
Hassan, Khalid al-: 104-5, 113, 117, 125, 130, 194
Hassan, King: 174-5
Hawatmeh, Nayef: 165, 179, 193-4
Hebron: 14
Herzl, Theodore: 31-2, 123
Histadrut: 37, 144-5, 156
Hitler, Adolf: 37

Other publications from Bookmarks

Revolution and Counter-revolution in Iran / *Phil Marshall*
From the oppression of the Shah to that of the Ayatollah—but why?
This book looks at the various forces acting during the Iranian revolution of
1979, particular the working class and the left. 128 pages. *£3.50 / $6.75*

Israel: The Hijack State / *John Rose*
A brief outline of Zionism and the role it plays in the world system.
80 pages. *£2.50 / $4.75*

Revolutionary Rehearsals / *edited by Colin Barker*
Five times in the past 20 years the working class has taken mass action:
France 1968, Chile 1972-3, Portugal 1974, Iran 1979 and Poland 1980-1.
This book gives the lie to those who say the working class is finished as a
political force. 272 pages. *£4.95 / $9.50*

South Africa between Reform and Revolution / *Alex Callinicos*
The crisis of white rule in South Africa has been at the centre of world
attention since the popular upsurge of 1984. Only swingeing emergency
powers hold the regime in place. This analysis looks at the stregths and
weaknesses of both sides. 230 pages. *£4.95 / $8.50*

The Fire last time: 1968 and after / *Chris Harman*
The year 1968 was a political watershed: the May events in France, the
Prague Spring in Czechoslovakia, ghetoo risings in the US. This book looks
at the contradictions in the world system which led to these
upheavals—and how the system reasserted its control. *£6.95 / $13.50*

The Quiet Revolutionary / *The autobiography of Margaret Dewar*
From schoolgirl in Petrograd during the 1917 revolution to become an
opponent of both Stalinism and Nazism in the Germany of the 1930s
—this is the story of one of the 'ordinary' people who are the real movers
of history. 224 pages. *£5.95 / $12.50*

Available from bookshops, or by post from Bookmarks
(add 10 per cent to cover postage, minimum 35p or $1).

 BOOKMARKS

265 Seven Sisters Road, Finsbury Park, London N4 2DE, England
PO Box 16085, Chicago, IL 60616, USA
GPO Box 1473N, Melbourne 3001, Australia